"These Are Written"

"These Are Written"

Toward a Cruciform Theology of Scripture

PETER H. NAFZGER

With a Foreword by Joel P. Okamoto

PICKWICK *Publications* · Eugene, Oregon

THESE ARE WRITTEN
Toward a Cruciform Theology of Scripture

Copyright © 2013 Peter H. Nafzger. All rights reserved. Except for brief quotations in critical publications or reviews, no part of this book may be reproduced in any manner without prior written permission from the publisher. Write: Permissions, Wipf and Stock Publishers, 199 W. 8th Ave., Suite 3, Eugene, OR 97401.

Scripture quotations are from *The Holy Bible, English Standard Version* (ESV), copyright 2001 by Crossway, a division of Good News Publishers. Used by permission. All rights reserved.

Pickwick Publications
An Imprint of Wipf and Stock Publishers
199 W. 8th Ave., Suite 3
Eugene, OR 97401

www.wipfandstock.com

ISBN 13: 978-1-61097-839-2

Cataloging-in-Publication data:

Nafzger, Peter H.

    These are written: toward a cruciform theology of scripture / Peter H. Nafzger ; with a Foreword by Joel P. Okamoto.

    xvi + 168 p. ; 23 cm—Includes bibliographical references.

    ISBN 13: 978-1-61097-839-2

    1. Bible—Hermeneutics. 2. Bible—Evidences, authority, etc. I. Title.

BS476 N25 2013

Manufactured in the USA.

For Katie

with Olivia, Johann, August, and Louisa

"Now Jesus did many other signs in the presence of his disciples, which are not recorded in this book; but these are written so that you may believe that Jesus is the Christ, the Son of God, and that by believing you may have life in his name."

John 20:30–31 (ESV)

Contents

Foreword by Joel P. Okamoto   ix
Preface   xiii
Abbreviations   xvii

Introduction   1

1   Where Modern Thinking about the Bible Went Wrong   9

2   Back to the Word: A Dogmatic Relocation   34

3   The Word of the "God of Word"   67

4   One Word, Many Forms   103

5   Meeting the Postmodern Challenge: Canon, Authority, Interpretation   114

Conclusion   159

Bibliography   163

Foreword

IN THIS BOOK PETER Nafzger deals with the question, "What is the Bible?" His answer is the traditional claim that the Bible is the Word of God. His account, however, differs from many in that it does not depend on the inspiration of the biblical authors and their words. He does not deny this claim, but he does not rely on it.

What, then, does he rely on? The short answer is "Jesus Christ." Of course, this is much too general a reply to stand on its own, but Nafzger's more specific answer is precise, clearly laid out, and thoroughly argued.

What kind of answer is this? One fitting response would compare it with Karl Barth's approach and answer to the question. Barth's approach stands out, because he diagnosed the modern situation well and developed a theological account of the Word within the doctrine of the Trinity. This was an impressive accomplishment, and Nafzger readily appreciates it and develops his own account with reference to it.

The difference in Nafzger's approach comes out most clearly in his insistence that the crucifixion and resurrection of Jesus must have constitutive significance for a theology of the Word. For all Christians, the question of whether God has spoken or is speaking is answered in Jesus Christ. But Nafzger reminds us forcefully that we come to this answer not only in what Jesus said and did but especially in the fact that his words and deeds led to his rejection and crucifixion. Although Jesus' words and actions did show that he was the Lord and the Son of God, others could question, deny, and explain away this identification, just as many did in his day and as many do in ours. This fact—which culminated in his crucifixion—has to be accounted for. When one does this, on what can faith in Jesus and his words and work stand? His resurrection on the third day. By raising him from the dead, God vindicated Jesus as Lord and as his Son, and he established that his word was indeed the divine Word. The resurrection also established Jesus' authority to send others to speak and act in his name, from which comes the preaching of the gospel, the administration of the means of grace, the teaching of the Christian faith, the continued authority and the proper interpretation of what we now call the "Old Testament," and the writings that would come to be regarded as the "New Testament." Out of this line of witness and reflection comes Nafzger's account of the Scriptures.

From this we can see another response to the question about Nafzger's approach: it focuses on the question of *authority*. Modern theological accounts of the Scriptures, including Barth's, have given little attention to authority as a theme for reflection. Nafzger, however, appreciates that the Gospel narrative makes it clear that Jesus' *authority* was a central claim. Those who recognized his authority looked to him (or, in the case of demons, looked out for him). Those who denied it looked for ways to kill him, and they found one. But Jesus' resurrection justified his authority, and the authority of the church, which derived from the risen Lord. As I have already suggested, more than a theology of the Scriptures arises from this. In fact, this is only one facet of a larger theological account of the Word of God. It is precisely this feature, however, that allows Nafzger to develop a closely-knit account of the Scriptures that deals clearly and consistently with questions about canonicity, authority, and interpretation.

Many readers will note a definite Lutheran accent throughout this book, and it calls for explanation. This accent is obvious in the repeated references to the Lutheran tradition and Lutheran theologians. It also comes through, but perhaps more subtly, in the way the account of the Word coheres with other features of Lutheran theology such as forensic justification, *sola fide*, and its focus on the one person of Jesus Christ. As such this book also serves as a concrete defense of the Lutheran confession of the faith and an illuminating look at the Lutheran way of doing theology.

But another reason for the Lutheran accent is that this book may be read as a suggestion for moving past a painful period for Concordia Seminary, where I teach and from which Nafzger submitted the initial version of this book as his doctoral dissertation, and the church body it serves, The Lutheran Church—Missouri Synod. In the 1960s and 1970s, Concordia and the Missouri Synod endured a bitter conflict over the Scriptures. The conflict was ended more than it was resolved. The willingness to think deeply about nature and interpretation of the Scriptures in the Missouri Synod has only returned over the last decade or so. This book testifies to and seeks to promote that willingness.

Understandably, this statement may puzzle readers who have no connection to or knowledge about the Missouri Synod. I would assure them that this book requires no prior knowledge about this conflict or its problems. Those, however, who do know about this conflict or about similar situations, and especially those whom this conflict affected personally, may be suspicious of a book that begins by criticizing the usual use of the doctrine of inspiration. I must assure them that there will be no great reversal, no theological turnaround to the doctrine of inspiration. But I would also assure them, and all readers, that out of this comes a theology of the Scriptures consistent with Martin Luther and Martin Chemnitz, with theologians of the ancient church, and, indeed, with the acknowledged testimony of the evangelists and the apostles. One might wish for more from a theological account of the Scriptures, but perhaps the clearest sign of this book's achievement is to show that no one should expect less.

Joel P. Okamoto

Preface

This book is the result of my own personal struggle to understand the Bible. My struggle has not been with a single passage or chapter—although there are plenty of passages and chapters that require some struggling—but rather with the nature and function of the Scriptures in the economy of salvation. Fifteen years ago, when serious questions about the Bible were beginning to surface for me, I would not have phrased it that way. But now, after more than a decade of trying to make sense of the Christian theology of Scripture, I have come to the conclusion that the writings of the Old and New Testaments are most appropriately understood in terms of the role they play in God's plan to save his fallen creation.

From as early as I can recall, I remember being taught and believing that the Bible is the inspired and inerrant Word of God. I believed it tells the truth about God, the universe, and me, and I looked to it for guidance and direction. My theology of Scripture could fit on a bumper sticker: "God said it. I believe it." When questions about the Bible occasionally arose, they were usually related to the application and interpretation of individual passages. As I began more formal theological studies, however, basic questions about the Bible became important to me. These questions did not arise from doubts that God could speak through a donkey or turn water into wine. And I did not question whether God could "inspire" sinful human beings to write sinless words. My struggle came from a sense of discomfort about the way in which I conceived of the Scriptures in the first place. My conception of these writings made it difficult for me to answer some fundamental questions. Some of these questions concerned the canon: "Why were these particular writings included in the canon and not others?" and "What do we do with New Testament writings that the early church was not sure about?" Other questions concerned authority: "What does it mean for the Scriptures to have authority in the church?" and "If the church canonized these writings, how should we understand the authority of the church in relation to the authority of the Scriptures?" Still other questions concerned interpretation: "How should we (or how *can* we) interpret the living and active Word of God?" and "Why do Christians disagree about so many interpretive issues?" Asking these questions made me uncomfortable because, with increasing frequency, I could not find satisfactory answers to them. The more these questions gnawed at me, the more I realized that I needed a more comprehensive *theological* account of why I believed that the Bible is the Word of God, including a clear explanation for how this belief was consistent with the rest of my faith—especially my faith in Jesus, the crucified and risen Son of God. My discomfort led me to a critical examination of the modern way of thinking about the Scriptures, especially the doctrine of inspiration. I reasoned that, if my way of thinking about the Bible is correct, I should not be afraid to put it to the test.

That is what I did. This is what I found.

Simply put, I have concluded that the modern framework in which the Bible has been considered has gone wrong. Neither side of the modern "battle for the Bible" offers a satisfactory account of the nature and function of the Scriptures in the biblical narrative. Both sides remain dogmatically detached from the rest of the Christian confession—especially from Christ and the gospel. Rather than trying to rehabilitate one of the two modern options, it seemed best to me to take a step back and approach the theology of Scripture with a different perspective, a new paradigm, a fresh start. I have taken comfort in the fact that I am not alone. Theologians from various backgrounds and traditions have recently come to the same conclusion, including theologians from my own background and tradition. The account of the Scriptures in this book is not the only way in which a theology of Scripture may be articulated. But as I will attempt to demonstrate, it flows from and is consistent with the trinitarian and soteriological narrative that undergirds the entire Christian faith. It is grounded in the church's one foundation, the crucified and risen Christ, and for that reason it is better able to handle contemporary questions about the canon, authority, and interpretation of the Scriptures.

There are many people who have helped me write this book—some more aware of it than others. This list begins appropriately with my parents. Before I was able to read a single word in the Bible, they spoke God's living and active Word to me and my siblings at home. My Christian faith is evidence of God's work through their faithful speaking, and I am thankful to them for serving as God's instruments in my life. I am also thankful for my brothers and sisters in Christ at New Life Church—Lutheran in Hugo, Minnesota. For the last five years I have been preaching and teaching the Word of God among them, and I am certain that I have learned much more than they. Ministry at New Life has given me many opportunities to witness firsthand God's use of the Scriptures in his plan of salvation.

I would also like to thank Christian Amondson, Chris Spinks, and the people at Wipf and Stock for working with me to make this book happen. I appreciate the opportunity they were willing to give me.

A number of my former professors have helped me a great deal by reading and commenting on versions of this book. Jeff Kloha and Leo Sanchez offered their helpful reflection and suggestions about the Scriptures in the early church and the relationship between Jesus and the Spirit. Robert Kolb helped me understand Luther's theology of the Word and how it functions in the church. He also provided some very helpful assistance in thinking through questions about publication. I would like to say a specific word of thanks to my father, Samuel Nafzger. He taught only one of my classes (on contemporary approaches to Bible, nonetheless), but he has been teaching me about Jesus and the Scriptures all my life. More recently, our conversations about the Bible have helped me refine my own thinking about God and his Word. In many ways I consider this book a continuation and expansion of his lifetime of engaging the Scriptures in the church. I am also extremely grateful to Joel Okamoto. It would be difficult for me to overstate his positive impact on this book. He has given generously of his time, critical reflection, and substantive support. The five years I spent working with him on the theology of Scripture shaped me as a pastor and a theologian. Our many conversations improved this work in countless ways. It would never have been written without his active engagement, and I continue to appreciate his support and friendship.

Finally, and most importantly, I am deeply thankful to (and for) my wife and children. To Olivia, Johann, August, and Louisa: I am sure you do not realize it, but the four of you have helped me think about the Scriptures and the Word of God with fresh eyes every time you sit on my lap for Bible stories and every time you gather around me for children's messages on Sunday mornings. My fervent hope and prayer is that you will always look to the Scriptures with faith in Jesus, our crucified and risen Savior, and that by believing in him you will have life in his name. To my wife, Katie: you have made countless sacrifices (several times) for me and this book. You have helped me think through the theology of Scripture in more ways than you realize. Our conversations about the Bible and preaching have helped me understand how and why we read the Scriptures. You are an indispensable part of my ministry and this work. On this, your birthday, I thank our Lord Jesus for the life he has given you, and for the life we share in him.

This book is dedicated to all five of you.

March 1, 2012
Peter H. Nafzger

Abbreviations

ANF   *The Ante-Nicene Father: Translations of the Fathers down to A.D. 325.* 10 vols. Edited by Alexander Roberts and James Donaldson. Peabody, MA: Hendrickson, 1994.

BC   *The Book of Concord: The Confessions of the Evangelical Lutheran Church.* Edited by Robert Kolb and Timothy J. Wengert. Minneapolis: Fortress, 2000.

        CA   Augsburg Confession (Confessio Augustana)
        Ap   Apology of the Augsburg Confession
        SA   Smalcald Articles
        SC   Luther's Small Catechism
        LC   Luther's Large Catechism
        FC   Formula of Concord
        SD   Solid Declaration of the Formula of Concord

CD   Karl Barth. *Church Dogmatics.* 4 vols. Translated by G. W. Bromiley. London: T. & T. Clark, 2004.

LCC   *Early Christian Fathers.* Translated by C. C. Richardson, Library of Christian Classics 1. Philadelphia: Westminster, 1953.

LW   *Luther's Works.* American Edition. 55 vols. Edited by Jaroslav Pelikan and Helmut T. Lehmann. Philadelphia: Muhlenberg and Fortress Press, St. Louis: Concordia, 1955–1986.

NPNF   *Nicene and Post-Nicene Fathers NPNF Nicene and Post-Nicene Fathers of the Christian Church.* Edited by Philip Shaaf. 28 vols. in two series. 1886–1890; reprint, Grand Rapids: Eerdmans, 1983–87.

TDNT   *Theological Dictionary of the New Testament.* Edited by G. Kittel and G. Friedrich. Translated by G. W. Bromiley. 10 vols. Grand Rapids: Eerdmans, 1964–1976.

WA   *Dr. Martin Luthers Werke.* Kritische Gesamtausgabe. Weimar: Böhlau, 1883.

Introduction

"To my mind it is Jesus Christ who is the original documents. The inviolable archives are his cross and death and his resurrection and the faith that came by him."

—Ignatius, *To the Philadelphians* 8.2 (ca. 110).[1]

Two things stand out in Ignatius' description of the relationship between Jesus and the Scriptures. First, the Scriptures are not simply *about* Jesus; in a serious way they *are* Jesus. Second, because his cross, death, resurrection, and faith in him are central to who Jesus is (and what he does), it follows that his cross, death, resurrection, and faith in him are also central to what the Scriptures are (and what they do).

The subject of this book is the Christian theology of Scripture. But because of the way the Scriptures have been thought of and talked about for the last several centuries, and because of the unique nature and function of the *Christian* understanding of Holy Scripture, this book is also very explicitly about Jesus. To be more specific, it is about Jesus Christ and him crucified, for the foundation of the Christian faith is the one who was crucified for our sins and raised for our salvation.

Perhaps that is the best place to start.

"Christ crucified." Thus the apostle Paul summarizes the Christian message to the Corinthians (1 Cor 1:23). "And I, when I came to you, brothers, did not come proclaiming to you the testimony of God with lofty speech or wisdom. For I decided to know nothing among you except Jesus

---

1. Ignatius, *LCC*, 1:110.

Christ and him crucified" (1 Cor 2:1–2). The cross appears foolish to human understanding, but Christians believe it is the wisdom of God and the power of salvation.[2] For this reason it has stood at the center of the Christian message since the very beginning. Each of the four of the canonical gospels highlights Jesus' death and resurrection as the climax and culmination of his life and ministry.[3] The apostolic preaching in the book of Acts and the apostolic message recorded in the New Testament epistles return repeatedly to the death and resurrection of Jesus as *the* constitutive Christian event. The earliest Christian creeds center around the cross,[4] and worship in the earliest Christian communities concluded with the celebration of the Lord's Supper as a proclamation of his death.[5]

Inseparable from Jesus' death and resurrection are the speaking and the writing of the prophets and apostles. The former foretold the coming of a promised Messiah—the "anointed one" who would deliver God's people from bondage (Isa 42:1). Jesus identified himself as this promised Messiah as he interpreted the prophetic writings in light of his own life and ministry (Luke 4:14–21; John 5:39). His mission and identity are bound together with the writings known as the "Old Testament"—he makes them intelligible and they make him intelligible. Jesus himself did not leave any written records, but he instructed his disciples to teach everything he had commanded them (Matt 28:20) and to speak on his behalf and with his authority (Luke 10:16). He did not leave them alone to do this, but rather promised to give them his Spirit of truth who would guide them (John 16:13–15, 20:21–23; Acts 2:1–4). They did this by speaking and by writing, and the definitive written versions of their message are found in the writings known today as the "New Testament." Together with those of the prophets, the apostolic writings are regarded in the church as Holy Scripture. They are read in worship, studied in the classroom, and meditated on at home. It is simply impossible

---

2. 1 Cor 1:22–30; Rom 1:1–4, 16.

3. At least a third of the chapters in the four gospels are dedicated to reporting the details surrounding the last week in Jesus' life. Martin Kähler famously described the Gospel of Mark as a "passion narrative with an extended introduction" (Kähler, *The So-Called Historical Jesus*, 80).

4. Kelly, *Early Christian Creeds*. In addition to the creedal statements in Scripture that focus on the death and resurrection of Christ (16–21), Kelly describes a number of early confessions of faith that do the same, such as the baptism profession of faith in Hippolytus' *Apostolic Tradition* (46), the creedal statements in the letters of Ignatius (68–69), and in Justin's *Apology* and *Dialogue with Trypho* (71–75).

5. 1 Cor 11:23–26. On the central place of the Lord's Supper in early Christian worship, see Elert, *Eucharist and Church Fellowship*.

to conceive of the Christian faith apart from these writings, and therefore it is appropriate to describe Christian history as an "ongoing encounter with Holy Scripture."[6]

Despite the central significance of Holy Scripture for the Christian faith, a great deal of confusion and disagreement exists, both inside and outside the church, about the nature and function of the Scriptures. In his historical survey of the theology of Scripture, Justin Holcomb asks some of the questions that have yet to be answered definitively:

> What is scripture? Is it divine? Human? Both? Is scripture authoritative? If so, how and for whom? What is the scope of its authority? Is scripture inspired by God? What about scriptural interpretation—is that inspired? Does God illuminate humans to understand scripture? Is there an appropriate method of interpreting scripture? What is its purpose? How *is* scripture used? How *ought* scripture to be used? How do scripture and tradition relate? Does scripture interpret tradition or does tradition interpret scripture? Or both? What does it mean for a Christian to call the Bible "the Word of God"? And if Jesus is also called the Word of God, how does Jesus as the Word of God relate to the Bible as the Word of God?[7]

Holcomb's questions show that there remains uncertainty and disagreement about many issues related to the Scriptures. This uncertainty reaches to the very existence of such a thing as "Holy Scripture" itself. Wilfred Cantwell Smith suggests: "Most of us hear the word 'scripture' without stumbling over it. Using it, we give the impression, even to ourselves . . . that we know what scripture is. On reflection, it turns out that it is hardly the case."[8] Smith challenges us to take another look at these well-known writings and ask ourselves a very fundamental question: "What is Scripture?"

Prior to the seventeenth century this question was easy to answer. Christians believed that the prophetic and apostolic writings were the written Word of God. In modern times, however, this belief was called into question in foundational ways. The advent of rationalism led some to begin reading the Scriptures from a critical perspective. Treating the Scriptures like any other ancient writing, they began questioning biblical reliability and authenticity; they began emphasizing the sinfulness of those who composed and transmitted these writings; they concluded that the traditional belief

---

6. Ebeling, *Word of God and Tradition*, 11–31.
7. Holcomb, *Christian Theologies of Scripture*, 1–2.
8. Smith, *What Is Scripture?*, 1.

that the Scriptures are the Word of God was no longer tenable. Not everyone accepted this approach to the Bible, of course. Many rejected it as a departure from historic Christianity. They went to great lengths to argue that the Scriptures are the inspired Word of God, completely free from error, finally and fully authoritative for Christian faith and life. The dispute between these two approaches became known as the modern "battle for the Bible,"[9] and the questions that framed the discussion several hundred years ago remain to this day.[10]

In his study of the theology of Scripture, Telford Work describes the modern debate as "the crisis of Scripture."[11] He compares it to the iconoclastic controversy that arose in the eighth century. Similar to the debate over the use of icons in the church, modernity brought about "a *wholesale* attack . . . from *inside* the Church, on the idea and use of Scripture."[12] He explains:

> [S]ince the Enlightenment the concept and practice of Scripture have been under unprecedented and sustained attack. From an ever-thickening stack of new hermeneutical proposals to radical uses of the historical-critical method (from both liberal Protestants and fundamentalists) and the "hermeneutics of suspicion," new ways of appreciating the Bible have challenged traditional concepts of Scripture in ways sometimes reminiscent of the era of Iconoclasm. "Formerly, people saw nothing but God" in Scripture, says Aidan Nichols. "Now they see nothing but humans." Protestants in general, and fundamentalists in particular, have been labeled bibliolaters by their rivals. In return, these movements have faulted Catholics, then modern Protestants, for adopting human traditions that usurped or denied Scripture's divinity. Liberals have been called adoptionists and ebionites, conservatives docetists and monophysites, neo-orthodox Nestorians—not because of their formal Christologies, but because of the Christological implications of their uses of Scripture. These charges and countercharges are reminiscent of the atmosphere in the eighth century.[13]

---

9. See Lindsell, *Battle for the Bible*.

10. The relationship between the Bible and the Word of God remains a significant topic in contemporary theology. The Lutheran World Federation met in February 2006 to consider whether the Bible can be equated with the Word of God (Lutheran World Federation, "Can the Bible?," 11).

11. Work, *Living and Active*, 6.

12. Ibid., 4. His emphasis.

13. Ibid., 4–5.

Work points out that resolution to the iconoclastic controversy required a comprehensive account of the nature and function of icons. He suggests that nothing less is necessary today for the theology of Scripture. If there is to be a "triumph of orthodoxy" with respect to the theology of Scripture, the church must move beyond the modern battle and articulate a comprehensive account of the nature and function of Scripture in the economy of salvation.[14]

Work is not alone in his dissatisfaction with the modern debate. A growing number of contemporary theologians from a variety of backgrounds and traditions are coming to the same conclusion. They have offered helpful suggestions about how to move beyond the modern battle and have made significant contributions toward a comprehensive theology of Scripture. Lacking in the contemporary discussion, however, is an account of the Scriptures that is grounded in and consistent with the biblical narrative's focus on the cross. If the heart of the Christian message is "Christ crucified," a comprehensive theological account of the Scriptures must have a distinctively cruciform shape and direction. That is the goal of this book: to offer a way of thinking about the Christian Scriptures that is grounded in Jesus' death and resurrection and directed toward the proclamation of Christ crucified.

The first two chapters are a critical evaluation of the concepts, categories, and assumptions that have governed modern thinking about the Bible. Chapter 1 takes a close look at both sides of the modern debate and notices that most of the conversation has amounted to an argument over the historical truthfulness of the biblical account. While the reliability of the Scriptures is fundamentally important for the validity of Christianity's central claims, much more needs to be said than that the Bible is reliable and true. This is where the traditional side of the modern debate falls short. As a result, contemporary Christians have a hard time speaking clearly and consistently about such things as the biblical canon, biblical authority, and biblical interpretation.

In order to move beyond the modern debate, chapter 2 examines Karl Barth's theology of Scripture as an important step in the right direction. Barth's dogmatic relocation of the Scriptures under the theology of Word of God provides a more comprehensive framework for considering the Scriptures in relation to the rest of the Christian confession, especially to Jesus and church proclamation. Barth's trinitarian perspective and his emphasis on the function of the Scriptures in the economy of salvation improve upon the modern debate, but his philosophical presuppositions keep him from following the biblical narrative in several important ways. Although

14. Ibid., 3–9.

he recognizes problems with the modern battle and points in some helpful directions, Barth's account of the theology of Scripture is finally insufficient.

Chapter 3 is my attempt to reorient the theology of Scripture around the cross. Rooted firmly in the biblical narrative, it examines the nature and function of the Word of God in the divine economy. It begins by noticing that the one true God is a *speaking* God. This God speaks his living and active Word at many times and in various ways, but he speaks *definitively, ultimately, decisively,* and *for all time* in his Son, Jesus Christ, the personal Word of God. In fulfillment of the Word that God had spoken by his prophets, this personal Word was sent in the power of the Spirit to do the Father's work and speak his Word for the salvation of humankind. Some who heard him accepted his message and believed in him. Others rejected and crucified him. But in the power of the same Spirit by whom he was conceived, he was raised from the dead and vindicated by the Father as the eternal Son of God. After completing his work of salvation, the personal Word sent his apostles with his Spirit to continue his ministry by proclaiming the Word of God. The apostolic writings that have been collected and circulated in the church are the definitive versions of their proclamation. Together with the written record of the prophets, Christians recognize them as the written form of the Word of God and the final rule and norm for Christian proclamation.

This account of the Word of God provides a solid foundation for the theology of Scripture that is addressed more specifically in chapters 4 and 5. Chapter 4 looks at the dogmatic ways in which recent theologians have tried to account for the various forms of the Word of God in the biblical narrative. It evaluates the popular "Analogy of the Word" and its comparison of the two natures of Christ with the two natures of the Bible; it reexamines Barth's threefold form of the Word and his understanding of the relationship between Jesus, the Scriptures, and church proclamation; and it takes a close look at Luther's understanding of the written and spoken forms of the Word of God as the means by which God relates to his human creatures. Chapter 4 concludes by offering a framework for thinking about the Word of God that is consistent with the biblical narrative and useful for teaching in the church today.

Chapter 5 examines, in preliminary ways, how this account of the Word of God provides more solid grounds for thinking about the canon, authority, and interpretation of the Scriptures. This final chapter is admittedly selective and incomplete. None of the issues are treated exhaustively. Indeed, there are many aspects of the theology of Scripture that are completely left out. The goal in chapter 5 is not to answer every question related to the Scriptures or to offer a comprehensive theology of Scripture. Instead, it aims to show how a cruciform understanding of the Word of God helps Christians understand the canon, authority, and interpretation of the Scriptures.

Almost fifty years ago Herman Sasse identified the need to articulate a theology of Scripture that moves beyond the modern concepts and categories: "Wir brauchen einen *neuen Konsensus über das Wesen und Authorität der Heiligen Schrift,* ein neues Verständnis des für die Kirche notwendigen Lehrstücks Sacra Scriptura."[15] More recently, and with a bit more creativity, N. T. Wright seeks the same thing:

> Writing a book about Scripture is like building a sandcastle in front of the Matterhorn. The best you can hope to do is to catch the eye of those who were looking down instead of up, or those who were so familiar with the skyline that they had stopped noticing its peculiar beauty. But as I have taken part in many discussions over the years about what the Bible is, and the place it should occupy in Christian mission and thinking, I have increasingly come to the conclusion that there are some, perhaps many, people both outside and inside the church who need to be nudged to look up once more, and this time with fresh eyes, not just at the foothills, but at the crags and crevasses, the cliffs and the snowfields, and ultimately at the dazzling and dangerous summit itself.[16]

The purpose of this book is to provide the kind of fresh perspective Sasse and Wright are seeking. It is not a *new* perspective, however. It attempts to unpack the Christian thinking that led Ignatius to identify the Scriptures so closely with Jesus and his cross, death, resurrection, and the faith that came by him. At its root, this account of the Scriptures approaches the task with John's description of own his writing in mind: "These are written so that you may believe that Jesus is the Christ, the Son of God, and that by believing you may have life in his name" (John 20:31).

---

15. "We need a new consensus over the nature and authority of Holy Scripture, a new understanding of the necessary article of faith, Holy Scripture" (Sasse, *Sacra Scriptura*, 8).

16. Wright, *Scripture*, xiii.

1

Where Modern Thinking about the Bible Went Wrong

There is little dispute that the Bible is the most influential book in history. Its writings have stood at the center of commentary and controversy ever since their composition. Debate has circulated inside and outside the church over its contents, its application, its meaning, even its proper "owner."[1] Although there has never been complete agreement among Christians about every issue related to the Scriptures, prior to the seventeenth century it was believed throughout the church that the writings of the prophets and apostles were the written Word of God. They were read with reverence and respect, and it was simply assumed that they were reliable and true.

In modern times these assumptions were called into question. Some theologians began subjecting the Scriptures to rational and scientific standards of investigation. They found contradictions, errors, and exaggerations, and they came to the conclusion that these writings were not as reliable and true as previous generations had thought. Not every theologian in modern times came to these same conclusions, however. Others rejected this critical approach and defended the traditional belief. They insisted that, as the written Word of God, these particular writings remained beyond the reach of human criticism. The ensuing debate became known as the "battle for the

---

1. See Pelikan, *Whose Bible Is It?*

Bible," and the lines that were drawn in the seventeenth century have divided Christianity ever since.[2]

A Debate about Historical Truthfulness

The rise of the modern world brought changes to every aspect of Western life and thought, including theology and the church.[3] Previously held beliefs and assumptions became the object of scrutiny and criticism, and the church of the Enlightenment found itself struggling to survive in a world increasingly dominated by philosophical rationalism. Van Austin Harvey describes the modern atmosphere as a clash of conflicting worldviews (or moralities). He explains that the old morality of faith and trust, which had characterized the church throughout its first seventeen hundred years, was threatened by the emergence of a new morality. This new morality was dominated by skepticism and distrust. Harvey explains:

> The old morality celebrated faith and belief as virtues and regarded doubt as sin. The new morality celebrates methodological skepticism and is distrustful of passion in matters of inquiry. If Pascal's belief that the heart has its reasons which the reason cannot know can be said of the old ethic, then Nietzsche's conviction that integrity in matters of the mind requires that one be severe against one's heart may be regarded as symbolic of the new one. The old morality was fond of the slogan "faith seeking understanding"; the new morality believes that every yes and no must be a matter of conscience.[4]

According to Harvey, the rise of modern skepticism presented Christians with two incompatible options. On the one hand was the traditional morality grounded in the premodern belief that God acts in history in miraculous ways. On the other hand was rationalism's inherent distrust of anything that cannot be verified by modern standards of reason or science. The battle between these two moralities manifested itself as a struggle between the "historian" and the "believer." Predictably, the first major struggle centered around the Bible. Harvey explains, "The first great conflict between the new

---

2. The "battle for the Bible" is not a Protestant phenomenon. Since Vatican II Rome has struggled to find its footing on questions about inspiration, inerrancy, and authority. See Hansen, "Rome's Battle."

3. Diogenes Allen suggests that modern philosophy started with René Descartes (1596–1650), (*Philosophy for Understanding Theology*, 171).

4. Harvey, *The Historian*, 103.

morality of historical knowledge and traditional Christian belief quite naturally occurred over the problem whether the Bible was to be subjected to the same methodological canons that were to be applied to other ancient and religious traditions and scriptures. The critic insisted on the right to be free and autonomous; the traditionalist insisted that the Bible was a holy and infallible book."[5] To the "historian" it became a matter of intellectual integrity that the Scriptures be treated like any other human composition. To the "believer" it became a matter of obedience to divine revelation that the Scriptures be exempt from rational criticism. They were separated by their answer to the question, "Is the Bible the Word of God?"[6]

The Critical Approach to the Scriptures

Theologians on the critical side of the debate accepted the basic tenets of modern rationalism. They abandoned the premodern belief that the biblical writings could be the Word of God, and they dismissed those who defended traditional views of the Bible as unenlightened and naïve. While critical theologians held a wide variety of positions, they shared a common belief that the Scriptures contain impossibilities, inconsistencies, and inaccuracies. Biblical miracles were more fictitious than factual, and many of the biblical commands were time- and culture-bound to ages long since gone. Harvey describes this approach to the Scriptures with legal imagery. The modern critic is like a prosecuting attorney and the Scriptures are like a witness under interrogation. "No witness can be permitted to go unexamined and no authority unquestioned. The historian does not accept the authority of his witnesses; rather he confers authority upon them, and he does this only after subjecting them to a rigorous and skeptical cross-examination."[7] In a world come of age, critical theologians found the traditional belief that the Scriptures are the Word of God to be rationally unacceptable and intellectually indefensible. Gordon Kaufman's 1971 essay, "What Shall We Do with the Bible?" summarizes the thinking:

> For centuries, as the very word of God to man, the Bible has provided the context of meaning with which Christian man—indeed, Western man generally—has appropriated and understood his existence and set his course in life . . . But this is all over with and

---

5. Ibid., 104.
6. See Nafzger, "Scripture and the Word of God," 107–26.
7. Harvey, *The Historian*, 107.

gone. Though we may recognize and be grateful for its contributions to our culture, the Bible no longer has unique authority for Western man. It has become a great but archaic monument in our midst. It is a reminder of where we once were—but no longer are. It contains glorious literature, important historical documents, exalted ethical teachings, but is no longer the word of God (if there is a God) to man.[8]

Although the Bible remains useful, Kaufman concludes, we must give up our traditional belief that it is the Word of God. "The Bible has become a theological problem for contemporary Christians with no traditional or pat answers acceptable."[9]

Similar conclusions were drawn by the Jesus Seminar. With modern rationalism as its standard, the Jesus Seminar examined the earliest accounts of Jesus' life and concluded that only ten of one hundred seventy-six events recorded in the four canonical gospels accurately reflect what really happened.[10] The result of their investigations yielded a "gospel" that can hardly be identified with the message of historic Christianity.[11] If Christianity is to continue, the seminar suggested, it must break free from the antiquated idea that the Scriptures are inspired by God and therefore inerrant. Robert Funk, in his introductory remarks to the first meeting of the Jesus Seminar in 1985, put it like this: "We need a new narrative of Jesus, a new gospel, if you will, that places Jesus differently in the grand scheme, the epic story . . . The fiction of revelation keeps many common folk in bondage to ignorance

---

8. Kaufman, "What Shall We Do?," 95–96.
9. Ibid., 96.
10. See Funk, *The Acts of Jesus*.

11. Robert Funk writes: "We no longer believe that Jesus was born of Mary without the benefit of male sperm. We no longer think of him literally as performing miracles like walking on the water or stilling the storm. We no longer believe that he fed 5,000 (not counting women and children, according to Matthew) with five loaves and two fish. We are relatively certain that the first reports of his resurrection were luminous apparitions prompted by grief. We think the empty tomb stories are a late and fictional attempt to certify a bodily resurrection. The ascension of Jesus into heaven can only be a fiction. We doubt that Jesus died to atone for the sins of the world, resulting from Adam's original error. We are convinced that Jesus did not intend to establish a new religion, appoint clergy, or inaugurate celibacy. In sum, there is little of the orthodox story that remains tenable. The essential dogmas of the television evangelists, Fundamentalists, and many Evangelicals are museum exhibits: the divinity of Jesus, the virgin birth, the blood atonement, the bodily resurrection, and the second coming. The decay of the old symbolic universe is so far advanced that many believers no longer find such dogmas interesting enough even to discuss" ("The Once and Future New Testament," 548).

and fear. We require a new, liberating fiction, one that squares with the best knowledge we can now accumulate and one that transcends self-serving ideologies. And we need a fiction that we recognize to be fictive."[12]

Despite the general acceptance of the critical approach in academia, not every critical theologian has been as consistent as Kaufman and the Jesus Seminar. Harvey notes that many modern theologians approach the Scriptures with a convenient *inconsistency*. Unwilling to accept the results that follow when rational criticism is carried to its logical conclusions, many modern theologians have "examined some of the New Testament traditions with the aid of accepted principles of criticism while they left others alone or handled them quite gingerly."[13] In order to affirm the "important" events in the life of Jesus, they pick and choose which miracles are credible and which miracles may be disregarded. For example, Harvey notes the common dismissal of an appearance of an angel at the empty tomb as "obviously legendary" by the same theologians who defend the resurrection of a dead man as historical and true.[14] He wonders about this double standard: "What is the warrant that excludes the one judgment but permits the other?"[15] As Marcus Borg observes, "The Bible does not come with footnotes that say, 'This passage reflects the will of God; the next does not,' or 'This passage is valid for all time; the previous passage is not.'"[16]

Despite its inconsistent application, Harvey concludes that the critical side of the modern battle has won. Biblical scholarship has become dominated by those who reject the traditional view of the Scriptures, and many mainstream denominations have moved on with a Bible that is no longer recognized as the Word of God.

The Doctrine of Inspiration

Theologians on the traditional side of the modern debate dispute Harvey's conclusion. They have responded with loud and repeated rebuttals, denouncing the use of critical methods of interpretation and defending their belief that the Bible is the inspired Word of God. Their defense of the traditional belief usually focuses on two related issues: the relationship between the Holy

---

12. Funk, "The Issue of Jesus," 11.
13. Harvey, *The Historian*, 106.
14. Ibid., 109–10.
15. Ibid., 110.
16. Borg, *Reading the Bible Again*, 27.

Spirit and the biblical texts, and the complete historical truthfulness (inerrancy) of the biblical record. This view of the Scriptures was fully articulated in dogmatic terms for the first time with the orthodox dogmaticians of the seventeenth century. They put into writing what became known in general terms as "the doctrine of inspiration."[17]

Proponents of the doctrine of inspiration typically argue that, although the human author physically moved the pen, the Holy Spirit is ultimately responsible for what has been written in the Bible. The prophets and apostles wrote according to their own particular style and disposition, but the Spirit worked alongside them in a supernatural way to ensure that their words were perfect and true. The Spirit gave them the impulse and the command to write and provided the inner revelation and information to be recorded. Abraham Calov, for instance, says the Spirit "accommodated himself at times to the ordinary manner of speaking, leaving to the writers their modes of speech. And yet we must not deny that the Holy Spirit inspired them in the very words."[18] Because the Holy Spirit is the ultimate author of the Scriptures, every jot and tittle in the Bible is equally and completely inspired—no matter how insignificant it might appear. Because every jot and tittle is *inspired*, they are all completely reliable and true. Indeed, the inspiration of the entire biblical account depends on the inspiration of every single word.[19] More recently Carl Henry has become a standard-bearer of the doctrine of inspiration. His focus on inerrancy is central to his understanding of what it means for the Bible to be inspired: "Inspiration is a supernatural influence upon divinely chosen prophets and apostles whereby the Spirit of God assures the truth and trustworthiness of their oral and written proclamation."[20]

The focus on biblical inerrancy as the first and more important corollary to biblical inspiration has resulted in a situation in which inerrancy is often (in practice, at least) the article on which the church stands or falls. Lindsell, in *The Battle for the Bible*, makes this point explicit by suggesting that the most fundamental question in Christian theology is this: "Is the Bible

---

17. There is no single "official" doctrine of inspiration. The following description follows Robert Preus' *The Inspiration of Scripture*, which is generally recognized as the definitive account of the doctrine of inspiration as it was developed by the orthodox dogmaticians of the seventeenth century. This account is consistent with current evangelical accounts of the doctrine of inspiration, including Carl Henry's six-volume account in *God, Revelation, and Authority*.

18. Quoted in Preus, *The Inspiration of Scripture*, 65.

19. Preus, *The Inspiration of Scripture*, 39.

20. Henry, *God, Revelation, and Authority*, 4:129.

trustworthy?"[21] To answer in the negative is not only to fall on the wrong side of the modern debate. It is ultimately a departure from historic Christianity itself.

The End of the Modern Battle

After centuries of fighting over the historical truthfulness of the Scriptures, it is becoming clear that there are problems with both modern ways of thinking about the Bible. Critical theologians, when they are consistent, are left with only one option: a rejection of historic Christianity and the adoption of what Funk calls a "new gospel." Many have become uneasy with this conclusion. Carl Braaten and Robert Jenson explain, "The historical-critical method was originally devised and welcomed as the great emancipator of the Bible from ecclesiastical dogma and blind faith. Some practitioners of the method now sense that the Bible may have meanwhile become its victim."[22] Joseph Ratzinger expressed a similar sentiment: "To speak of the crisis of the historical-critical method today is practically a truism. This despite the fact that it had gotten off to so optimistic a start."[23] Despite its initial and widespread acceptance, the growing consensus among Christian scholars is that historic Christianity is incompatible with a consistently critical approach to the Scriptures.[24]

On the other side of the debate is the doctrine of inspiration. It is also inadequate, but for different reasons. The first problem is that, in response to the critical claims that the Scriptures contain errors, proponents of the doctrine of inspiration have conceived of the Spirit's "inspiring" as little more than guaranteeing propositional inerrancy. They have paid little attention to the work of the Spirit in relation to Jesus and proclamation of his Gospel.[25] Robert Preus acknowledges, "Yes, the powerful emphasis of a Luther upon the centrality of justification is wanting in some of the theological literature of the seventeenth century . . . It is true that their treatment of the *sola scriptura* is more detached from the article of justification than

---

21. Lindsell, *Battle*, 18.
22. Braaten and Jenson, *Reclaiming the Bible*, ix.
23. Ratzinger, "Foundations and Approaches," 593.
24. Gerhard Maier discusses some of the fatal problems with the critical approach to the Scriptures. See *The End of the Historical-Critical Method*, 11–49.
25. Carl Henry's eight theses describing biblical inspiration are a clear example of this. See *God, Revelation, Authority*, 144–61.

it might have been."²⁶ This detachment from Christ and the Gospel has led proponents of the doctrine of inspiration to focus far too much attention on issues peripheral to the church's mission of proclaiming Christ crucified.²⁷

A second problem with the doctrine of inspiration is that, in order to justify the Scriptures as the source and norm of dogmatic theology, dogmatic accounts of the Scriptures have migrated to the prolegomena. Theologically detached from the rest of the Christian confession, the doctrine of inspiration has been imagined, not as an article of faith, but as an *a priori* foundation outside the realm of belief. This dogmatic separation of the Scriptures from Christ and the gospel has contributed to widespread confusion about the nature and function of the Scriptures in the economy of salvation. Many proponents of the traditional belief think of the Bible as little more than a collection of divinely inspired pieces of information. The message of the cross has been viewed, not as the center and foundation of the Christian faith, but as one more of God's many revealed truths. In addition, the migration of the Scriptures to the prolegomena has forced the doctrine of inspiration to provide the epistemological warrant for the rest of the Christian confession. The entire Christian faith has been thought to depend on the inspiration (and inerrancy) of every single word.

Harvey suggests that the problems with the doctrine of inspiration began with the initial response of the "believers" to the criticism of the "historians." Faced with challenges to the traditional view, believers had three options: "(1) They could appeal to the state to repress the new and dangerous doctrines; (2) they could retreat from discussion and hold up to ridicule the occasional inconsistencies and extravagances of the new science; and (3) they could step into the arena of debate and attempt to vindicate their own view."²⁸ At great cost, Harvey argues, they chose the third option:

> The only really viable alternative was to enter the lists of the debate and to attempt to vindicate the truth of the sacred narratives. To do this, however, it was necessary to pay a costly price: it was necessary to accept the general canons and criteria of just those one

---

26. Preus, *Inspiration*, 209–10. Preus recognizes this problem with the doctrine of inspiration, but he does not offer a solution.

27. Hermann Sasse criticizes those who focus on obscure details (such as ventilation in the belly of the great fish in the book of Jonah) in order to defend biblical inerrancy. He notes a 1927 study published in the *Princeton Theological Review* that argues that the temperature inside the great fish was 104–7 degrees Fahrenheit. See Feuerhahn and Kloha, *Scripture and the Church*, 99–100.

28. Harvey, *The Historian*, 104–5.

desired to refute. One had, so to speak, to step onto the ground that the critics occupied. This was fatal to the traditionalist's cause, because he could no longer appeal to the eye of faith or to any special warrants. The arguments had to stand or fall on their own merits.[29]

As Harvey sees it, the doctrine of inspiration was in trouble from the start. The seventeenth-century dogmaticians allowed the debate over the Scriptures to become an argument over whether or not the Scriptures are historically true, and in doing so they sacrificed their ability to articulate a theology of Scripture on their own terms.

The Impact on the Theology of Scripture

The doctrine of inspiration is not necessarily *wrong*. But is not the most helpful way of thinking about the Bible. This can be seen as we take a closer look at three fundamental biblical issues: canon, authority, and interpretation.[30]

Canon

For all the debate about the Scriptures in modern times, the question of the canon has played a surprisingly minor role. Traditional accounts of the doctrine of inspiration make little mention of the canon,[31] and with the exception of an occasional ecclesiastical controversy,[32] the canonical question has been a nonissue in modern theology. In recent decades, however, this

---

29. Ibid., 105–6. Harvey's claim that it was *necessary* for conservative theologians to accept the general canons and criteria of the critics may be debated. Indeed, the purpose of this book to offer a more helpful way of articulating a theology of Scripture that is consistent the traditional Christian confession.

30. These three aspects of the theology of Scripture are inseparably connected. In many ways they are three different ways of looking at the same issue. The canonicity of a book, for example, is based on and helps determine its authority, which is grounded in and exercised through its interpretation. Although they are distinguished here for heuristic purposes, canon, authority, and interpretation cannot be separated.

31. Robert Preus discusses the question of the canon only briefly in the preface. *Inspiration*, xi–xv.

32. A dispute arose in the Lutheran Church—Missouri Synod (LCMS) in the 1850s, for example, when a pastor named Roebbelen was charged with false teaching for stating that, with Luther, he did not consider the book of Revelation to be the inspired Word of God. Roebbelen was exonerated by the president of the LCMS, C. F. W. Walther, with extensive quotations from Martin Chemnitz's examination of the Council of Trent. See Pieper, *Christian Dogmatics*, 1:331–32.

has begun to change. There has been an increasing interest in the historical and theological issues involved in the process of canonization. In order to understand why the canon question has been missing from most of the modern debate, it is helpful to investigate the point at which it faded from the discussion. This requires a return to the sixteenth century.

On April 5, 1546 the Council of Trent officially established the biblical canon in Roman Catholic theology.[33] Trent listed the contents of the Old and New Testaments, "lest doubt should arise in anyone's mind which the books are that are received by this synod."[34] On this list are the thirty-nine Old Testament and twenty-seven New Testament books that traditionally make up the Protestant Bible, as well as seven additional books commonly known as the Apocrypha.[35] Trent makes no mention of the distinctions made since the fourth century between the *homologoumena* and *antilegomena*.[36] It simply decrees, "If anyone does not accept these books whole, with all their parts, as they have customarily been read in the Catholic Church and are contained in the old Vulgate Latin edition, as sacred and canonical, and knowingly and intentionally despises the above-named traditions, let him be anathema."[37] With this decree the Council of Trent marked a turning point in the history of the biblical canon. For fifteen hundred years the exact boundaries of the canon had not been decisively determined. By closing the canon with a conciliar decree so late in the process, Rome sidestepped the historical witness of the early church. In his comprehensive *Examination of the Council of Trent* (1565–1573) Martin Chemnitz sharply criticizes this move:

> Can the present church make those writings concerning which the most ancient church had doubts because of the contradiction of some, because the witness of the primitive church concerning

---

33. The text of the decrees concerning Scripture in the Council of Trent can be found in Martin Chemnitz, *Examination of the Council of Trent*.

34. Chemnitz, *Examination*, 168.

35. The Apocrypha includes Tobit, Judith, Wisdom, Ecclesiasticus, Baruch, and First and Second Maccabees.

36. The *homolegoumena* (literally, "agreed upon") were books that were universally recognized as canonical Scripture in the early church. Eusebius included in this group the four Gospels and Acts, the Pauline letters (including Hebrews), 1 Peter, and 1 John. The *antilegomena* (literally, "spoken against") were books whose canonicity was disputed in some circles at the time of Eusebius. He includes James, Jude, 2 Peter, 2 and 3 John, and Revelation in this group. For a discussion of these distinctions see Bruce, *The Canon of Scripture*, 197–207 and Everett R. Kalin, "The New Testament Canon of Eusebius" in MacDonald and Sanders, *The Canon Debate*, 386–404.

37. Chemnitz, *Examination*, 168.

them did not agree—can the present church, I ask, make those writings canonical, catholic, and equal to those which are of the first class? The papalists not only argue that they can do this, but they, in fact usurp this authority in that they totally obliterate the necessary distinction of the primitive and most ancient church between the canonical and apocryphal, or ecclesiastical, books.[38]

Chemnitz's point is simple. The church does not have the authority to change the historical record. The exact boundaries of the canon were never firmly settled in the early church. If Rome is able to canonize books that were not universally recognized as canonical in the first few centuries, Chemnitz asks, what should stop it from canonizing the likes of Aesop's fables?[39] He concludes, "The church does not have such power, that it can make true writings out of false, false out of true, out of doubtful and uncertain, certain, canonical and legitimate."[40]

Despite Chemnitz's critique, Trent had spoken and the canon was closed in Rome. It was not long before Reformed churches followed suit by closing the canon in their confessional writings. The Thirty-Nine Articles (1571) listed the books of the Old Testament, explicitly rejecting the apocryphal books that had been canonized by Trent. The Belgic Confession, adopted in revised form at the Synod of Dordt in 1618, listed all sixty-six books of the Protestant canon with the assertion that there can be no quarrel about their authority as Holy Scripture. The Westminster Confession of Faith (1646) similarly named the sixty-six books of the Protestant canon as the written Word of God, insisting that all of them were given by divine inspiration. Much like the Council of Trent, these confessional statements closed the canon within the Reformed traditions.

Unlike the Catholics and the Reformed, the sixteenth-century Lutherans insisted on leaving the question of the canon open. They did not list the books of the Old or New Testament in the Book of Concord (1580) and, with Chemnitz, they retained the historic distinctions between the New Testament *homologoumena* and *antilegomena*. They acknowledged the lack of certainty in the early church surrounding a few of the biblical books and they emphasized the primary authority of the undisputed books.[41] Early in the

38. Ibid., 180.
39. Ibid., 181.
40. Ibid.
41. One of the ways in which the distinctions between the *homolegoumena* and the *antilegomena* were maintained involved the order in which the books of the New Testament were arranged. Luther, for instance, placed James, Jude, Hebrews and Revelation

seventeenth century, however, the distinctions between the *homologoumena* and the *antilegomena* gradually disappeared among the Lutherans. J. A. O. Preus identifies Johann Gerhard (1582–1637) as the turning point: "Gerhard marks a definite change in thinking among Lutherans on this subject . . . [A]fter his time the dogmaticians, while still paying lip-service to Chemnitz, for all practical purposes abolished the distinction between homolegoumena and antilegomena."[42] With a gradual shift away from Luther and Chemnitz's thinking about the canon, it was not far into the seventeenth century before the Lutherans (in practice, at least) had adopted the Reformed position and began operating with a closed canon.

Before examining the consequences of these developments, it is useful to ask why the Lutheran dogmaticians moved away from Luther and Chemnitz on the question of the canon. To answer this question it is helpful to recall the focus of the modern battle for the Bible. As Rome questioned the sole authority of the Scriptures, and as early rationalists attacked the reliability of the biblical writings, defenders of the traditional view focused their attention on the Holy Spirit's relationship to biblical texts and the implications this had for their historical truthfulness. It became important to those who defended the traditional belief to insist upon full, verbal inspiration of the Bible *as a whole*. Because the battle was being waged over the Bible as a single entity, many traditionalists seemed to have thought that questioning any portion of the Scriptures would concede victory to the critics. As Robert Preus puts it, "If the inspiration of only one verse is denied, then all Scripture is not inspired."[43] Acknowledging uncertainties about the exact boundaries of the canon seemed to have put inspiration itself at risk. It did not help, of course, that some of Luther's more striking statements about James were highlighted by critics to support their attacks against the Bible.[44] J. A. O. Preus writes, "Luther's position on James in particular and the early Lutheran position on the *antilegomena* in general were unpleasant and embarrassing to the Lutherans."[45]

---

at the end of his German translation after a blank page, clearly separating them from the rest of the New Testament. See Bruce, *The Canon of Scripture*, 243.

42. Preus, "New Testament Canon," 21.

43. Preus, *Inspiration*, 39.

44. It is commonly known that in his first preface to James, Luther describes it as "an epistle of straw." In 1542 Luther wrote, "I almost feel like throwing Jimmy in the stove." See Mark Thompson, *A Sure Ground*, 132–38.

45. Preus, "New Testament Canon," 24.

In addition to ignoring the differences between books that *did* exist in the early church, the Lutheran dogmaticians of the seventeenth century introduced a new distinction to support their doctrine of inspiration. In place of the historic distinctions between *homologoumena* and *antilegomena*, they began speaking of differences between the "primary" and "secondary" authors of the Scriptures. The primary author was the Holy Spirit. The secondary author was the human writer. Gerhard explains:

> There have been noted certain books of the New Testament called apocryphal, but almost for no other reason than that there was doubt concerning them—not whether they were written by the inspiration of the Holy Ghost, but whether they were published by the apostles by whom they had been signed. But because there was no doubt concerning the more important of their authors, namely, the Holy Ghost (but only concerning their writers or ministering authors), and because despite this doubtful authority of these books certain outstanding ancients of the church had raised them to a high level, they have obtained equal authority with the canonical books in the opinion of many people. Indeed, in order that a certain book be regarded as canonical, it is not necessarily required that there be agreement concerning the secondary author or writer. It is sufficient if there be agreement concerning the primary author, or dictator, who is the Holy Ghost.[46]

This distinction between primary and secondary authorship was an invention of the seventeenth-century dogmaticians. It had no basis in the early church or the Reformation.[47] Although it was intended to safeguard the inspiration of every book in the Bible (including the *antilegomena*), the cost was a disregard for the historical record. Robert Preus summarizes, "The views of the dogmaticians regarding canonicity seem to misunderstand and therefore fail to meet the issues of the question in the ancient church."[48]

Partially because of Lutheranism's tacit acceptance of the Reformed position, the question of the canon has been largely ignored for the last three hundred years.[49] Recent questions about the formation of the New Testament, however, have forced defenders of the traditional view to revisit the matter. Ben Witherington III summarizes some of the issues involved in his

---

46. Quoted in ibid., 19.
47. Ibid.; see also Preus, *Inspiration*, xiii.
48. Preus, *Inspiration*, xi.
49. J. A. O. Preus notes that the question of the canon among Lutherans has not changed since 1700 ("The New Testament Canon," 24).

article, "Why the Lost Gospels Lost Out."[50] He begins by reviewing a scene in Dan Brown's best-selling novel, *The DaVinci Code*. In what has become an infamous fictional discussion, one of Brown's main characters challenged the traditional account of the canonization process. He asserted that Emperor Constantine commissioned the writing of a new Bible to support his view of Christ's divinity. Although there were actually some eighty different gospels that had equal claims to the truth about Jesus, Constantine chose to canonize four that served his agenda. These four were included in the Bible in the fourth century and have remained there to this day. The other gospel accounts, the story goes, were unjustly outlawed and destroyed.[51] What ultimately determined the shape of the canon in this view was not that some books were "inspired" and others were not, but that a number of books fell victim to an ecclesio-political power play. Brown's fictional conversation reflects a number of recent proposals by scholars such as Elaine Pagels and Bart Ehrman. Together with recent archeological discoveries of documents like the *Gospel of Judas*, they have challenged the traditional view of the canon and contributed to a renewed interest (among Christians and non-Christians alike) about the contents of the biblical canon.

The question for our purposes is this: "How helpful is the doctrine of inspiration for responding to these challenges?" One way of answering this question is to examine how defenders of the traditional view of the Bible have responded. Witherington is a ready example. In order to defend the traditional canon, he highlights the historical record. He argues that such writings as *The Gospel of Thomas*, *The Gospel of Philip*, and other noncanonical gospels were never recognized as equals to the four canonical gospels. As evidence he points to the early church's practice of collecting and circulating texts that were recognized as genuinely apostolic. He highlights 2 Peter 3:16, which indicates Paul's letters were known as a collection at the end of the first century. He refers to Harry Gamble's *Books and Readers in the Early Church*, which argues that a Pauline collection circulated as the earliest and most authentic interpretation of the Christian faith. He points to Martin Hengel's *Four Gospels and the One Gospel of Jesus Christ*, which shows that the four canonical gospels appeared together early in the second century as one of the first collections to circulate in codex form. With these historical studies as his support, Witherington concludes: "[B]y the New Testament period, there was already a core of documents and ideas by which Christians could evaluate

---

50. Witherington, "Why," 26–32.
51. Brown, *DaVinci Code*, 231.

other documents . . . There was never a time when a wide selection of books, including gnostic ones, were widely deemed acceptable."[52]

My purpose at this point is not to evaluate how well Witherington defends the traditional canon but to consider the role of the doctrine of inspiration in his defense of the traditional canon. It is significant that Witherington bases his defense of the traditional canon almost entirely on the historical record. He points to a core of New Testament documents that were recognized as uniquely authoritative already in the first century. He cites examinations of the way in which early Christians collected and circulated the four canonical gospels and the Pauline epistles. He highlights the writings of Irenaeus and Justin and other church fathers, and concludes that recent conspiracy theories about "lost gospels" are inconsistent with the history of the early church. Importantly, he does not mention the doctrine of inspiration. Neither the internal testimony of the Spirit nor biblical inerrancy appears anywhere in his argument. The reason is simple: the doctrine of inspiration is unable to provide any real support for the traditional understanding of the canon. Its focus on the Holy Spirit's supernatural relationship to the text offers no foundation for handling serious questions about the canonization process. Not only does the doctrine of inspiration fail to meet the issues of the early church[53]—it also fails to meet the needs of the twenty-first-century church.

Authority

A central and explicit issue in the modern battle for the Bible has been biblical authority. In a collection of essays written by some of the most prominent defenders of doctrine of inspiration in the twentieth century, Carl Henry summarizes the heart of the struggle: "In assessing the fortunes of Christianity in our century, we all agreed that authority, particularly the authority of Scripture, is the watershed of Christian conviction." He goes on, "We concurred, too, that the Christian impact in our lifetime had suffered immeasurably from liberal Protestant deletion of authority from biblical religion."[54] Those who defend biblical inspiration view the use of critical tools of investigation in the study of the Scriptures as a direct attack on biblical authority. They view the liberal rejection of biblical authority as *the* central problem in modern theology, lamenting the fact that "the notion of the Bible as the

---

52. Witherington, "Why," 29.
53. Preus, *Inspiration*, xi.
54. Henry, *Revelation and the Bible*, 7.

authoritative word for everyone has long since vanished."⁵⁵ On the other side of the modern debate, critical theologians have concluded that the idea of biblical authority is a thing of the past. The Bible may no longer be considered inspired nor inerrant; many of its stories are fictional; its commands cannot apply to people of all times and places. It remains a useful book in many ways, but the Bible is no more authoritative than any other significant human composition.⁵⁶

Despite all the energy that has been spent debating biblical authority in modern times, proponents of the doctrine of inspiration have actually said surprisingly little about the substance of biblical authority. They have focused attention on explaining and defending its *basis*, which is "its divine origin . . . its inspiration."⁵⁷ They point to Paul's description of the Scriptures as *theopneustos* (2 Tim 3:16) and 2 Peter's comment that the prophets were "carried along by the Holy Spirit" (2 Pet 1:21). They conclude that the inevitable result of the divine origin of the Scriptures is that they are completely inerrant. The logic goes something like this: (a) the Scriptures are authoritative because they are inspired by the Holy Spirit; (b) because they are inspired they are historically true; (c) their authority, therefore, stands or falls with their historical truthfulness. Lindsell argues, "The authority of the Bible is viable only if the Bible itself is true. Destroy the trustworthiness of the Bible, and its authority goes with it. Accept its trustworthiness and authority becomes normative . . . Infallibility and authority stand or fall together."⁵⁸ The supposed strength of this approach is its defense of the belief *that* the Bible is authoritative. The problem is that it offers very little direction for thinking about *how* the Bible is authoritative.

N. T. Wright points out that this is a significant deficiency. He notes that, for all the talk among proponents of the doctrine of inspiration *about* the Bible's authority, few have explained what they understand the phrase "authority of Scripture" actually to mean. This is a problem, Wright notes, because the phrase "authority of Scripture" is a slogan. It is shorthand, and as such does not do nearly as much as it first appears. He compares it to a suitcase:

> Slogans and clichés are often shorthand ways of making more complex statements. In Christian theology, such phrases regularly act as

---

55. Freitheim and Froehlich, *The Bible as the Word of God*, 11.
56. See Borg, *Reading the Bible*, 26.
57. Preus, *Inspiration*, 89.
58. Lindsell, *Battle*, 39.

"portable stories," that is, ways of packing up longer narratives about God, Jesus, the church and the world, folding them away into convenient suitcases, and then carrying them about with us . . . Shorthands, in other words, are useful in the same way that suitcases are. They enable us to pick up lots of complicated things and carry them around all together. But we should never forget the point of doing so, like the point of carrying belongings in a suitcase, is that they can then be unpacked and put to use in the new location. Too much debate about scriptural authority has had the form of people hitting one another over the head with locked suitcases. It is time to unpack our shorthand doctrines, to lay them out and inspect them. Long years in a suitcase may have made some of the contents go moldy. They will benefit from fresh air, and perhaps a hot iron.[59]

Wright unpacks "the authority of Scripture" by identifying an important gap in the doctrine of inspiration. All authority belongs to God alone (Rom 13:1; see also John 19:11). God exercises his authority on earth through his Son: "All authority in heaven and on earth has been given to me" (Matt 28:18). If there is such a thing as scriptural authority, Wright reasons, it must be shown how it is related to the authority given to Jesus. "The phrase 'authority of Scripture' can only make Christian sense if it is shorthand for 'the authority of the Triune God exercised somehow *through* Scripture.'"[60]

Standing behind Wright's concerns about the doctrine of inspiration is the idea that authority is a functional concept. David Kelsey makes this point in *Proving Doctrine: The Uses of Scripture in Modern Theology*. He observes that "global affirmations of the Bible's authority, which were commonplace in [modern] doctrines of scripture, were so vague as to be nearly meaningless."[61] In order to dig deeper, Kelsey ignores what modern theologians *say* about scriptural authority and instead investigates the ways in which the Scriptures *function* in their theological proposals. Contrary to the claims of Lindsell (that authority stands or falls with inerrancy), he argues that virtually every modern theologian assigns some sort of authority to the Scriptures, no matter how critical they may be of inspiration and inerrancy. Kelsey's study of the use of the Scriptures is helpful because it demonstrates the confusion that surrounds the (still) unpacked phrase, "the authority of Scripture." He shows that blanket denials or affirmations of biblical authority are less helpful than they first appear. In fact, they are virtually meaningless,

---

59. Wright, *Scripture*, 18.
60. Ibid., 17.
61. Kelsey, *Proving Doctrine*, xi.

for inherent in the identification of a writing as "scripture" in the first place is the assignment of at least some sort of authority. He explains:

> "Authoritative" is part of the meaning of "scripture"; it is not a *contingent* judgment made about "scripture" on other grounds, such as their age, authorship, miraculous inspiration, etc . . . To call certain texts "scripture" is, in part, to say that they ought to be *used* in the common life of the church in normative ways such that they decisively rule its form of life and forms of speech. Thus part of what it means to call certain texts "scripture" is that they are authoritative for the common life of the church. It is to say of them that they *ought* to be used in certain ways to certain ends in that life.[62]

Simply put, the phrase "authority of Scripture" can only make theological sense if it is understood in functional terms. We must ask not only *if* the Scriptures are authoritative, but more importantly we must also ask *how* the Scriptures function authoritatively in the church.[63]

Interpretation

In the introduction I described Christian history as an "ongoing encounter with Holy Scripture." At this point we might revise that description by speaking of Christian history as "the history of the *interpretation* of Scriptures." Beginning with Jesus, who interpreted the prophetic writings as referring to himself (e.g., Luke 24:25–27, 44–47; John 5:39), the history of Christianity could be written in terms of the developments that have occurred in biblical interpretation. Debates in the early church between Alexandria and Antioch revolved around the use of allegory and typology; interpretation in the Middle Ages was governed by the fourfold method; the Reformation was, in part, a struggle to identify the rightful interpreter of the Scriptures—the papacy or ordinary Christians; and in modern times attention has focused on the propriety of historical-critical methods of interpretation. That leads us to the contemporary situation. It has recently been said that "the 'hermeneutical

---

62. Ibid., 97–98.

63. See Wenz, *Das Wort Gottes*, 11. He writes, "Strittig ist nicht ob, sondern, 'wie' die Schrift 'Autorität sei und normierende Kraft gegenüber allen christlich-theologischen Aussagen besitze.'" ("The point at hand is not whether, but 'how' the Scriptures are the authority and possess norming force over against all Christian theological assertions.'")

issue' has surfaced with a vengeance"[64] and that the interpretation of the Scriptures is "the soul of theology."[65]

There are many different directions a discussion about biblical interpretation in contemporary theology might take, for the number of interpretative issues has grown significantly in recent decades. In a study of the current situation, the Pontifical Biblical Commission summarizes the landscape by dividing the various methods and approaches into six categories: (1) historical-criticism (including textual, form, and redaction criticism), (2) literary criticism (including rhetorical, narrative, and semiotic analysis), (3) approaches based on tradition (including canonical criticism, recourse to Jewish tradition, and *Wirkungsgeschichte*), (4) approaches that use the human sciences (including sociology, cultural anthropology, and psychology), (5) contextual approaches (including liberationist and feminist perspectives), and (6) fundamentalist interpretation.[66] Each of these are part of the postmodern hermeneutical context, resulting in what John Webster has appropriately called "a great tangle of issues."[67] Rather than attempting to untangle all of these issues, my goal is to consider the modern approach to biblical interpretation.

Until recently, proponents of the doctrine of inspiration have said relatively little about the interpretation of the Scriptures. What they have said has usually been limited to a rejection of the historical-critical method. This is not actually as helpful as it first appears, however, primarily because historical criticism lacks a precise definition. Rather than being a single method, it is more like a "shifting set of conventions, never clearly defined and constantly under negotiation."[68] Instead of joining the attack against historical criticism, therefore, it seems more helpful to take a step back and examine how modern theology has conceived of biblical interpretation in the first place. For all their differences regarding the historical truthfulness of the Scriptures, modern theologians on both sides of the debate tend to conceive of biblical interpretation in remarkably similar ways. Webster suggests that the modern conception of interpretation flows from a distinctively modern anthropology. This anthropology is shaped by two fundamental

---

64. Silva, *Has the Church Misread the Bible?*, 2.
65. Vanhoozer, "Lost in Interpretation?," 89.
66. Pontifical Biblical Commission, "The Interpretation of the Bible," 497–524.
67. Webster, "Hermeneutics in Modern Theology," 307.
68. Watson, "A Response," 518. For this reason outright rejections of historical-criticism as a single method of interpretation are not very helpful.

ideas about humankind: "immediacy and autonomy."[69] These two underlying themes govern modern interpretation, regardless of a given interpreter's belief about whether or not the Scriptures are historically true. These ideas about humankind manifest themselves in biblical interpretation as scholars approach the Scriptures with attitudes of individualism and objectivism.

Much like modernity in general, modern interpretation of the Scriptures has been characterized by a spirit of individualism. This can be seen among traditional and critical theologians alike. Stanley Hauerwas suggests that this individualistic spirit has been detrimental to the communal nature of biblical interpretation. "Indeed literalistic-fundamentalism and the critical approaches to the Bible are but two sides of the same coin, insofar as each assumes that the text should be accessible to anyone without the necessary mediation by the church. The reformation doctrine *sola scriptura*, joined to the invention of the printing press and underwritten by the democratic trust in the intelligence of the 'common person,' has created the situation that now makes people believe they can read the Bible 'on their own.'"[70] William Willimon agrees. He argues that both sides of the modern debate have "assumed that it is possible for the Bible to make sense apart from the living, breathing community which makes it make sense. Both groups assumed that it was possible to understand the Bible, the church's book, without being converted into the church's faith."[71]

Statements like these of Hauerwas and Willimon raise eyebrows among those who consider themselves heirs of the Reformation. At the center of debate in the sixteenth century was the ability of ordinary Christians to interpret the Scriptures without the controlling supervision of the Roman magisterium. Luther's immortalized confession at the Diet of Worms captures the Reformation interpretive spirit: "Unless I am convinced by the testimony of the Scriptures or by clear reason (for I do not trust either in the pope or in councils alone, since it is well known that they have often erred and contradicted themselves) I am bound by the Scriptures I have quoted and my conscience is captive to the Word of God."[72] Luther's interpretative declaration of independence has lived on in Protestant theology, causing Hauerwas' and Willimon's insistence on bringing interpretation back into the church to sound suspiciously reminiscent of Rome's response to Luther in the Council of Trent:

69. Webster, *Holy Scripture*, 73.
70. Hauerwas, *Unleashing the Scripture*, 17.
71. Willimon, *Shaped by the Bible*, 26.
72. Luther, *LW* 32, 112.

> Furthermore, in order to restrain willful spirits, the synod decrees that no one, relying on his own wisdom in matters of faith and morals that pertain to the upbuilding of Christian doctrine, may twist the Holy Scripture according to his own opinions or presume to interpret Holy Scripture contrary to that sense which holy mother Church has held and holds, whose right it is to judge concerning the true sense and interpretation of the Holy Scriptures, or contrary to the unanimous consensus of the fathers, even though such interpretations should at no time be intended for publication. Those acting contrary to this shall be reported by the ordinaries and be punished with the penalties appointed by law.[73]

On guard against this kind of magisterial supervision, and consistent with modernity's emphasis on the autonomous individual, many modern Protestants have run away from the idea that the church has a necessary role in the proper interpretation of the Scriptures.

It must be acknowledge that the seventeenth-century dogmaticians were not to blame for this. They did not advocate the kind of individualism that has come to characterize modern interpretation. To the contrary, they insisted that the Scriptures are properly interpreted *within* the church. Robert Preus explains: "The orthodox teachers hold that the Church is the interpreter of Scripture, but in such a way that each Christian searches and interprets Scripture himself."[74] The difference between the individualism that governs modern interpretation and the dogmaticians' rejection of Rome's control is that, for the dogmaticians, interpretation belongs to individuals *in the church*. All Christians, they argued, are involved in the interpretation of the Scriptures—but being a Christian necessarily involves being a part of the church. The Reformation emphasis on *sola scriptura* must be seen in these terms. The reformers did not intend for the interpretation of the Scriptures to occur in isolation from the church or from its historic understanding of Christian faith. D. H. Williams explains,

> Magisterial Reformers such as Luther and Calvin did not think of *sola scriptura* as something that could be properly understood apart from the church or the foundational tradition of the church, even while they were opposing some of the institutions of the church . . . The early Reformers declared the Word of God, as it is communicated in Scripture, to be the final judge of all teaching in the church. But functioning as the norm of faith and practice did

---

73. Quoted in Chemnitz, *Examination*, 38.
74. Preus, *Inspiration*, 156.

not mean that Scripture was the sole resource of the Christian faith. As its own history attests, Scripture is never really "alone."[75]

Reinhard Hütter puts it another way: "The Reformation *sola scriptura* does not make the Church superfluous; rather, it implies the Church since it functions as intra-ecclesial criterion, something very different from later, banalized 'thin' version of *sola scriptura*."[76] This "thin" view of *sola scriptura*, coupled with modernity's overall rejection of external authority, has led modern interpreters on both sides of the debate to act as though "Scripture alone" means "my interpretation of Scripture alone." This "hyper-individualism" has led to a "great number of Christians today who think of the Bible as the believer's Bible, not the church's Bible."[77] Hauerwas identifies the result: "Fundamentalists and biblical critics make the Church incidental."[78]

Along with this individualistic attitude, modern theologians tend to think of biblical interpretation as an objective exercise. Charles Hodge, a leading Reformed proponent of the doctrine of inspiration in the nineteenth century, compared biblical interpretation to scientific observation: "If natural science be concerned with the facts and laws of nature, theology is concerned with the facts and laws of the Bible. If the object of the one would be to arrange and systematize the facts of the external world, and to ascertain the laws by which they are determined; the object of the other is to systematize the facts of the Bible, the ascertaining of principles or general truths which those facts involve."[79] Hodge reasons that because the Scriptures are the inspired Word of God and without error, their truth should be clear to any rational person who reads them. R. C. Sproul continues this line of thought today. He suggests that any reasonable person who reads the Bible must come to the conclusion that Jesus is the incarnate Son of God.[80] Willimon describes this objective conception of biblical interpretation: "Common sense, when confronted with the 'facts' of Scripture, could rightly interpret Scripture."[81]

There are a number of problems with viewing the interpretation of the Scriptures in such objective terms. First, the idea that anyone is able to

---

75. Williams, *Evangelicals and Tradition*, 97.
76. Quoted in Hauerwas, *Unleashing the Scripture*, 27n17.
77. Williams, *Evangelicals and Tradition*, 99.
78. Hauerwas, *Unleashing the Scripture*, 26.
79. Quoted in Willimon, *Shaped*, 25.
80. Sproul, *Scripture Alone*, 75.
81. Willimon, *Shaped*, 25.

interpret the Scriptures from a neutral standpoint is no longer defensible. Alister McGrath explains, "As someone who began his academic career as a natural scientist, I am intensely aware of the fact that allegedly neutral 'observation' is actually theory laden . . . [S]ince Bultmann, we have all learned to wonder if there is any such thing as a 'presuppositionless exegesis,' whether in the academy or in the church." He concludes, "The demand for detachment is quite simply an illicit claim to an objectivity that cannot be held in practice."[82] There is no such thing as reading any text, much less the Scriptures, without bias or preconception. This leads to a second problem. An objective view of scriptural interpretation makes faith in Christ and the enlightening work of the Holy Spirit irrelevant. Hauerwas speaks of this problem in a sermon called "The Insufficiency of Scripture":

> To claim that if Jesus had joined us on the Emmaus road, we would have recognized him is not unlike claiming that in order to understand the Scripture all we have to do is pick it up and read it. Both claims assume that "the facts are just there" and that reasonable people are able to see the facts if their minds are not clouded. Yet as we shall see, the story of the Emmaus road makes clear that knowing the Scripture does little good unless we know it as part of a people constituted by the practices of a resurrected Lord. So Scripture will not be self-interpreting or plain in its meaning unless we have been transformed in order to be capable of reading it.[83]

Consistent with the individualism and objectivism that governs modern thinking about interpretation is a particularly modern understanding of the perspicuity of the Scriptures. A standard tenet of the doctrine of inspiration, biblical perspicuity is the affirmation that, because it is God's Word, the Bible's meaning must be understandable by anyone. Robert Preus identifies the key question: "How can we be saved through faith in the message of Scripture if that message is not clear?"[84] The seventeen-century dogmaticians unpacked their understanding of biblical perspicuity with a number of important nuances that are often lost among modern interpreters. First, the dogmaticians insisted that the clarity of the Scriptures applies only to matters of salvation: "It clearly sets forth all we need to know to be saved."[85] Second, and more importantly, they emphasized that true understanding

---

82. McGrath, "Reclaiming Our Roots," 64.
83. Hauerwas, *Unleashing the Scripture*, 49.
84. Preus, *Inspiration*, 156.
85. Ibid.

requires the enlightening work of the Holy Spirit. Again Preus: "A true spiritual understanding, a *noticia Spiritus*, of Scripture is attained only by the regenerate and only by means of illumination which the Holy Spirit bestows through Scripture."[86] The true understanding of the Scriptures can only be brought about by the same Spirit who inspired it. For this reason the dogmaticians emphasized the need for the Holy Spirit to illuminate the reader and enable proper interpretation—an emphasis that is absent among many modern theologians. Even when it is retained in theory, Stephen Fowl observes, it rarely figures prominently in any practical way. "All Christians give some place to the Spirit in interpretation. In fact, however, this often amounts only to lip service."[87]

Summary

To say that the Bible is reliable and true is an important and necessary thing to say. But it is not enough. Konrad Hoffmann explains, "Wenn diese Schrift nichts anderes wäre als ein irrtumsloses Buch, wäre sie wenig... Die Schrift aber ist mehr als ein irrtumsloses Buch... Der treue Gott spricht in diesem Buche... Fehllos, truglos, irrtumslos, ist alles viel zu wenig."[88] Throughout this chapter I have argued that the church needs a theology of Scripture that is able to address serious questions about the canon, authority, and interpretation. In this respect I agree with Gordon Kaufman: the traditional way of speaking about the Bible is no longer acceptable.[89] The time has come for a comprehensive examination of the nature and function of the Scriptures in the economy of salvation that goes beyond modern conceptions and categories. Alister McGrath is hopeful:

> In the recent past, we have been overwhelmed by the force of a rhetoric that has sought to persuade us that there are no other options than an obscurantist fundamentalism and a culturally and intellectually sophisticated liberalism. But that viewpoint now seems to belong to a different world—a world that is now definitely located in the past. The rise of postliberalism and postmodernism

---

86. Ibid., 158.

87. Fowl, *Engaging Scripture*, 11.

88. "If these Scriptures are nothing other than an inerrant book, this would be too little... The true God speaks in this book... 'Free from mistakes,' 'without blemish,' 'inerrant'—these are all too small" (Quoted in Schöne, "Die Irrlehre des Fundamentalismus," 183).

89. Kaufman, "What Shall We Do?," 96.

symbolize—even if they do not resolve—the collapse of confidence in these certainties of yesteryear. We can now begin to work toward the reconstruction and retrieval of our heritage, by reclaiming the Bible for the church.[90]

If there is to be a "triumph of orthodoxy" in the crisis of Scripture, if the Bible is to be reclaimed for the church, we must reconsider of the assumptions, concepts, and categories that have governed the modern debate. This requires a return to the biblical narrative and its focus on Christ crucified.

---

90. McGrath, "Reclaiming Our Roots," 87.

2

Back to the Word
A Dogmatic Relocation

In March of 2005 N. T. Wright published a book in London called *Scripture and the Authority of God*. Eight months the same book appeared in the United States, but this time it had a new name: *The Last Word: Beyond the Bible Wars to a New Understanding of the Authority of Scripture*. Whether the change was an improvement can be debated. Beyond debate is the fact that the revised title better reflects the growing consensus that there are problems with the modern battle over the Bible. An increasing number of contemporary theologians are expressing dissatisfaction with the concepts and categories that have governed modern thinking about the Scriptures. Instead of focusing exclusively on whether or not the Bible is historically true, they are examining the Scriptures in terms of the role they play in God's plan of salvation. Instead of concentrating solely on the relationship between the Holy Spirit and the original texts, they are looking at the Scriptures from a trinitarian perspective. This growing desire to move "beyond the Bible wars" is resulting in a comprehensive reconsideration of the nature and function of the Scriptures in the economy of salvation.

Although widespread interest in the theology of Scripture is a relatively recent development, the move beyond the modern battle began almost a century ago. Karl Barth entered the conversation at a time when the battle for the Bible was at its peak. Rather than joining one side or the other, he saw and addressed problems with both modern approaches. He rejected Protestant liberalism for dismissing the possibility of divine revelation. But he also rejected what he saw to be the doctrine of inspiration's exclusive identification of revelation with the Scriptures. Barth insisted that divine revelation is absolutely necessary for the Christian faith, but that it encompasses more than just the biblical texts.[1] In order to move beyond the modern debate, he shifted the conversation away from a narrow debate about inerrancy toward a fuller consideration of a broader theological concept: the Word of God.

BACK TO THE WORD OF GOD

The cover of the April 20, 1962 issue of *Time* pictures a seventy-five-year-old Swiss theologian standing in front of an empty tomb. Religion editor John Elson introduces him in the feature article:

> On a hill outside Jerusalem, a carpenter from Nazareth, condemned by the Roman Procurator of Judea and the high priest of the Jews, died upon a cross. Four historians of the time soberly reported that he was buried, and that on the third day the carpenter, Jesus, rose from the dead. Since that first Easter, his followers have defied all reason to proclaim that the Jew of Nazareth was the Son of God, who, by dying for man's sin, reconciled the world to its Creator and returned to life in his glory. Christians have always been content to stand by this paradox, this mystery, this unfathomable truth. "If Christ has not been raised," wrote St. Paul to the young church at Corinth, "then our preaching is in vain, and your faith is in vain. If Christ has not been raised, your faith is futile and you are still in your sins." In the 20th century, no man has been a stronger witness to the continuing significance of Christ's death and Christ's return than the world's ranking Protestant theologian, Swiss-born Karl Barth.[2]

Arguably the most influential theologian of the twentieth century,[3] Barth has stood at the center of the theological conversation ever since his 1919 Romans commentary dropped like a bombshell on the playground of liberal theology.[4] He instigated a "real turning point in man's theological thinking,"

---

1. This was nothing new, of course. Christians have always recognized that divine revelation encompasses more than the Scriptures. In terms of the dogmatic treatment of the theology of Scripture in modern theology (especially the doctrine of inspiration), however, revelation and Scripture have often been treated as one and the same.

2. Elson, "Witness to an Ancient Truth," 59.

3. Pope Pius the XII is said to have described Barth as the most important theologian since Thomas Aquinas.

4. Anderson, *A Journey*, 162.

taking his stand "on a new point of departure for the whole problem of theology, a point of departure diametrically opposed to that of most of the other Protestant theologians since the Reformation, so that his theology may be said to represent a Copernican turn in the history of human thought."[5] The heart of this turning point is his doctrine of the Word of God—the subject of his first volume in *Church Dogmatics*.[6]

The origins of Barth's thinking about the Word of God stemmed from a decade of pastoral ministry in the small Swiss town of Safenwil (1911–1921). As a pastor Barth took seriously his duty of proclaiming the Word of God. Because of his high respect for divine transcendence, this fundamental pastoral task created for him an existential dilemma. Like Kierkegaard, he saw an "infinite qualitative difference" between human beings and God. He believed that God's otherness stood at odds with the possibility of human beings actually speaking God's Word. "We are human," he reasoned, "and so cannot speak of God."[7] The only way for humans to speak the Word of God is for God himself to intervene in some miraculous way. "To speak of God seriously," he insisted, "would mean to speak in the realm of revelation and faith. To speak of God would be to speak God's words, the words which can come only from him."[8] In order to make sense of his regular pastoral duty of proclaiming the Word of God, Barth came to depend entirely on the miracle of divine revelation. He believed that if God did not act to reveal himself through human preaching, church proclamation (and Christian theology in general) would be impossible.

Barth's belief in the necessity of divine revelation stands in sharp contrast with the liberal theology of his day. Ever since Schleiermacher made the religious consciousness the center of theology, mainstream Protestant theology found increasingly little room for divine revelation. Continental theology had become the human search for the divine, and Barth's teachers—Wilhelm Herrmann, Adolf von Harnack, Ernst Troeltsch—left the Christian preacher with little more than his own thoughts about God. Klaas Runia summarizes the result: "This means that there is no message from

---

5. Hartwell, *The Theology of Karl Barth*, 1–2.

6. While Barth wrote about the Word of God throughout his career, I will focus primarily on his mature theology of the Word of God as it appears in the first volume of *Church Dogmatics*. For an overview of his earlier writing on the Scriptures and the Word of God, see Bromiley, "The Authority of Scripture," 276–82.

7. Barth, *Word of God and the Word of Man*, 198.

8. Ibid.

God any more, but pious man speaks to himself about himself."[9] When Barth took this liberal theology into the community of the believers at Safenwil, he quickly recognized its bankruptcy. The only option he saw was a complete rejection of everything he had learned and a radical return to the biblical theology of the Reformation.

Despite his rejection of the critical side of the modern debate, Barth was unable to accept the only other modern alternative. "Of the history of the doctrine of inspiration as such, it must still be said that in the Evangelical Church it finally made the statement incomprehensible. After a promising start it was for the most part a chapter of accidents."[10] In Barth's opinion the doctrine of inspiration was significantly flawed, but not because it taught something new about the Scriptures. He acknowledged that it was "merely the development and systematization of statements which had been heard in the Church since the first centuries."[11] Neither did he fault the doctrine of inspiration for being too "supranatural." The opposite was, in fact, the case—the doctrine of inspiration was not "supranatural enough."[12]

In Barth's view the doctrine of inspiration identified revelation directly and exclusively with the Bible. This resulted in a number of significant problems. It led to a "freezing" of the work of the Holy Spirit in the original composition of the texts; it separated the Scriptures from church proclamation; it restricted divine revelation to the conveyance of propositional information; it failed to account for God's continuing work of revelation *through* the Bible; and, most importantly for Barth, it limited God's freedom and grace. In short, Barth thought the doctrine of inspiration dissolved the mystery of the Word of God by denying "the sovereignty of the Word of God and therefore the Word of God itself."[13] He explains what went wrong: "The statement that the Bible is the Word of God was now transformed . . . from a statement about the free grace of God into a statement about the nature of the Bible as exposed to human inquiry brought under human control. The Bible as the Word of God surreptitiously became a part of the natural knowledge of God, i.e., of that knowledge of God which man can have without the free grace of God, by his own power, and with direct insight and assurance."[14] As part of the natural knowledge of God "the Bible was now grounded upon itself apart from the

9. Runia, *Karl Barth and the Word of God*, 1.
10. Barth, *CD* 1/2:526.
11. Ibid., 1/2:525.
12. Ibid.
13. Ibid., 1/2:522.
14. Ibid., 1/2:522–23.

mystery of Christ and the Holy Ghost . . . It was no longer a free and spiritual force, but an instrument of human power."[15]

Starting with Jesus

In order to correct the mistakes of both sides of the modern debate, Barth set about the task of rethinking theology from the ground up. *Church Dogmatics*, as he envisioned it, was an attempt to recover divine revelation and all that it entailed. In contrast to liberalism's reduction of Christian theology to human talk about God, he stressed the necessity of divine revelation as the starting point for all Christian theology. Runia explains his thinking: "Revelation is not a human, but only a divine possibility. God is both the subject and the object of revelation. Even though revelation comes to us in the words of men, it is not these men who are the revealers, but *God Himself reveals Himself* through these men."[16] The only possibility for Christian theology is the reality of divine revelation. Knowledge of God is knowledge of what God has revealed.[17]

To Barth, divine revelation is one and the same as the Word of God. The Word of God, however, is not mere information. It is better understood as an event, a mysterious and miraculous work of God reconciling the world to himself. This gets to the heart of the Christian faith for Barth. The content of revelation (the Word of God) is not information *about* God; it is God himself. "Revelation in fact does not differ from the person Jesus Christ nor from the reconciliation accomplished in Him. To say revelation is to say 'The Word became flesh.'"[18] Simply put, "God's revelation is Jesus Christ, the Son of God."[19] Here we see the central significance of Christology for Barth's theology. As divine revelation and the Word of God, Christ is the substance of all Christian dogmatics. "The content of the New Testament is solely the name Jesus Christ, which, of course, also and above all involves the truth of his God-manhood. Quite by itself this name signifies the objective reality of revelation."[20] Dogmatic theology, therefore, including the dogmatic theology of Scripture, is ultimately nothing more and nothing less than

---

15. Ibid., 1/2:525.
16. Runia, *Karl Barth and the Word of God*, 2. His emphasis.
17. Barth, *CD* 1/1:187.
18. Ibid., 1/1:119.
19. Ibid., 1/1:137.
20. Ibid., 1/2:15.

Christology. "A church dogmatics must, of course, be christologically determined as a whole and in all its parts, as surely as the revealed Word of God, attested by Holy Scripture and proclaimed by the Church, is its one and only criterion, and as surely as this revealed Word is identical with Jesus Christ. If dogmatics cannot regard itself and cause itself to be regarded as fundamentally Christology, it has assuredly succumbed to some alien sway and is already on the verge of losing its character as church dogmatics."[21] The christological center of dogmatic theology reflects the christological center of the biblical narrative. Barth noticed that the entire biblical narrative, both Old and New Testaments, declares the Word of God made flesh:

> Every statement in the New Testament originates in the fact that the Word was made flesh. God's covenant with man, the covenant which God made with Abraham, with Moses and David, finds its reality solely, but completely and finally, in the fact that God was made man, in order that as man He might do what man as such never does, what even Israel never did, appropriate God's grace and fulfill God's law. This is what God did Himself as man in Jesus Christ. For that very reason in Jesus Christ the kingdom of God is at hand, as nigh as it can get while time has not yet become eternity. So the New Testament declares. It declares nothing else, it declares, broadly speaking, nothing more than the Old Testament. But it declares it in a different way, because it is looking back at fulfillment.[22]

For Barth, Christ is the beginning, the end, and the main subject of all Christian theology.[23] Elson summarizes, "Above all [Barth] writes of the mysterious history of Christ. Knowledge of God is knowledge of God through Christ. Faith is faith in Christ; the church is the Church of Christ; the Bible

21. Ibid., 1/2:123.

22. Ibid., 1/2:124.

23. George Hunsinger suggests that Barth's theology is best understood in light of six motifs, or modes of thought. At the heart of all six of them is Jesus. He writes, "In short, as the living reality to whom his scriptural depiction analogically points, and as the divine rationality by whom the understanding sought by faith is warranted, Jesus Christ is the center of the foundational motifs. As the event of the absolute miracle of grace and as the absolute mystery of its content, Jesus Christ is the center of the structural motifs. And as the objective Mediator of revelation and salvation, in whom the truth of God may be known and the reality of humanity found, and as the Word of personal address encountered in fellowship, attested in witness and appropriated by prayer, he is the center of the freestanding motifs. Realism, rationalism, actualism, particularism, objectivism, and personalism, as they shape Karl Barth's theology, are directed toward Christ the center" (*How to Read Karl Barth*, 233).

is the witness of Christ. Theologian Hans Frei calls him a 'Christ-intoxicated man.'"[24]

The Triune Word of the Triune God

Barth's emphasis on the Word made flesh as the focus and starting point for all Christian theology does not limit his conception of the Word of God to Christ alone. In addition to the Word made flesh, he identified the Scriptures as the written Word of God and church proclamation as the spoken Word of God. Similar to the relationship between the Father, the Son, and the Holy Spirit, these three forms of the Word of God (Christ, the Scriptures, and church proclamation) may be distinguished, but not separated. In this respect the Word of God makes up the only true vestige of the Trinity.[25] Barth explains:

> There is only one analogy to this doctrine of the Word of God. Or, more accurately, the doctrine of the Word of God is itself the only analogy to the doctrine which will be our fundamental concern as we develop the concept of revelation. This is the doctrine of the triunity of God. In the fact that we can substitute for revelation, Scripture and proclamation the names of the divine persons Father, Son and Holy Spirit and *vice versa*, that in the one case as in the other we shall encounter the same basic determinations and mutual relationships, and that the decisive difficulty and also the decisive clarity is the same in both—in all this one may see specific support for the inner necessity and correctness of our present exposition of the Word of God.[26]

As Barth saw it, real proclamation of the Word of God should be heard as God's direct address to human beings. "Proclamation is human speech in and by which God Himself speaks like a king through the mouth of his herald, and which is meant to be heard and accepted as speech in and by which God Himself speaks, and therefore heard and accepted in faith as a divine decision concerning life and death, as divine judgment and pardon, eternal Law and eternal Gospel both together."[27] The foundation for church proclamation is God's commission to speak. God calls people to speak on

---

24. Elson, "Witness," 60.
25. Barth, *CD* 1/1:347.
26. Ibid., 1/1:121.
27. Ibid., 1/1:52.

his behalf. He quotes Luther: "If it is to be God's Word, it must be sent."[28] The Word God sends to be proclaimed is not just any word. It is the Word of Christ, the revelation of God, a miracle worked only by God himself. This is an important qualifier for Barth. In order to protect God from being manipulated or controlled by human creatures (including the church), God retains the free decision to (or not to) reveal himself through human proclamation. Proclamation in the church becomes the divine Word only where and when God chooses to speak through it. "The Word of God is the event itself in which proclamation becomes real proclamation."[29] Here is how it works: from time to time God, in his divine freedom, chooses to exalt human speech and speak about himself through the words of his commissioned spokesmen.[30] But because he is sovereign, he is never bound to make human proclamation become "real" proclamation.[31] For this miraculous event the church speaks in hopeful expectation.

This does not mean that God works through just any preaching or speaking in the church, regardless of its content. There is a criterion by which proclamation of the Word is to be judged. This criterion is the church's canon, which is the Bible. For Barth the Scriptures are nothing other than the prophetic and apostolic proclamation put into writing, the "deposit of what was once proclamation by human lips."[32] The Scriptures and proclamation "may thus be set initially under a single genus, Scripture as the commencement and present-day preaching as the continuation of one and the same event, Jeremiah and Paul at the beginning and the modern preacher of the Gospel at the end of one and the same series."[33]

Despite this unity, the Scriptures and proclamation remain distinct as two forms of the Word of God. The difference between them is in the order in which they relate to each other—the "supremacy, the absolutely constitutive significance of the former [Scripture] for the latter [proclamation], the determination of the reality of present day proclamation by its foundation upon Holy Scripture and its relation to this, the basic singling out of the written word of the prophets and apostles over all the later words of men

---

28. Ibid., 1/1:90.

29. Ibid., 1/1:93.

30. Ibid., 1/1:95.

31. By "real" proclamation Barth means human proclamation through which God directly encounters human beings through Christ, the revealed Word.

32. Barth, *CD* 1/1:102.

33. Ibid.

which have been spoken and are to be spoken to-day in the Church."[34] As the church's canon, the Scriptures are the "necessary rule of every word that is valid in the Church."[35] Apostolic succession means that the church is guided by the writings of the apostles.[36]

The Scriptures exist in the church as the canon and written Word of God because they testify to the incarnate Word of God. "The prophetic and apostolic word is the word, witness, proclamation, and preaching of Jesus Christ."[37] They are not only *about* Jesus (who is God's revelation), but like proclamation, from time to time they, too, *become* divine revelation. As they become the Word of God, they impose themselves on the church as the only canon and final authority in the church.[38] Similar to the proclaimed Word of God, the Bible becomes the Word of God *in the event* that God chooses to reveal himself through it. Barth summarizes, "The Bible, then, is not in itself and as such the expected future revelation, just as Church proclamation is not in itself and as such the expected future revelation. The Bible, speaking to us and heard by us as God's Word, bears witness to past revelation. Proclamation, speaking to us and heard by us as God's Word, promises future revelation. The Bible is God's Word as it really bears witness to revelation, and proclamation is God's Word as it really promises revelation."[39]

Barth argues that biblical inspiration must be understood in this context. Instead of thinking of inspiration as a past event or a guarantee of ontological perfection, it is better understood as the work of the Holy Spirit in and through the Scriptures. This includes (especially) the present-day work of the Spirit to enlighten those who read and hear it. This leads Barth away from the *sedes doctrinae* of the doctrine of inspiration (2 Tim 3:16 and 2 Pet 1:21). Instead, he highlights instead Paul's words to the Corinthians:

> So also no one comprehends the thoughts of God except the Spirit of God. Now we have received not the spirit of the world, but the Spirit who is from God, that we might understand the things freely given us by God. And we impart this in words not taught by human wisdom but taught by the Spirit, interpreting spiritual truths to those who are spiritual. The natural person does not accept the things of the Spirit of God, for they are folly to him, and he is

---

34. Ibid.
35. Ibid.,1/1:104.
36. Ibid.,1/1:103.
37. Ibid., 1/1:107.
38. Ibid.; cf. 1/2:540.
39. Ibid., 1/1:111.

not able to understand them because they are spiritually discerned (1 Cor 2:11–14).

Barth does not deny that the biblical writings are inspired. But he insists that inspiration must not be confused with "permanent inspiredness," which is what he sees in the doctrine of inspiration.[40] In contrast, he maintains, a correct understanding of inspiration includes the entire work of the Spirit, from original composition to the reader's illumination. "It is only spiritually, on the basis of the same work of the same Spirit, by which he can know and therefore speak of these benefits, that they can be known and therefore received."[41] He points to 2 Corinthians:

> Such is the confidence that we have through Christ toward God. Not that we are sufficient in ourselves to claim anything as coming from us, but our sufficiency is from God, who has made us competent to be ministers of a new covenant, not of the letter but of the Spirit. For the letter kills, but the Spirit gives life . . . Since we have such a hope, we are very bold, not like Moses, who would put a veil over his face so that the Israelites might not gaze at the outcome of what was being brought to an end. But their minds were hardened. For to this day, when they read the old covenant, that same veil remains unlifted, because only through Christ is it taken away. Yes, to this day whenever Moses is read a veil lies over their hearts. But when one turns to the Lord, the veil is removed. Now the Lord is the Spirit, and where the Spirit of the Lord is, there is freedom. And we all, with unveiled face, beholding the glory of the Lord, are being transformed into the same image from one degree of glory to another. For this comes from the Lord who is the Spirit (2 Cor 3:4–18).

In the end, the key event in biblical inspiration is *not* what the Spirit did when the biblical writings were first composed, but rather what the Spirit does here and now among those who hear and read it. "Everything depends on the fact that without this work of the Spirit Scripture is veiled, however great its glory may be and whatever its origin."[42]

After considering the Scriptures and church proclamation, Barth comes to the third and most important form of the Word of God: Jesus Christ, the "primary" and "absolute" form of the Word.[43] Here he begins to unpack his understanding of revelation in trinitarian terms by identify-

---

40. Ibid., 1/1:112.
41. Ibid., 1/2:516.
42. Ibid., 1/2:515.
43. Ibid., 1/1:290.

ing the Father as the Revealer, Jesus as his Revelation, and the Spirit as the Revealedness.[44] "*God* reveals Himself. He reveals Himself *through Himself*. He reveals *Himself*."[45] It is only in relation to this miracle of divine revelation that proclamation and the Scriptures are properly recognized as the Word of God. To illustrate how this works Barth compares the Word of God to the Pool of Bethesda (see John 5:2–7). As he did with the waters in the Pool of Bethesda, God periodically "stirs" the reading of Scripture and the proclamation of the church so that it might become the Word of God.[46] In this event God encounters human beings through his Word, while at the same time remaining completely free in his decision to (or not to) reveal himself. Proclamation and the Scriptures become the Word of God only where and when it pleases God (*ubi et quando visum est Deo*).[47] "When we speak about revelation we are confronted by the divine act itself and as such . . . [R]evelation is simply the freedom of God's grace."[48] Against the dogmaticians who claim that the Bible is the Word of God even when it is not being used (*extra usum*), Barth restricts the Word of God to the event in which God speaks through it to humankind.[49]

When God chooses *not* speak through the Bible or church proclamation, it would be inaccurate to describe either of them as the Word of God *directly*. Instead, because they must become the Word of God, the Scriptures and proclamation are better understood to be the Word of God *indirectly*. "We know [revelation] only indirectly, from Scripture and proclamation. The direct Word of God meets us only in this twofold mediacy."[50] This does not mean, however, that the Bible and proclamation are anything *less* than the Word of God. Barth explains:

> It is one and the same whether we understand it as revelation, Bible, or proclamation. There is no distinction of degree or value between the three forms. For to the extent that proclamation really rests on recollection of the revelation attested in the Bible and is thus obedient repetition of the biblical witness, it is no less the Word of God than the Bible. And to the extent that the Bible really attests revelation it is no less the Word of God than revelation

---

44. Ibid., 1/1:295.
45. Ibid., 1/1:296. His emphasis.
46. Ibid., 1/1:111; 1/2:530.
47. Ibid., 1/1:117; 1/1:120.
48. Ibid., 1/1:117.
49. Ibid., 1/1:110.
50. Ibid., 1/1:121.

itself. As the Bible and proclamation become God's Word in virtue of the actuality of revelation they are God's Word: the one Word of God within which there can be neither a more nor a less. Nor should we ever try to understand the three forms of the Word of God in isolation.[51]

But is the Bible the Word of God?

At this point many readers of Barth shake their heads in frustration and conclude that the first volume (both parts) of *Church Dogmatics* is a prolonged series of theological contradictions. Despite his frequent affirmations that the Bible is the Word of God, Barth seems to deny the very same thing with such comments as: "There are obvious overlappings and contradictions—e.g., between the Law and the prophets, between John and the Synoptics, between Paul and James";[52] "[The Bible] only 'holds,' encloses, limits and surrounds [God's Word]";[53] "On the one hand *Deus dixit*, on the other *Paulus dixit*. These are two different things."[54] In addition, his frequent insistence the Scriptures must "become" the Word of God,[55] and that the Bible is only a "witness" to the Word create doubt about his statements that the Scriptures are the Word of God.[56] While proponents of the doctrine of inspiration find this apparent inconsistency troubling, many critical theologians have found it attractive. John Morrison explains, "Through Barth, many were attracted to the possibility of substantially 'orthodox' faith commitment and confession without the need wholly to follow the pre-modern Reformers and, even more, pre-modern Protestant Scholasticism's location of present historical authority in the actual concrete text of Holy Scripture as verbally inspired, written Word of God."[57] Many recognized "Barthians" think that Barth separates the Scriptures from the Word of God.[58] Is the Bible the Word of God for Karl Barth? Critics and proponents of the doctrine of inspiration often agree: "no."

51. Ibid., 1/1:120.
52. Ibid.,1/2:509.
53. Ibid., 1/2:492.
54. Ibid., 1/1:113.
55. Ibid., 1/1:110; 1/1:123–24.
56. Ibid., 1/2:463; 1/2:507.
57. Morrison, "Barth, Barthians, and Evangelicals," 188.
58. Ibid., 187.

Despite its widespread acceptance, this reading of Barth's theology of Scripture has recently been called into question. Bruce McCormack argues that many readers of *Church Dogmatics* have not adequately considered the theological ontology that undergirds Barth's doctrine of the Word of God. They have not taken into account his unique understanding of the nature of being. McCormack points to this key statement toward the beginning of the first volume of *Church Dogmatics*:

> The statement that the Bible is God's Word is a confession of faith, a statement of faith that hears God himself speak through the biblical word of humankind. To be sure it is a statement which, when venturing it in faith, we accept as true even apart from our faith and beyond all our faith and even in face of our lack of faith. We do not accept it as a description of our experience of the Bible. We accept it as a description of God's action in the Bible, whatever may be the experiences we have or do not have in this connection. But this is precisely the faith which in this way sees and reaches beyond itself and all related or unrelated experiences to God's action, namely, to the fact that God's action on man has become an event, and not therefore that man has grasped at the Bible but that the Bible has grasped at man. *The Bible, then, becomes God's Word in this event, and in the statement that the Bible is God's Word the little word "is" refers to its being in this becoming.* It does not become God's Word because we accord it faith but in the fact that it becomes revelation to us.[59]

McCormack argues that the Bible *is* the Word of God for Barth, but "is" in this statement refers to a unique understanding of the nature of being. This was not a defensive move, as if he found errors throughout the Scriptures and sought to salvage biblical authority by redefining its ontology. To the contrary, Barth viewed essences as relations, and he believed relations have the character of events.[60] His insistence that the Bible must become the Word of God is based on his belief that *everything* has its being in becoming.[61] McCormack explains, "Barth's understanding of the being-in-becoming of Holy Scripture was a function of his commitment to the being-in-becoming of the God-human, his actualizing of the doctrine of the incarnation, which brought in its wake the necessity of affirming the being-in-becoming of the Trinity, of human beings and, ultimately, of everything that is."[62] George

---

59. Barth, *CD* 1/1:110. Emphasis added.
60. McCormack, "Being," 69.
61. Ibid., 63.
62. Ibid., 64.

Hunsinger calls this aspect of Barth's theology "actualism."[63] To Barth "being" is always "being-in-act." Because God's being occurs in a constant state of activity, God cannot be defined in static terms. He is love; he is grace; he is freedom. He is active in himself as the Father loves the Son, and the Son loves the Father in the unity of the Spirit, and he is active in his relationship with creation as he draws human beings into relationship with him. Human beings, for their part, are completely incapable of establishing fellowship with God. Their salvation depends entirely upon God's gracious act of condescension. Hunsinger summarizes, "Barth's theology of active relations is therefore a theology which stresses the sovereignty of grace, the incapacity of the creature, and the miraculous history whereby grace grants what the creature lacks for the sake of love and freedom."[64] This motif of "actualism" can be seen throughout Barth's doctrine of the Word of God as he repeatedly describes God's Word with the language of event.[65] Morrison explains, "Revelation is that event in which the being of God comes to word, and revelation is, too, God's free decision in eternity to be *our* God, and so to bring himself to speech for us."[66] God's essence does not undergo any kind of change. He exists as he becomes *for us*. His being-in-becoming is his existence as a gracious God.

Human being to Barth is also being-in-becoming, but not in an absolute sense as it is with God. Because of sin, act and being in humans fall apart.[67] God is completely free; humans are only relatively free. God is pure love; humans are love in a contingent sense. God determines his own existence; humans depend on God for their existence.[68] The difference between *divine* being-in-becoming and *human* being-in-becoming comes from two fundamental ideas about the relationship between God and human beings. The first (and most important to Barth's theology) is his emphasis on the ontological chasm that separates God from humanity—the Kierkegaardian "infinite qualitative difference" that separates the Creator from the creatures. Because God is "wholly other," his being-in-becoming is distinct from human being-in-becoming. The second is the presence of sin in human beings, which makes humankind unable to know God. Because they are creatures, and sinful creatures at that, human beings are utterly dependent upon God's

---

63. Hunsinger, *How to Read*, 30.
64. Ibid., 31.
65. Barth, *CD* 1/1:109; 1/1:143; 1/2:503; 1/2:527.
66. Morrison, "Barth," 190. His emphasis.
67. McCormack, "Being," 66.
68. Ibid., 65.

free and gracious decision to restore them to what they truly are: beings in relation to God.

With this activist ontology in mind, Barth's view of the Scriptures must be understood in terms of the event it occasions. McCormack explains,

> First, what the Bible *is*, is defined by the will of God as expressed in his act of giving it to the church. And this means that where and when the Bible *becomes* the Word of God, it is only becoming what it already is. But second, where and when the Bible does *not* become the Word of God, there God has chosen provisionally, for the time being, not to bear witness to himself in and through its witness *to this particular reader or this particular set of readers of it*. This changes nothing whatsoever as to the true nature of the Bible as defined by the divine will which came to expression in the giving of the Bible to the church. It only means that God does not will, for the time being, that the Bible should *become* what it is for these readers.[69]

McCormack points out that Barth's view of the unity between the divine and the human in Scripture is similar to his understanding of the person of Christ. The Bible is neither human only nor divine only, and neither is it a mixture of the two or a *tertium quid*. In its own way and to its own degree it is very God and very man, a witness to revelation which itself belongs to revelation and at the same time is fully human.[70] The union that occurs between God's Word and the human word in the Scriptures does not result in a divinization of the human writings any more than the incarnation results in a divinization of Jesus' humanity. Again McCormack: "If Christ's humanity is true humanity—and it is—then the hypostatic union may not be thought to result in a divinization of the human nature. So, too, in this case, where something a good deal less intimate than hypostatic union is at work: the relation between the divine element and the human element is a relation that Barth describes by means of the metaphor of an 'indirect identity.'"[71] He quotes Barth: "It is quite impossible that there should be a direct identity between the human word of Holy Scripture and the Word of God, and therefore between the creaturely reality in itself and as such and the reality of God the Creator. It is impossible that there should have been a transmutation of the one into the other or an admixture of the one with the other. *This is not*

---

69. Ibid., 66. His emphasis.
70. Barth, *CD* 1/2:501.
71. McCormack, "Being," 68.

even the case in the person of Christ."⁷² McCormack suggests this clarification of Barth's theological ontology enables us to understand what Barth means when he says, "The Bible is not in itself and as such God's past revelation."⁷³ Barth's refusal to identify directly the Scriptures as God's Word or revelation comes from his belief that human realities are unable to contain the divine. Here, McCormack concludes, is the root of the conservative unease with Barth's theology of Scripture:

> At this point, it has to be frankly acknowledged that Barth's denial that the Bible has either an intrinsic or a permanently bestowed capacity to be an adequate bearer of the Word of God is, in large measure, simply a function of the Reformed character of his Christology. If there was a constant in Reformed treatments of the person of Christ, it was that the divine and the human natures of Christ remain undistinct and unimpaired in their original integrity *after* their union in one Person. The writers of the Reformed confessions insisted on this point in order to render impossible the Lutheran affirmation of a communication of the attributes of the "divine majesty" (divine attributes like omnipotence, omniscience and omnipresence) to the human nature of Christ, resulting in a "divinization" of the human nature. If the human nature of Christ is not divinized through the hypostatic union, how much less are the human words of the prophets and apostles divinized through the sacramental union by which God joins them to the Word of God . . . So when evangelical Christians stumble over the claim that human language has no capacity in itself for bearing adequate witness to the Word of God, my suspicion is that they are stumbling not because they are evangelicals, but because they are not *Reformed* evangelicals.⁷⁴

According to McCormack, the source of Barth's refusal to identify the Scriptures as the Word of God is his commitment to a fundamental presupposition in classic Reformed Christology: the finite cannot contain the infinite (*finitum non capax est infiniti*).

Because he views the Word of God as an event, Barth reacts strongly against the seventeenth-century dogmaticians who claimed that the Bible is the Word of God when it is not in use (*extra usum*). Barth considers this a "divinization" of part of creation. In contrast he emphasizes God's being-in-act, claiming that the Word of God does not exist in abstraction or in static terms.

72. Barth, *CD* 1/2:499. Emphasis added.
73. Ibid., 1/1:111.
74. McCormack, "Being," 70. His emphasis.

"It is the divine will and act that make the Bible to be what it is 'essentially.'"[75] This means the book called *The Holy Bible* that is sitting on my desk right now is not directly the Word of God because God is not working through it to reveal himself to me. Therefore it cannot be the Word of God. Even when I pick it up and read it, however, it does not for that reason alone become God's Word, for God is not obligated to reveal himself through it when it is read. When God does not choose to reveal himself, it does not become what it is—but that does not change what it *essentially* is.

With Barth's theological ontology in mind, we might return to the question posed above. Is the Bible the Word of God for Barth? According to McCormack and Morrison, the correct answer to this question is a bit more complicated than simply saying "no." It would be more accurate to answer it like this: "no *and* yes"—and in that order. Apart from God's actualization of it, the book sitting on my desk right now is not the Word of God, for it is not being what it essentially is. It is only what it truly is *where and when* God chooses to reveal himself through it. When God does this, it is entirely accurate to say that the Bible *is* the Word of God.[76]

If McCormack and Morrison are correct, theologians who identify Barth as a critic of the Scriptures have not taken into account his unique theological ontology. While their concerns about some of his more striking statements about the Scriptures are justified, they have not read Barth's theology of Scripture within his particular way of thinking. His activist ontology determines not only the way he views the Scriptures, but more importantly the way he imagines God, the nature of humankind, and the infinite chasm that separates them. If there are problems with his view of the relationship between Scripture and the Word of God, therefore, engagement must begin by taking a closer look at the one who bridged that chasm. We must begin with the person and work of Jesus Christ.

Barth's Impact on the Contemporary Theology of Scripture

Barth's move beyond the modern debate over the Bible has been widely influential in the contemporary theology of Scripture. Telford Work explains, "[Barth's] treatment of the Word of God in its threefold form, with Scripture occupying the place of the second person of the Trinity, has been so

---

75. Ibid.

76. Dietrich Bonhoeffer advised that the only way to understand Barth's theology is temporarily to forget everything you have ever learned (Hartwell, *The Theology of Karl Barth*, 2). When it comes to Barth's theological ontology, that is probably sound advice.

influential that it has set the terms for the twentieth-century discussion of Christology's relevance for bibliology."[77] By offering an alternative way of thinking about the theology of Scripture, Barth changed the way in which the Bible has been imagined in Christian theology. Before we evaluate Barth's theology of Scripture, therefore, it is helpful to take a brief look at the effect he has had on the contemporary discussion.

There are two specific aspects of Barth's doctrine of the Word of God that have been especially influential in the contemporary theology of Scripture. First, theologians have begun investigating more specifically the work that God does *through* the Scriptures. They have moved away from a narrow concentration on whether or not the information in the Bible is historically true and have begun considering more fully its function in the economy of salvation. Second, consistent with the overall revival of the Trinity in twentieth-century Christian theology, Barth offers ways of applying the old rule *opera trinitatis ad extra indivisa sunt* to the theology of Scripture in comprehensive and tangible ways. Rather than focusing exclusively on the relationship between the text and the Holy Spirit, contemporary theologians are following his lead by exploring the various ways in which the Scriptures are related to all three members of the Trinity.

The Function of Scripture

Viewing it primarily as a means of providing information about the past (either about what God has said and done, or about what early Christian communities believed he has said and done), theologians in the modern debate tend to treat the Bible as an object to be studied. This is true for both critics and proponents of the doctrine of inspiration, suggests Willimon. He concludes that the two modern ways of conceiving of the Scriptures are actually two sides of the same coin.[78] Both sides "believe that 'facts,' defined by the prevailing empirical methods of the modern age, are what make any document important."[79] With the focus on the information conveyed in the Bible, God's active work through it has been left out of the discussion. Willimon explains: "The Bible becomes fragmented, uninteresting. The story and its political claim upon us is lost in debates over 'what really happened.'

---

77. Work, *Living and Active*, 19. "Bibliology" is the term that Work uses to describe the doctrine of Scripture.

78. Willimon, *Shaped*, 24. Hauerwas makes a similar claim in *Unleashing the Scripture*, 17.

79. Willimon, *Shaped*, 25.

Modern infatuations—historicism, science, life based only upon what I can know and prove through empirical means—are applied to the Bible in ways that have little to do with the Bible's original intent."[80] John Webster offers a similar criticism. He suggests that modernity's narrow concentration on the historical truthfulness of the Scriptures has resulted in a flattening of the doctrine of revelation. Many proponents of the doctrine of inspiration have identified revelation exclusively with the facts recorded in the Bible. As a result "revelation was transposed rather readily into a feature of generally 'theistic' metaphysical outlooks."[81] Without material reference to soteriology, revelation was conceived of as little more than the sending of divine information. "Understood in this dogmatically minimalistic way, language about revelation became a way of talking, not about the life-giving and loving presence of God the Father of our Lord Jesus Christ in the Spirit's power among the worshipping and witnessing assembly, but instead of an arcane process of causality whereby persons acquire knowledge through opaque, non-natural operations."[82] N. T. Wright comes to the same conclusion. He faults modernity for adopting a "shrunken version" of revelation, "a picture of God merely conveying true religious, theological, or ethical information."[83] The result has been "the false antithesis of seeing scripture either as a convenient repository of timeless truth, a vehicle for imparting 'true information,' or as a take-it-or-leave-it resource."[84] Wright insists, "Scripture is more than simply 'revelation' in the sense of 'conveying information'; more even than 'divine self-communication'; more, certainly, than simply a 'record of revelation.' Those categories come to us today primarily from an older framework of thought, in which the key question was conceived to be about a mostly absent God choosing to send the world certain messages about himself and his purposes."[85] As Willimon, Webster, and Wright maintain, the modern debate has narrowed the function of the Scriptures to the conveyance of information. The writings of the prophets and apostles have been thought of as little more than deposits of true (or partially true) statements *about* God and what he has done, rather than instruments through which God continues to accomplish his work of salvation.

---

80. Ibid., 25–26.
81. Webster, *Holy Scripture*, 11.
82. Ibid., 12.
83. Wright, *Scripture*, 23.
84. Ibid.
85. Ibid., 22.

In order to move beyond the modern conception, David Kelsey argues that the informative function of the Scriptures must not be the only (or primary) way of thinking about what God does with the Bible. "It may be perfectly correct to say, in a *theological* proposal, that one of the things that God is 'using' the Bible for is to 'say' certain things to men. But that is at most only *one* sort of the thing Christians have tended to say God is 'doing' with the Bible."[86] Wright agrees: "It is enormously important that we see the role of Scripture not simply as being to provide *true information about*, or even an accurate running commentary upon, the work of God in salvation and new creation, but as taking an active part *within* that ongoing purpose ... Scripture is there to be a means of God's action in and through us—which will include, but go far beyond, the mere conveying of information."[87] Kelsey suggests this alternative: "Instead of taking 'God saying' as the overarching image for all the various things Christians are inclined to say God 'does' with the Bible, we have proposed 'shaping identity': Speaking *theologically*, God 'uses' the church's various uses of scripture in her common life to nurture and reform the self-identity both of the community and of the individual persons who comprise it."[88] The Bible, according to Kelsey, shapes the community and individuals who read it. Willimon argues much the same in his book *Shaped by the Bible*, maintaining that the distinctiveness of the church consists in the fact that it is formed and continually *re*formed by the Scriptures. "A congregation is Christian to the degree that it is confronted by and attempts to form its life in response to the Word of God."[89]

The recognition that the Scriptures must be viewed in terms of their function in the economy of salvation has been a helpful move in the contemporary theology of Scripture, and Barth deserves much of the credit for turning the discussion in this direction.

Scripture in Trinitarian Perspective

Karl Rahner famously observed that one could dispense with the doctrine of the Trinity and the majority of modern religious literature would remain

---

86. Kelsey, *Proving Doctrine*, 214. His emphasis.

87. Wright, *Scripture*, 22. His emphasis.

88. Kelsey, *Proving Doctrine*, 214. His emphasis. Kelsey is correct in saying that God does more than convey information through the Scriptures. But as I will try to show in the next chapter, it is precisely *through* God's "saying" (his Word) that he "shapes identity."

89. Willimon, *Shaped by the Bible*, 11.

virtually unchanged.⁹⁰ When it comes to the doctrine of inspiration, he is probably right. Rather than unpacking how the Scriptures are the Word of the *Triune* God, the doctrine of inspiration focuses almost exclusively on the relationship between the biblical texts and the Holy Spirit. Although the seventeenth-century dogmaticians affirmed the rule *opera Trinitatis ad extra sunt indivisa* and formally ascribed inspiration to all three members of the Godhead, neither Jesus nor the Father played a significant role. David Scaer explains, "Though the dogmaticians affirmed a Trinitarian inspiration, their exegetical exposition of the doctrine centered on the Spirit's relation to the biblical authors. In terms of the cliché, inspiration was Third Article matter."⁹¹ As a result contemporary theologians find themselves "caught between a doctrine of biblical inspiration which is offered without serious reference to the Second Article and certain historical-critical methods which have a Jesus-history in which the *incarnatus* has no role."⁹² This lack of attention to Christology in the modern debate is ironic, given the christological name calling that has characterized much of the discussion.⁹³ It is also problematic. Scaer concludes: "Without the Trinitarian perspective, no doctrine can be considered fully presented."⁹⁴

The revival of the Trinity in twentieth-century theology has led to a reconsideration of the Scriptures from a trinitarian perspective. Work explains: "If Scripture is God's Word then in some sense it reflects God's character; and if God's character is Triune, then the Bible reflects the Triunity of God in some significant way."⁹⁵ Because the Triune God acts to save, this trinitarian perspective moves beyond a consideration of the *nature* of the Scriptures to an examination of their trinitarian *function*. Webster explains, "Holy Scripture is dogmatically explicated in terms of its role in God's self-communication, that is, the acts of Father, Son and Spirit which establish and maintain that saving fellowship with humankind in which God makes himself known to us and by us."⁹⁶

Barth explored the relationship between the Trinity and the Scriptures by taking a closer look at the functional relationship between Christ and the

---

90. Rahner, *The Trinity*, 11.

91. Scaer, "Biblical Inspiration," 148.

92. Ibid., 160.

93. Critics refer to traditionalists as docetists and monophysites, and traditionalists accuse critics of being ebionites and adoptionists.

94. Scaer, "Biblical Inspiration," 143.

95. Work, *Living and Active*, 10.

96. Webster, *Holy Scripture*, 8; see also Slenczka, "Die Heilige Schrift," 189.

Bible. His frequent comparison of the Bible to the finger of John the Baptist in Matthias Grünewald's *Crucifixion* emphasizes that the Scriptures were written so that people might believe in Jesus (see John 20:31).[97] Alister McGrath notes this Christological direction: "Christology and biblical authority are inextricably linked in that it is Scripture that brings us to a knowledge of Jesus Christ . . . Scripture is read in order to encounter Christ; it is like a lens through which Christ is brought into focus."[98] When it comes to the role of the Holy Spirit, then, increasing interest in Spirit-Christology has added additional trinitarian insights. Work describes, "The rise of Spirit-Christology has helped recover the relevance of the Holy Spirit as One who conceives, anoints, and empowers Jesus' work in the created order, not just the One who points to it and carries it on in Jesus' absence."[99] Viewed from the perspective of Spirit-Christology, inspiration becomes an activity that involves Jesus as much as it involves the Spirit. Again Scaer: "A Christological view of inspiration would require that the words inspired by the Spirit are those of Jesus and ultimately of the Father."[100] He summarizes, "Inspiration is not derived baldly from the Spirit of the Trinity, but from the one whom the Creed describes as *crucifixus*. It is not an inward, mystical experience but is historical because it comes from the one who took on flesh and lived among us. The Scriptures are Christological because they originate with him; and the Spirit of Jesus is the Spirit who inspires them."[101]

Barth's Limitations

Barth's influence in the contemporary theology of Scripture has been far-reaching. His emphasis on the function of the Scriptures in the economy of salvation and his trinitarian perspective have been adopted and developed in a variety of helpful ways. His relocation of the Scriptures under the theology of the Word of God has helped liberate Scripture from its "prolegomenal ghetto,"[102] and his threefold form of the Word of God has provided a much needed framework for unpacking the theological relationship between the Scriptures and the rest of the dogmatic corpus. Despite these positive con-

---

97. Barth, *CD* 1/1:112; 1/1:262; 1/2:125.
98. McGrath, "Reclaiming Our Roots," 66–67.
99. Work, *Living and Active*, 111.
100. Scaer, "Biblical Inspiration," 151.
101. Ibid., 154.
102. Work, *Living and Active*, 9.

tributions, however, there remain several significant problems in Barth's theology of the Word of God.

A Limited Conception of Jesus

The strength of Barth's doctrine of the Word of God is that it is grounded firmly in the doctrine of Christ. The weakness is that his doctrine of Christ is inadequate. This can be seen in two specific ways. First, Barth's understanding of the person of Jesus Christ—including his relationship to the Father and the Spirit—is undermined by the same problems of the ancient Nestorian heresy. Second, his account of the work of Christ, which focuses disproportionately on the incarnation, makes the death and resurrection of Jesus theologically inconsequential for his understanding of the Word of God.

In the previous section we considered McCormack's suggestion that the problem with Barth's theology of Scripture (and therefore the problem with his theology of the Word of God) is ultimately a christological problem. As Barth put it, "It is quite impossible that there should be a direct identity between the human word of Holy Scripture and the Word of God, and therefore between the creaturely reality in itself and as such and the reality of God the Creator. It is impossible that there should have been a transmutation of the one into the other or an admixture of the one with the other. *This is not even the case in the person of Christ.*"[103]

Barth's unwavering commitment to the "infinite qualitative distance" between God and humankind is clear in his repeated defense of God's sovereign freedom and absolute transcendence. Gustav Wingren suggests that this insistence on divine freedom stems from a worldview that is governed by a "*Gott-Mensch* antithesis" in which the primary opposition in reality is between God as Creator and human beings as creatures.[104] The divine and human natures are so vastly different that it would be impossible for God to *become* flesh. "The gulf between God and man gapes unabridged even in the Incarnation."[105] The implications of this understanding of the person of Christ for the doctrine of the Word of God and for the theology of Scripture are obvious. By refusing to allow the divine and human to come together even in the person of Christ, Barth rules out the possibility of God's Word being united with human words in any direct way, whether they be

103. Barth, *CD* 1/2:499. Emphasis added.
104. Wingren, *Theology in Conflict*, 23–44.
105. Wingren, "'The Word' in Barth and Luther," 266.

spoken or written. Wingren explains, "The opposition between the divine and the human remains in the Incarnation in spite of the unity, and the same division comes again between God's Word and man's word in the Scriptures, to be carried over in exactly the same sense into Barth's view of preaching."[106]

Barth's emphasis on the opposition between Creator and creatures surfaces again in his view of Christ's work. The most basic problem facing humankind in Barth's theology is that it has been created. As creatures, human beings are completely incapable of reaching God on their own. Sin is a lack of knowledge about God, which can only be overcome through God's own self-presentation. Wingren observes, "There is in Barth's theology no active power of sin, no tyrannical, demonic power that subjects men to slavery and which God destroys in his work of redemption. There is no devil in Barth's theology."[107] It is here that the importance of divine revelation for Barth's theology of the Word of God can be seen. Barth recognized liberalism's rejection of divine revelation as a departure from historic Christianity. He sought to restore Christianity to its original form by emphasizing the need for God to reveal himself to his creatures. In the incarnation he finds this revelation—a revelation that makes possible reconciliation between sinful human creatures and their transcendent Creator. Barth explains: "'Incarnation of the Word' asserts the presence of God in our world and as a member of this world, as a Man among men. It is thus God's revelation to us, and our reconciliation with him. That this revelation and reconciliation have already taken place is the content of the Christmas message."[108] Again, "The Word of God as the Word of reconciliation directed to us is the Word by which God announces Himself to man, i.e., by which He promises Himself as the content of man's future, as the One who meets him on his way through time as the end of all time, as the hidden Lord of all times."[109] To Barth revelation *is* reconciliation—they are "two sides of the same coin."[110] And because the incarnation is the miracle of divine revelation, it follows that the *incarnation* is reconciliation. In terms of the biblical narrative, then, salvation took place at Christmas. God reconciled the world to himself as he manifested himself to his creation in the babe in the manger.

---

106. Ibid., 269.

107. Wingren, *Theology in Conflict*, 25. Wingren suggests that the absence of evil in Barth's theology is a hold-over from his liberal education.

108. Barth, *CD* 1/2:173.

109. Ibid., 1/1:142.

110. Runia, "Karl Barth and the Word of God," 6.

The problem with Barth's (over-)emphasis on the incarnation is that makes the death and resurrection of Jesus theologically inconsequential. Despite his frequent affirmation of the "theology of the cross," Jesus' crucifixion has no constitutive significance for his Christology or his doctrine of the Word of God. Even when he addresses Christ's death and resurrection more fully in volume 4, he rejects the idea that justification should stand at the center of Christian theology.[111] Runia explains, "Barth does not deny the reality of the cross and the resurrection. But in a sense they are relegated to a secondary place. The cross is only the consequence of the incarnation."[112] By speaking of "revelation" and "God's presence" in place of "justification" and "forgiveness of sins," Barth deviates from the central thrust of the biblical account and its emphasis on "Christ crucified." As Wingren points out, "The birth of Jesus plays a relatively minor part in the New Testament kerygma. The cross and the resurrection dominate the four gospels, even quantitatively, while some of them do not even relate the story of his birth."[113] For all the attention Barth gives John the Baptist's finger, he seems to have missed the fact that John is pointing to the Jesus who was hanging on the cross.[114]

A Limited Conception of God Speaking

To Barth the Word of God and the revelation of God are identical. This leads to a second problem with Barth's understanding of Scripture and the Word. Nicholas Wolterstorff helps explain this problem in his philosophical investigation into the claim that God speaks by arguing that "speaking is not revealing."[115] These two activities share a number of important traits, and they are often treated as one and the same idea (especially in modern theology). But in fact, says Wolterstorff, speech and revelation are distinct in some important ways. He illustrates this with an anecdote:

> When I mentioned to various friends and acquaintances that I had resolved to reflect and write on the topic of divine discourse, further conversation almost always revealed that they assumed my topic was divine revelation, and that my conversation partners would be a sampling from that vast number of thinkers who have written on

---

111. Barth, *CD* 4/1:581–89.
112. Runia, "Karl Barth and the Word of God," 12.
113. Wingren, *Theology in Conflict*, 120.
114. See Work, *Living and Active*, 99.
115. Wolterstorff, *Divine Discourse*, 19.

the topic of revelation. "Is there anything new to be said on revelation?" a rather skeptical theologian friend remarked. I replied that my topic was divine *discourse*, not divine *revelation*. His response was like that of almost everyone else: "What's the difference?"[116]

To Barth there is no difference. To speak of revelation is to speak of the Word of God, and vice versa.

Wolterstorff suggests this is a problem. At its very basic revelation informs. "Revelation occurs when ignorance is dispelled—or when something is done which *would* dispel ignorance if attention and interpretive skills were adequate."[117] While there are a variety of kinds of revealing and different agents of revelation, the act of revelation itself consists in the transmission of knowledge. It occurs when information that was previously unknown is made known—or, to be more precise, when information that was previously *unknowable* is made known. Wolterstorff explains, "Dispelling ignorance becomes *revelation* when it has, to some degree or in some way, the character of unveiling the veiled, of uncovering the covered, of exposing the obscured to view. The counterpart of the revealed is the hidden."[118] Although it is true that speaking may reveal certain things (about the speaker, for example), Wolterstorff maintains that the essence of speaking is *not* the transmission of knowledge. To support this claim he recalls the speech-act theory of J. L. Austin.[119] Fundamental to Austin's account of language is the distinction between two different kinds of speech-acts: locutionary acts and illocutionary acts. A locutionary act occurs when words are uttered or inscribed. It consists of sounds or symbols. An illocutionary act occurs when a something is performed *by means* of uttering or inscribing. In other words, a speaker performs an act as he speaks. He does such things as asserting, commanding, promising, or asking a question by uttering sounds or writing symbols (locutionary acts) to an addressee. While speech-acts *also* inform (and thus reveal things), that is not all they do, and that is not even the most important thing they do. "Asserting, commanding, promising, and asking," Wolterstorff explains, "do not *consist in* the transmission of knowledge."[120] Through speaking people relate to one another in ways that go beyond the giving and receiving of information. "The intended function of promising

116. Ibid.
117. Ibid., 23.
118. Ibid.
119. Wolterstorff briefly reviews Austin's speech-act theory in his first chapter (*Divine Discourse*, 13; see also 33). See Austin, *How to Do Things with Words*.
120. Wolterstorff, *Divine Discourse*, 33.

and commanding is not to inform us of what we don't know but to take on duties *toward* us and to require things *of* us; trust and obedience are the appropriate responses."[121]

Why does this distinction matter for the theology of the Word of God? The key question in modern theology (and philosophy) is the question of epistemology: how does one know God (or anything)? While this has always been an important issue in the Western world, the question of knowing has been elevated in modern times to "the point of pathology."[122] Epistemology has become the only (or at least, the first and most important) question in philosophy, making revelation and the transmission of divine knowledge the central theological topic. Wolterstorff summarizes, "Thus it is that the topic of revelation has assumed looming, structural significance in the theologies of the West."[123] It is in this context that we should understand Barth's attempt to move beyond the modern debate over the Scriptures. While he recognizes the centrality of the Word of God in the biblical narrative, the key question for Barth remains epistemological. The modern fascination with knowing shapes his conception of what God does with his Word.[124]

Epistemology and revelation are significant theological concepts. No one doubts they have an important place in Christian theology and the theology of the Word of God. But the biblical narrative describes God primarily as one who *speaks* to his people. Much more than simply transmitting information, God issues commands and makes promises. When the Word of God is considered within the framework of revelation, as it is with Barth, God's speaking loses its distinctively relational nature and becomes the means by which ignorance is dispelled. This would suggest that Barth's account of the Word of God is not as "post-Enlightenment" or "postmodern" as it is often thought. Reminiscent of Enlightenment Deism, Barth's conception of the Word of God (and God himself) remains impersonal and distant.[125]

Barth's equation of revealing and "Word of God" is not the only problem with his understanding of God's speech. There is a second aspect of Wolterstorff's investigation into divine discourse that warrants consideration. It is

121. Ibid., 35.
122. Ibid., 36.
123. Ibid.
124. Remember that Barth conceives of the Father as Revealer, the Son as Revelation, and the Spirit as Revealedness (*CD* 1/1:295).
125. Barth is not the only modern theologian to conceive of the Word of God as revelation. Many proponents of the doctrine of inspiration have treated the Word of God in a similar way.

the concept he calls "deputized discourse."[126] Most instances of human speaking occur when the speaker utters sounds with his own mouth or inscribes symbols with his own hand. There are times, however, when a speaker says something that is uttered or inscribed by someone else. Wolterstorff calls this "double agency discourse." By way of example he describes the common practice of a secretary writing a letter for an executive. The executive does not write the words on the page, but when she signs it, the words that were written by the secretary become the words of the executive. The key factor in "double agency discourse" is that the secretary "knows the mind" of the executive and communicates on her behalf.[127] The secretary writes a message that corresponds to the thoughts and intentions of the executive, and the executive makes the message her own by signing her name to it.

This example can be stretched further to the situation in which the same executive "authorizes" the secretary not only to write the letter for her, but also to sign her name to it. Wolterstorff describes this act with a more specific term. He calls this "deputized discourse."[128] When the secretary has been "deputized" to write and sign for the executive, the secretary's signature *counts as* the signature of the executive. In this case the executive has granted authority to the secretary to write on her behalf and with her authority. Wolterstorff explains:

> To deputize to someone else some authority that one has in one's own person is not to surrender that authority and hand it over to that other person; it is to bring it about that one exercises that authority by way of actions performed by that other person acting as one's deputy. That's what happens when the executive deputizes the secretary to sign the letters "for" her. The act which generates the executive's authorizing signing, and which thereby generates the executive's discourse, is the secretary's act of producing an inscription of the executive's name.[129]

To be deputized, therefore, is to write (or speak) in the name of someone else in order to communicate his or her message.

At this point Wolterstorff turns to the biblical account to show how prophetic speech is an instance of deputized discourse. Much like an ambassador sent to speak in the name of a head of state, God sent prophets

---

126. Wolterstorff, *Divine Discourse*, 42.
127. Ibid., 39.
128. Ibid., 42.
129. Ibid.

to speak in his name. Wolterstorff describes what happened: "Those who hear the prophet speaking, when he is speaking in his prophetic capacity, are confronted with that which counts as God speaking; the utterances of the prophet are the medium of God's discourse."[130] The deputized speaking does not originate with the prophet himself; it comes from God. "Speaking in the name of God is not something that a person just undertakes to do; God will 'raise up' the prophet, as God raised up Moses. To be a prophet requires being deputized to speak in God's name. In addition, God will tell the prophet what he is to say, putting words in his mouth; the prophet does not devise the words by himself. The prophet is commissioned to communicate a message from God, and God will give that message to the prophet."[131]

With this concept of "deputized discourse" in mind, Barth's doctrine of the spoken Word of God runs into a related problem. Although God's speaking takes center stage in Barth's theology, Wolterstorff notes that there is really only one form in which God can truly be said to speak. In order to demonstrate this point he examines Barth's concept of "witness." In his description of Jesus as the revealed Word of God, Barth is clear that Jesus is God's *original* (or direct) speech in which God reveals himself. Proclamation and the Bible are God's *derivative* (or indirect) speech. They reveal God only where and when it pleases God.[132] This is an important distinction. To Barth the prophets and apostles (in their proclamation and in their writing) do not, in and of themselves, reveal God. Instead, they are *witnesses* to revelation. They are witnesses to "the revelatory speech of God which is Jesus Christ."[133]

Wolterstorff observes several significant aspects of Barth's understanding of a witness. First, Barth insists that a witness to revelation is *not* revelation itself: "In the Bible we meet with human words written by human speech, and in these words, and therefore by means of them, we hear of the lordship of the triune God. Therefore when we have to do with the Bible, we have to do primarily with this means, with these words, with the witness which as such is not itself revelation."[134] The implications for divine speech are clear. "The prophets and apostles are not ones who speak *in the name of* God; rather, they are ones who have *witnessed* God's revelatory speech

---

130. Ibid., 48.
131. Ibid.
132. Ibid., 64.
133. Ibid., 67.
134. Barth, *CD* 1/2:463

and who, then, in turn, *witness* to that."[135] This also means that neither the prophets nor the apostles were truly deputized by God to speak his Word. Because they are finite human beings, they are simply incapable of uttering divine words. "Witnessing is human speech, nothing more."[136] This means that, apart from God's active revelation in Christ, there is actually no divine discourse in Barth's theology.[137] Despite Barth's occasional descriptions of the Scriptures (and proclamation) as the Word of God, Wolterstorff concludes that it would be a mistake "to interpret him as saying thereby that Scripture is a medium of divine discourse."[138]

Wolterstorff completes his examination of Barth's doctrine of the Word of God by wondering why there is less of God speaking than it first appears in Barth's theology. "It is surprising," he admits. "Barth is the great theologian of the Word of God. One gets the impression upon first reading him that many are the episodes of human speech which are the media for divine discourse. But close scrutiny proves that to be not true."[139] Why is this so? Wolterstorff offers a likely answer: "Barth regarded the claim that God speaks by way of authoring Scripture as compromising the freedom of God. God and God alone speaks for God."[140] For God to allow human beings to speak his Word on their terms would limit God's freedom, and that is something that Barth cannot accept. Wolterstorff responds to Barth with a suggestion: "If it is indeed a limitation on God's freedom that God would commission a human being to speak 'in the name of' God, then perhaps we have to take seriously the possibility that God is willing, on occasion to limit God's freedom in that way—or alternatively, consider the possibility that we are working with an alien and inapplicable concept of freedom."[141]

A Contemporary Barthian Approach to Scripture

As I have tried to demonstrate, Barth's doctrine of the Word of God is inadequate in a number of significant ways. He disallows a hypostatic union

---

135. Wolterstorff, *Divine Discourse*, 67–68.

136. Ibid., 68.

137. As McCormack notes, this does not mean that the Scriptures and proclamation are *not* the Word of God to Barth. It means that they are the Word of God *only* when God speaks through them.

138. Wolterstorff, *Divine Discourse*, 282.

139. Ibid., 73.

140. Ibid., 73–74.

141. Ibid., 74.

between the two natures of Christ; he neglects the theological significance of the death and resurrection of Jesus; and he limits God's ability to speak through his prophets and apostles through deputized discourse. These shortcomings create problems for his theology of Scripture, and an examination of a contemporary Barthian approach to the theology of Scripture helps demonstrate how these problems have persisted to the present day.

Much like Barth, John Webster grounds his dogmatic account of the Scriptures in divine revelation. "Revelation," Webster maintains, "is the self-presentation of the triune God, the free work of sovereign mercy in which God wills, establishes and perfects saving fellowship with himself in which humankind comes to know, love, and fear him."[142] Quoting Barth, Webster argues that "revelation is . . . divine presence"[143]—it is God manifesting himself to sinful human begins. This establishment of fellowship with God accomplishes salvation because it enables creatures to know their Creator—it bridges the gap between finite and infinite. "Revelation is the self-giving presence of God which overthrows opposition to God, and, in reconciling, brings us into the light of the knowledge of God."[144] Revelation saves by removing "human blindness and ignorance."[145]

In order to describe God's self-revelation through the Scriptures, Webster speaks in terms of God's "sanctification" of the Bible. "At its most basic," he explains, "the biblical texts are creaturely realities set apart by the triune God to serve his self-presence."[146] Webster suggests that God "sanctifies" the Scriptures in order to use them in his reconciling work of revelation: "A sanctified text is creaturely, not divine. Scripture's place in the economy of saving grace does not need to be secured by its divinization through the unambiguous ascription of divine properties to the text . . . Sanctification is not transubstantiation. Nor is it an exclusively natural product arbitrarily commandeered by a supernatural agent. Sanctification is the Spirit's act of ordering creaturely history and being to the end of acting as *ancilla Domini*."[147] Sanctification is a fitting term to describe God's use of the Scriptures, Webster suggests, because it affirms divine action through these writings without having to ascribe divine qualities directly to the texts. The Scriptures are

---

142. Webster, *Holy Scripture*, 13.
143. Ibid.
144. Ibid., 16.
145. Ibid., 17.
146. Ibid., 22.
147. Ibid., 28.

used by God, but they remain part of his finite creation. "Once again, the rule is: sanctification *establishes* and does not abolish creatureliness."[148]

Several Barthian themes appear in Webster's dogmatic account of the Scriptures. First, the absolute distinction between Creator and creature comes through clearly in Webster's conception of how God works through the Scriptures. His description of God's work through the Scriptures in terms of "sanctification" protects the sovereign freedom of God as he reconciles creatures to himself through his Word. "A sanctified text is creaturely, not divine,"[149] Webster insists, thereby guarding the infinite against the control of finite human creatures. Second, by grounding his conception of the Scriptures in revelation, Webster leaves little room to consider the Word God speaks through his deputized prophets and apostles. He seems to recognize the importance of the proclamation of the Word, but he confuses it with the Scriptures. This passage is instructive: "Holy Scripture is the location of a struggle for the proper externality of the church, for true hearing of the *viva vox Dei*, for true attention to the sanctified and inspired servant through which God announces the judgment and promise of the gospel, above all, for faith as the end of defiance and false confidence and the beginning of humble listening."[150] Webster recognizes the importance of speaking (*viva vox Dei*) and the human response of "humble listening," but it appears that he is thinking of the Bible, and not the human proclaimer of the Word, as the "sanctified and inspired servant." The third and most problematic similarity between Webster and Barth is the absence of the cross. Salvation in Webster's account consists primarily in terms of God's "saving self-manifestation" and "presence."[151] Like it was with Barth, the cross and the message of Christ crucified are almost entirely absent. Webster explains his view of salvation: "As the gracious presence of God, revelation is itself the establishment of fellowship. It is . . . a way of indicating the communicative force of God's saving, fellowship-creating presence. God is present as our savior, and so communicatively present."[152] Although Webster speaks with regularity about the presence of the "risen Christ,"[153] the death of Jesus, as well as the theological necessity of his resurrection, is nowhere to be found.

---

148. Ibid., 30. His emphasis.
149. Webster, *Holy Scripture*, 28.
150. Ibid., 47.
151. Ibid., 40; cf. 97.
152. Ibid., 16.
153. Ibid., 18, 38, 50.

Summary

Karl Barth's relocation of the theology of Scripture under the theology of the Word of God was an important step beyond the modern battle for the Bible. His trinitarian and soteriological focus has helped provide a more comprehensive framework for understanding the nature and function of the Scriptures in the economy of salvation. Still, his insistence on maintaining the infinite qualitative difference between God and humankind limits his understanding of the Word of God in all its forms, and his neglect of the cross moves him away from the central thrust of the biblical narrative.

In order to build on what is helpful in Barth, but to avoid his limitations, it is necessary to reexamine the nature and function of the Word of God in the biblical narrative. This examination will recognize God's frequent use of deputized discourse, and it will take into account the foundational and central significance of Jesus' death and resurrection. In other words, it will result in a decidedly "cruciform" account of the Scriptures and the Word of God. As Wingren reminds us, "To understand God we must always return to this, that Christ was crucified."[154]

---

154. Wingren, "'The Word' in Barth and Luther," 268.

3

The Word of the "God of Word"

From the beginning of the biblical narrative to the end, the one true God is a "God of Word."[1] Hermann Sasse observes, "Der Gott der Bibel ist der redende Gott, von dem 'Und Gott sprach: es werde Licht' auf dem ersten Blatt der Bibel bis zu dem 'Es spricht, der solches bezeugt: Ja, ich komme bald' auf ihrem lezten Blatt."[2] Speaking is not incidental to God, as if it were simply one more thing he happens to do. It is central to who he is, what he does, and how he relates to his creation.[3]

The Speaking God and His Deputies

The biblical narrative revolves around the Word of God. It is God's primary means for communicating and accomplishing his will. Through his creative Word he brings all things into existence; through his spoken and written Word he establishes and maintains relationships with his human creatures; and through his incarnate, crucified, and resurrected Word he accomplishes salvation for his fallen creation. In contrast to the false gods who cannot speak, the one true God is known by what he says (see Ps 115:4–5; Jer 10:5; Hab 2:18–19; 1 Cor 12:2). Sasse notes, "Die Götzen sind stumm, aber der Herr redet . . . Niemand kann die biblische Lehre vom Reden Gottes, von

---

1. Work, *Living and Active*, 33. Cf. Barth, *CD* 1/1:132.
2. "The God of the Bible is the speaking God, from 'and God said: let there be light' on the first page of the Bible to 'he speaks, the one who witnesses: yes, I am coming soon' on the last page" (Sasse, *Sacra Scriptura*, 11).
3. Cf. Ringleben, "Die Bibel als Wort Gottes," 21.

seinem gesprochenen und geschriebenen Wort verstehen, der sich nicht darüber klar ist, daß das Reden ein Merkmal des einen wahren Gottes ist im Unterschied von den 'andern Göttern,' deren Verehrung im Ersten Gebot verboten ist."[4] Occasionally God speaks directly to his human creatures, but his most common way of communicating in the biblical narrative is to speak to his people by speaking *through* his people. In the previous chapter we briefly considered Nicholas Wolterstorff's philosophical investigations into the claim that God speaks. At this point his thoughts require closer attention.

At the foundation of the claim that God speaks is a more general phenomenon that Wolterstorff calls "deputized discourse." "Deputized discourse" occurs when one person speaks *in the name of* another person. In order for this to take place, two specific elements must be in effect. The first involves the content of the message to be conveyed. The one who sends a messenger to speak on his behalf is responsible for telling the messenger what to say. Wolterstorff calls this element "superintendence." A few examples explain what this means. A low degree of superintendence is in effect when a student asks a classmate to make up an excuse to the teacher for his absence. The classmate has been sent to deliver a message, but he has been given very little direction for what exactly he should say. With this low degree of superintendence he is free to give the teacher any excuse that comes to mind. In contrast, a high degree of superintendence is in effect when an executive dictates a letter for her secretary. The secretary does the actual writing, but the executive provides every single word to be written. The second essential element in "deputized discourse" is the authority given to the deputy by the sender. Deputizing someone involves more than simply asking this person to relay information. It is what happens when one person is authorized to speak *on behalf of* another.[5] Wolterstorff calls this element "authorization." He explains, "Being asked to communicate a message for someone is not the same as being deputized to speak in the name of someone . . . The deputy has, as it were, 'power of attorney.'"[6] One who has been "authorized" to speak as a deputy speaks with the sender's authority, regardless of whether or not the sender gives the deputy the specific words to say. For "deputized discourse" to occur there must be at least some degree of superintendence *and* some

---

4. "The false gods are dumb, but the Lord speaks. . . No one can understand the biblical teaching of God's speaking, whether it be his spoken or written Word, if he is not clear that speaking is a characteristic of the true God in contrast to other false gods, whose worship is forbidden in the First Commandment" (Sasse, *Sacra Scriptura*, 11).

5. Wolterstorff, *Divine Discourse*, 38–42.

6. Ibid., 44.

degree of authorization. When both of these elements are in effect "deputized discourse" occurs.

In order to illustrate how this works, Wolterstorff describes the relationship between an ambassador and a head of state. Using President Harry Truman and his ambassador to Russia, George Kennen, as his examples, Wolterstorff describes a situation in which Truman sends Kennen to issue a warning to Joseph Stalin about Berlin. As one who has been deputized to speak *in the name of* President Truman, Kennen physically goes to meet with Stalin. Kennen utters the sounds (the locutionary act) that have the effect of warning (the illocutionary act) Stalin. But because Kennen has been sent with Truman's message (superintendence) and authority (authorization), the words Kennen speaks as Truman's deputy *count as* the words of Truman himself. Wolterstorff explains, "If the ambassador was deputized to say what he did in the name of his head of state, then the head of state speaks (discourses) by way of the utterings of the ambassador; locutionary acts of the ambassador count as illocutionary acts of the head of state."[7] It will be important, of course, for Stalin to understand that Kennen has been deputized to speak *in the name of* Truman—that Kennen has Truman's superintendence and authorization. But if Kennen has been so deputized, Stalin is confronted with Truman's warning through Kennen's speech—whether he acknowledges it or not.

Wolterstorff notes that the instance of an ambassador speaking *in the name of* a head of state is analogous to the way that God usually speaks in the biblical narrative. Rather than speaking directly to his people with his own mouth, God normally speaks to his human creatures through one of his chosen "deputies." In the Old Testament these deputies are known as prophets. Wolterstorff identifies Deuteronomy 18 as the *locus classicus* of the biblical prophet.[8]

> The LORD your God will raise up for you a prophet like me from among you, from your brothers—it is to him you shall listen—just as you desired of the LORD your God at Horeb on the day of the assembly, when you said, "Let me not hear again the voice of the LORD my God or see this great fire any more, lest I die." And the LORD said to me, "They are right in what they have spoken. I will raise up for them a prophet like you from among their brothers. And I will put my words in his mouth, and he shall speak to them all that I command him. And whoever will not listen to my words

7. Ibid., 45.
8. Ibid., 47.

> that he shall speak in my name, I myself will require it of him. But the prophet who presumes to speak a word in my name that I have not commanded him to speak, or who speaks in the name of other gods, that same prophet shall die." And if you say in your heart, "How may we know the word that the Lord has not spoken?"—when a prophet speaks in the name of the Lord, if the word does not come to pass or come true, that is a word that the Lord has not spoken. (Deut 18:15–22)

Wolterstorff points out that God's promise to raise up a prophet like Moses contains the two essential components necessary for deputized discourse: authorization and superintendence. The prophet receives the commission to speak for God ("He shall speak in my name"—authorization), and God gives the prophet his own Word to speak ("I will put my words in his mouth"—superintendence). To depart from Wolterstorff's terminology, speaking *in the name of* God as a deputy depends on the prophet's reception of two things: the commission to speak and the Word to be spoken.

The commission to speak is important because no true prophet takes up the responsibility of speaking for God on his own. The prophet must be sent (or commissioned) by God. This is what it means to be "raised up."[9] Barth recognizes this and points out that human proclamation of the Word of God depends on "God's own direction, which fundamentally transcends all human causation."[10] He gets this from Luther: "Let none think that God's Word cometh to earth of man's device. If it is to be God's Word, it must be sent."[11] Instances of this sending can be found throughout the Old Testament. Isaiah, for example, describes his commission: "And I heard the voice of the Lord saying, 'Whom shall I send, and who will go for us?' Then I said, 'Here am I! Send me.' And he said, 'Go, and *say* to this people . . .'" (Isa 6:8–9, emphasis added).

Equally important as the commission to speak is the content of the message God sends his prophet to communicate. In the biblical narrative the message of the prophet is known as the "Word of God." Rendtorff explains, "The decisive feature in OT prophecy is the *dabhar*, the word. The prophet

---

9. Rolf Rendtorff describes the work of the prophet as one who "speaks on the commission of a superior." See "*Nabi* in the Old Testament" in *TDNT* 6:803.

10. Barth, *CD* 1/1:90.

11. Quoted in Barth, *CD* 1/1:90. See Luther, *LW* 22:477: "These two facts are entirely logical: that those who preach the Word of God must necessarily be sent by God; and conversely, that those who are sent by God cannot proclaim anything but the Word of God. It is impossible to derive the Word of God from reason; it must be given from above."

has to pass on the *dahbar Yahweh* which he receives."[12] Throughout the Old Testament the prophets affirm, often times at the beginning of their proclamation, that they have been sent to speak the Word of God (cf. Hos 1:1; Joel 1:1; Jonah 1:1; Micah 1:1; Zeph 1:1; Hag 1:1; Zech 1:1). Jeremiah explicitly describes how God gave him this Word: "Then the Lord put out his hand and touched my mouth. And the Lord said to me, 'Behold, I have put my words in your mouth'" (Jer 1:9). Ezekiel records an even more vivid image of his reception of the Word: "And [God] said to me, 'Son of man, eat whatever you find here. Eat this scroll, and go, speak to the house of Israel.' So I opened my mouth, and he gave me this scroll to eat. And he said to me, 'Son of man, feed your belly with this scroll that I give you and fill your stomach with it.' Then I ate it, and it was in my mouth as sweet as honey. And he said to me, 'Son of man, go to the house of Israel and speak with my words to them'" (Ezek 3:1–4). When God's prophets speak messages from God, they speak the Word of God *in the name of* God as divinely appointed deputies. Wingren explains, "The messenger and he whose messenger he is are bound together. When the messenger speaks, he who sent him speaks."[13]

A "Normative" Word

Wolterstorff's definition of "deputized discourse" is a helpful and significant contribution to the theology of the Word of God. But it is not his only significant contribution. After considering God's way of speaking through his prophets, Wolterstorff takes a step back and investigates what actually happens when one person speaks to another. In order to describe the phenomena involved in this process he offers a "normative theory of discourse."[14] Unlike revelation, which is either received or not received (in an impersonal way), Wolterstorff argues that "speaking" involves the establishment of a relationship between at least two parties. Austinian speech-act theory comes back into play at this point. By means of uttering sounds (a locutionary act) a speaker issues a command or makes a promise (an illocutionary act). When that command or promise has been made, a "normative stance" has been established between the speaker and the hearer. Wolterstorff gives the example of a person who promises to write a letter of recommendation for another person. The one who makes the promise (the illocutionary act)

---

12. Rendtorff, *TDNT* 6:810.
13. Wingren, *Living Word*, 96.
14. Wolterstorff, *Divine Discourse*, 76.

takes on a moral obligation (takes a "normative stance") toward the one who requested the letter. If the promiser fails to fulfill the promise, he has failed in his moral obligation and the communicative relationship between them breaks down. If this becomes a pattern of behavior for a certain person, he or she loses credibility. If this becomes a pattern of behavior for an entire society, the existence of meaningful communication is jeopardized. Again Wolterstorff: "When a single boy too often cries 'wolf' in the absence of wolves, we disregard *his* speech. When it becomes a habit on the part of many to cry 'wolf' in the absence of wolves, our system of speaking itself is undermined."[15] For interpersonal communication to function properly, both parties must operate on the basis of trust. The promiser must be trustworthy and the promisee must trust the promiser.

A similar dynamic occurs when one person issues a command to another. Like the moral obligation that the promiser accepts in making a promise, the one who receives a command is morally obligated to obey the commander. This does not mean, however, that everyone is in the position of making morally binding commands. For a command to be in effect (and therefore establish a moral obligation on the hearer), the one making the command must have the proper authority. Wolterstorff calls the one who possesses this authority a "qualified party."[16] He offers several obvious examples: only a judge can *pronounce* someone guilty; only Congress can *declare* war; only the umpire can *call* a runner out. Those who are not in the appropriate position of authority in a given context are unable to issue morally binding commands. A prosecuting attorney, for example, does not have authority to pronounce guilt; a mayor does not have authority to declare war; and a fan does not have the authority to call a runner out. One of these individuals may attempt to issue a command—a fan might try to call a runner out, for example—but the addressee (the runner in this case) is not morally obliged to obey because the fan is not qualified to make such a command. If, on the other hand, the one who makes the command is a "qualified party" (the umpire), the addressee (the runner) is morally obligated to obey that command—whether or not he agrees with it.

Wolterstorff's normative theory of discourse is helpful for the theology of the Word of God because, throughout the biblical narrative, God communicates with his people by issuing commands and making promises. He morally obligates himself with his promises, he morally obligates his creatures with his commands. And as he reminds Moses, he has the authority

---

15. Ibid., 89.
16. Ibid., 91.

to do so because he is the ultimate "qualified party." "Who has made man's mouth? Who makes him mute, or deaf, or seeing, or blind? Is it not I, the LORD? Now therefore go, and I will be with your mouth and teach you what you shall speak" (Exod 4:11–12). As the Creator, God has the authority to issue commands that morally obligate his human creatures. As the Almighty, he is capable of fulfilling every promise that he makes. If human beings are to have a meaningful relationship with him—if we are able to rely upon his communication to us—he must be entirely trustworthy.[17]

Living and Active Words

The Word God speaks through his prophets is a unique kind of "deputized discourse." God's promises and commands do more than simply impose moral obligations.[18] Beginning at creation, God uses his Word as his primary instrument for accomplishing his will. It is "living and active, sharper than any two-edged sword" (Heb 4:12). Philip Edgcumbe Hughes explains, "It is no dead letter, no utterance lost as soon as spoken in an unresponding void. As the word of the living God it cannot fail itself to be living. And as God is the God who acts with power, his word cannot fail to be active and powerful."[19] This is what Isaiah is speaking about in his description of the Word of God: "As the rain and the snow come down from heaven, and do not return to it without watering the earth and making it bud and flourish, so that it yields seed for the sower and bread for the eater, so is my word that goes out from my mouth. It will not return to me empty, but will accomplish what I desire and achieve the purpose for which I sent it" (Isa 55:10–11; see also 1 Thess 1:5). God's work and Word are so closely related that Barth was able to conclude: "To say 'the Word of God' is to say the work of God."[20]

---

17. This is one of the reasons why the truth of the Word of God is so important. If God cannot be trusted, our "system of speaking" with God will be undermined and our relationship with him will break down. So the prophets repeatedly affirm the truth of God's Word. Samuel prays, "And now, O Lord God, you are God, and your words are true" (2 Sam 7:28). The psalmist proclaims, "The sum of your word is truth, and every one of your righteous rules endures forever" (Ps 119:160; see also 2 Sam 22:31; Neh 9:13; Pss 18:30, 19:9, 119:142; Prov 30:5; Isa 45:19; Dan 10:1).

18. At this point we are moving beyond Austinian speech-act theory. God is able to do more with his words than human beings.

19. Hughes, *Hebrews*, 164.

20. Barth, *CD* 1/2:527. See also Lotz, "Proclamation of the Word" 348–54. Lotz says that for Luther, "*Verbum Dei est opus Dei:* The Word of God *is* the deed of God" (353).

As a "two-edged sword" the Word of God performs a dual work. It cuts in two directions, having "an edge of life and an edge of death."[21] God summarized them both in his commissioning of the prophet Jeremiah: "Behold, I have put my words in your mouth. See, I have set you this day over nations and over kingdoms, to pluck up and to break down, to destroy and to overthrow, to build and to plant" (Jer 1:9–10). Psalm 29 paints a vivid picture of the power of God's Word in creation:

> The voice of the Lord is over the waters; the God of glory thunders, the Lord, over many waters. The voice of the Lord is powerful; the voice of the Lord is full of majesty. The voice of the Lord breaks the cedars; the Lord breaks the cedars of Lebanon. He makes Lebanon to skip like a calf, and Sirion like a young wild ox. The voice of the Lord flashes forth flames of fire. The voice of the Lord shakes the wilderness; the Lord shakes the wilderness of Kadesh. The voice of the Lord makes the deer give birth and strips the forests bare (Ps 29:3–9).

When spoken to human beings, the Word's "edge of death" is always a response to sin and disobedience. God speaks a Word of judgment to those who have failed in their moral obligation to obey his commands. He sends Jeremiah, for example, to speak against the false prophets who had misled his people: "Behold, I am making my words in your mouth a fire, and this people wood, and the fire shall consume them" (Jer 5:14). Again: "Is not my word like fire, declares the Lord, and like a hammer that breaks the rock in pieces?" (Jer 23:29). Through Hosea God speaks about those who continue to break his commands: "Therefore I have hewn them by the prophets; I have slain them by the words of my mouth, and my judgment goes forth as the light" (Hos 6:5). Luther summarizes the destructive edge of God's Word: "Now this is the thunderbolt of God, by means of which he destroys both the open sinner and the false saint."[22]

The Word of God also has the power to create life. Ezekiel's journey to the valley of dry bones in chapter 37 illustrates the Word's other "edge." After showing Ezekiel a valley full of dry bones God asked him if the bones could ever live again. The obvious answer was no—they were completely dead. But God wanted them to live again, so he deputized Ezekiel to speak his life-giving Word: "Prophesy over these bones, and say to them, O dry

---

21. Hughes, *Hebrews*, 165.

22. SA 3.2. Luther's description of God's Word of judgment as a "thunderbolt" is found throughout the Old Testament as the prophets describe God's judgment through his Word. See Job 37:1–13; Ps 18:12–15; Isa 30:30–33; Jer 25:30–31.

bones, hear the word of the Lord (*dahbar Yahweh*). Thus says the Lord God to these bones: Behold, I will cause breath (*ruah*) to enter you, and you shall live. And I will lay sinews upon you, and will cause flesh to come upon you, and cover you with skin, and put breath in you, and you shall live, and you shall know that I am the Lord" (Ezek 37:4–6). As an obedient deputy, Ezekiel proclaimed the Word that God had given him and the dry bones took on flesh and blood. He prophesied again and the breath (*ruah*) of God entered into them and they were brought from death to life. Here in Ezekiel we get a glimpse of the *trinitarian* work of the Word of God. God gives life to those who are dead through his Word and his Spirit. As Webster puts it, "The 'Word' from which the church has its being is thus the lordly creativity of the one who, as Father, Son and Holy Spirit, *calls* into being the things that are not."[23]

We could summarize what God does through his living and active Word in this way: through his Spirit and his Word, God tears down and builds up, condemns and forgives, kills and makes alive. In the Old Testament he accomplishes these things through the deputized proclamation of his prophets. But when the fullness of time had come, God spoke *definitively, ultimately, decisively,* and *for all time* in the life, death, and resurrection of Jesus Christ, the Spirit-anointed personal Word of God made flesh.

THE PERSONAL WORD

"Long ago, at many times and in many ways, God spoke to our fathers by the prophets, but in these last days he has spoken to us by his Son, whom he appointed the heir of all things, through whom also he created the world" (Heb 1:1–2). Up to this point we have focused primarily on the Word that God spoke through his prophets before the birth of Christ. But the heart and foundation of the Christian faith is Jesus Christ, the "Word in the Word."[24] As John begins his gospel: "In the beginning was the Word, and the Word was with God, and the Word was God. He was in the beginning with God. All things were made through him, and without him was not any thing made that was made . . . And the Word became flesh and dwelt among us" (John 1:1–3, 14). The personal Word is the "image of the invisible God" for whom and through whom "all things were created" and in whom the "fullness of God was pleased to dwell" (Col 1:15–19). So Barth writes, "It is beyond question that whenever

---

23. Webster, *Holy Scripture*, 44.
24. Roehrs, "The Word in the Word," 81–108.

the *Nic. Const.* spoke of the Son of God it always meant the Word of God too. The Word is the one Lord. The Word is spoken by the Father before all time. The Word is light of light, very God of very God. The Word is spoken by God, not made . . . As the Word which God thinks or speaks eternally by Himself and whose content can thus be no other than God Himself."[25]

As Barth notes, the theology of the Word of God is fundamentally a christological doctrine. But it is also a Christology deeply connected to and framed within the broader trinitarian economy of salvation. For this reason classic Logos-Christology (with its focus on the two natures and their hypostatic union) is not the most helpful way of understanding Jesus' identity as the Word of God. Although it was necessary for the church of the fourth and fifth centuries to articulate the doctrine of Christ especially in terms of his divine essence (against Arius) and his personal constitution (against Nestorius), Jesus' identity is most frequently described in the biblical narrative in terms of his mission. Oscar Cullman points out, "The New Testament hardly ever speaks of the person of Christ without at the same time speaking of his work . . . When it is asked in the New Testament 'Who is Christ?', the question never means exclusively, or even primarily, 'What is his nature?', but first of all, 'What is his function?'"[26]

When considering the function of the personal Word of God, Jesus' prophetic office stands out. In continuity with the prophets who preceded him, Jesus was sent by the Father to speak his Word in the power of the Holy Spirit. To use Wolterstorff's terminology, he was "deputized" to speak in the name of the Father. Jesus was not simply another prophet in a long line of God's chosen spokesmen, however. Cullman notes, "Jesus appears not only as *a* prophet but as *the* prophet."[27] He is *the* divinely appointed deputy, *the* Word of God who accomplishes the will of God in what he says and how he acts and who he is. Unlike the prophets who were led by the Spirit (1 Pet 1:11; 2 Pet 3:16), the Spirit *remained* on Jesus (John 1:32). Unlike the prophets who received the Spirit, Jesus *baptized* with the Spirit (John 1:33) and *gave* the Spirit to his disciples (John 20:22). Unlike the prophets who pointed towards the suffering and glorification of the Christ (Luke 24:47; 1 Pet 1:10–11), Jesus pointed to *himself*. It was *his* words that were "Spirit and life" (John 6:63); *he* is the one with "words of eternal life" (John 6:68); *he* is the "resurrection and the life" so that those who believe in *him* will never die (John 11:25–26).

25. Barth, *CD* 1/1:436.
26. Cullman, *Christology*, 3–4.
27. Ibid., 13.

Sent by the Father

Throughout John's gospel Jesus identifies himself as the one sent to do the Father's will and speak the Father's word. "I have come down from heaven," he told the crowd in Capernaum, "not to do my own will but the will of him who sent me" (John 6:38). In a dispute with the Jews he insisted, "I came from God and I am here. I came not of my own accord, but he sent me" (John 8:42). John the Baptist prepared his way by announcing, "He who comes from heaven is above all. He bears witness to what he has seen and heard, yet no one receives his testimony. Whoever receives his testimony sets his seal to this, that God is true. For *he whom God has sent utters the words of God*, for he gives the Spirit without measure" (John 3:31–34, emphasis added). Jesus repeatedly affirmed his commission from the Father: "My teaching is not mine, but his who sent me" (John 7:16; see also John 8:26–29; 14:24; 15:15; 17:6–8).

Although the prophetic work of Christ is stated more explicitly in John's gospel than in the Synoptics, the other evangelists also portray Jesus in terms of his prophetic office. After recording his account of Jesus' baptism in the Jordan and temptation in the desert, Luke describes the beginning of Jesus' prophetic ministry:

> And he came to Nazareth, where he had been brought up. And as was his custom, he went to the synagogue on the Sabbath day, and he stood up to read. And the scroll of the prophet Isaiah was given to him. He unrolled the scroll and found the place where it was written, "The Spirit of the Lord is upon me, because *he has anointed me to proclaim good news to the poor. He has sent me to proclaim liberty to the captives and recovering of sight to the blind, to set at liberty those who are oppressed, to proclaim the year of the Lord's favor.*" And he rolled up the scroll and gave it back to the attendant and sat down. And the eyes of all in the synagogue were fixed on him. And he began to say to them, "Today this Scripture has been fulfilled in your hearing." (Luke 4:16–21, emphasis added)

Throughout the Gospel of Luke Jesus identifies himself and his mission in terms of prophetic proclamation (Luke 4:43; 5:32; 7:22; 11:28; 13:33), and each of the Synoptic Gospels portray Jesus' words as uniquely divine (e.g., Matt 7:28–29; 8:23–27; Mark 1:22–27; Luke 4:32–36). Luther says of this prophetic work of Christ: "Now whenever I hear the Man Christ, I conclude that the Word which I hear is also that of the Father, proceeds from the heart of the Father, and is identical with that of the Father . . . For Christ's will and Christ's Word and work are the Father's will, yes, also the Father's Word and work."[28] To return to Wolterstorff's terminology, Jesus is *the* deputy who speaks with absolute superintendence and complete authorization as the Word of God in person.

On the Mount of Transfiguration the Father explicitly affirms Jesus' identity as his Son and deputy: "This is my beloved Son, with whom I am well pleased; *listen to him*" (Matt 17:5, emphasis added; cf. Mark 9:7; Luke 9:35). As one who is sent by the Father to do his will and speak his words, Jesus demonstrates his unity with the Father. When Philip asked Jesus to show him the Father, Jesus responded:

> Have I been with you so long, and you still do not know me, Philip? Whoever has seen me has seen the Father. How can you say, "Show us the Father"? Do you not believe that I am in the Father and the Father is in me? *The words that I say to you I do not speak on my own authority, but the Father who dwells in me does his works.* Believe me that I am in the Father and the Father is in me, or else believe on account of the works themselves (John 14:9–11, emphasis added; cf. also John 7:28–29; 8:16–18; 10:30–38; 17:21–22).

Jesus' oneness and mutual indwelling (perichoresis) with the Father is intimately connected to the Word that he speaks in the power of the Spirit. Central to this work is the giving of life. "For as the Father raises the dead and gives them life," Jesus explains, "so also the Son gives life to whom he will" (John 5:21). He goes on: "Truly, truly, I say to you, whoever hears my word and believes him who sent me has eternal life. He does not come into judgment, but has passed from death to life. Truly, truly, I say to you, an hour is coming, and is now here, when the dead will hear the voice of the Son of God, and those who hear will live. For as the Father has life in himself, so he has granted the Son also to have life in himself" (John 5:24–26). This is what it means for Jesus to have "words of eternal life" (John 6:68). He tells his disciples, "For this is the will of my Father, that everyone who looks on the Son and believes in him should have eternal life, and I will raise him up on the last day." (John 6:40)

Sent in the Spirit

The personal Word, who was sent by the Father to give life to those who believe, conducted his mission in the power of God's Spirit. A closer look

---

28. Luther, *LW* 23:64.

at the relationship between the Spirit and the Word reminds us that the old rule *opera trinitatis ad extra sunt indivisa* is more than just an old rule.

The joint work between the Spirit and the Word can be seen throughout the biblical narrative, beginning already at creation. In the beginning the Spirit (*ruah*) of God, who was hovering over the waters (Gen 1:2), accompanied the Word in his work of creation. The psalmist notes, "By the word (*dabhar*) of the Lord the heavens were made, and by the breath (*ruah*) of his mouth all their host" (Ps 33:6). Irenaeus describes the Word of God and the Holy Spirit as the two hands by which God brings into existence all things: "For with him were always present the Word and Wisdom, the Son and the Spirit, by whom and in whom, freely and spontaneously, He made all things, to whom he also speaks, saying, 'Let Us make man after Our image and likeness.'"[29] After forming the first man from the dust of the earth, God "breathed into his nostrils the breath of life, and the man became a living creature" (Gen 2:7). Gustav Wingren describes the joint work of the Spirit and the Word: "God's creation by the Word and God's 'breathing in' of the breath of life (Gen 2:7) are, basically, one and the same. Man's life is from God's Word or from God's Spirit: man lives from that which cometh out of the mouth of God (Deut 8:3)."[30]

The close connection between the Spirit and the Word continues throughout the Old Testament.[31] This same Spirit who empowered Moses' prophetic ministry (Num 11:17) was given by God to subsequent prophets so that they could speak his Word in his name (see Num 11:25–30; 2 Sam 23:2; 2 Chr 15:1; Ezek 11:5; Neh 9:30; Zech 7:12). The prophets spoke "not by might, nor by power, but by my Spirit, says the Lord of hosts" (Zech 4:6; cf. Luke 1:67). Felix Porsch notes the connection between the Spirit and the Word of the prophets, "Wie Gott seinen Geist auf den Propheten legt, so legt er auch sein Wort in dessen Mund."[32] The Formula of Concord recognizes the unity between the Spirit and the Word in the continued proclamation of the church: "The Word of God, when preached and heard, is a function and

---

29. *Against Heresies* 4.20.1 in *ANF* 1:487–88.

30. Wingren, *The Living Word*, 74.

31. Felix Porsch writes, "Die enge Bezogenheit von Wort und ruah Jahwehs zeigt sich nicht nur in den 'Schöpfersberichten,' sie wird auch in dem 'pneumatischen Vorgang' des Wortemphanges durch den Propheten erkennbar." ("The close relationship between between Word and *ruah* of Yahweh shows itself not only in the creation account, but it is also recognizable in the pneumatic procession of the Word through the prophet.") (*Pneuma und Wort*, 196).

32. "As God lays his Spirit on the prophet, so also he lays his Word in the prophet's mouth" (Porsch, *Pneuma und Wort*, 197).

work of the Holy Spirit, through which he is certainly present in our hearts and exercises his power there."[33]

This joint mission of the Word and the Spirit becomes even more explicit when we take a closer look at the personal Word of God. Luke records the angel's annunciation to Mary: "The Holy Spirit will come upon you, and the power of the Most High will overshadow you; therefore the child to be born will be called holy—the Son of God" (Luke 1:35; cf. Matt 1:18). The participation of the Spirit in the birth of Jesus does not diminish the unique nature of the incarnation, but rather shows that even in his birth the Word of God remains a trinitarian Word. Leopoldo Sánchez explains, "Indeed, the Word alone *assumes* and *becomes* flesh, but he does so *in the Spirit,* namely, in a way that the preexistent Son gladly receives from the Father in the economy of salvation the Spirit who creates and makes holy what he at once assumes."[34]

The connection between the personal Word of God and the Holy Spirit did not end at Christmas. At his baptism Jesus received the same Spirit by which he was conceived (Matt 3:16; Mark 1:10; Luke 3:22; cf. Acts 10:38). This anointing confirmed Jesus' identity as the Son of God, identified him as the one who would baptize with the Spirit (John 1:33–34), and inaugurated his prophetic ministry. While the Spirit was with Jesus from the moment of conception, it was not until after he was anointed with the Spirit in the Jordan that he began his prophetic ministry of preaching repentance and forgiveness of sins. After being led into temptation by the Spirit, Jesus began his ministry in "in the power of the Spirit" (Luke 4:14). In light of what took place at his baptism, we might say that Jesus' identity as Christ "does not become a concrete reality *for us* until the Father anoints *him* at the Jordan with his [i.e., the Father's] Spirit for mission."[35]

In John 6 we get a glimpse into the connection between Jesus' bearing of the Spirit *for us* and his prophetic work as the personal Word of God. After announcing his mission to do the will of the Father, many of his disciples had second thoughts: "This is a hard saying; who can listen to it?" (John 6:60). Knowing their hearts, Jesus replied, "Do you take offense at this? . . . It is the Spirit who gives life; the flesh is no help at all. The words that I have spoken to you are *spirit and life*" (John 6:61–63, emphasis added). John records two specific episodes that shed light on what it means that Jesus' words are "spirit and life." Two chapters earlier, after Jesus had returned to Galilee

---

33. *FC SD* II, 56.

34. Sánchez M., "Receiver, Bearer, and Giver," 52.

35. Ibid., 54.

from Samaria, an official from Capernaum approached him and asked him to heal his son who was "at the point of death" (John 4:47). Jesus listened to his request and responded with a command and a promise: "Go, your son will live" (John 4:49). Trusting Jesus' words, the official returned to his son. While he was still on the way he learned that his son had been healed at the very hour that Jesus had spoken.[36] The second episode occurs in chapter 11 with the death of Lazarus. Several days after Lazarus had died and been buried, Jesus arrived and mourned with the survivors. He went to the grave and spoke words that brought the dead man back to life: "Lazarus, come out!" (John 11:43). Much as he had done with the official's son, Jesus gave life to Lazarus simply by speaking.

As the anointed one (the "Christ") who bears the Spirit without measure (John 3:34), Jesus performed miraculous signs and wonders in the Spirit's power (Matt 12:28). He taught with authority and cast out demons by speaking (Mark 1:21–28). But the personal Word of God was not sent to forgive, heal, and raise to life only a few select individuals. He was sent to forgive, heal, and bring life to *all people*. John the Baptist recognized the scope of his mission: "Behold, the Lamb of God, who takes away the sin *of the world*" (John 1:29, emphasis added). As Moses lifted up the snake in the desert so that all who looked on it would be saved, so Jesus was lifted up so that all who look on him with faith would be saved (John 3:14–16). The "lifting up" took place ultimately on the cross. Jesus explains, "For this reason the Father loves me, because I lay down my life that I may take it up again. No one takes it from me, but I lay it down of my own accord. I have authority to lay it down, and I have authority to take it up again. This charge I have received from my Father" (John 10:17–18). The mission of the personal Word of God that began with his anointing with the Spirit and continued with his preaching, teaching, forgiving, and healing, was not complete (*tetelestai*) until he took the place of sinful humanity on the cross and gave up his *pneuma* (John 19:30).[37] In his crucifixion the personal Word of God glorified the Father (John 17:1–5), and after three days he "was declared to be the Son of God in power according to the Spirit of holiness by his resurrection from the dead" (Rom 1:4; cf. 1 Pet 3:18).

---

36. It is noteworthy that John introduces this episode by identifying Jesus as a prophet (John 4:44).

37. This giving of the Spirit by the Son on the cross points toward the Son's giving of the Spirit after the resurrection to the disciples for their ministry. Just as he had done by the power of the Spirit, he would send them to retain and forgive sins in his name (see John 20:20–23).

The Rejected and Crucified Word

At the heart of the biblical narrative is the suffering and death of the personal Word of God. His death was foretold by the prophets (Luke 24:25–27, 44–47) and proclaimed by the apostles (1 Cor 1:23; 2:2). Any attempt to make sense of the Word of God in the divine economy must account for the fact that Jesus was rejected and crucified. It must answer the question: what did Jesus say and do to get himself killed?[38]

Throughout the biblical narrative we see evidence that validates Wolterstorff's normative theory of discourse. Already in the garden of Eden God established a normative relationship with his human creatures by issuing commands that were morally binding. When Adam and Eve disobeyed this command ("Did God actually say . . . ?"), the death that God had warned (promised) came to pass as he spoke words of judgment (Gen 3:19). This pattern—God speaking clear commands, the people disobeying, God speaking words of judgment—is a recurring theme throughout the Old Testament narrative. Again and again God's people strayed from his commands and "did what was right in their own eyes" (see Judg 17:6; 21:25). God responded by sending prophets to remind the people of God's commands and to call them to repentance. Despite their repeated warnings, the people of God continually failed in their moral obligation to obey. Isaiah summarizes their story:

> They are a rebellious people, lying children, children unwilling to hear the instruction of the Lord; who say to the seers, "Do not see," and to the prophets, "Do not prophesy to us what is right; speak to us smooth things, prophesy illusions, leave the way, turn aside from the path, let us hear no more about the Holy One of Israel." Therefore thus says the Holy One of Israel, "Because you despise this word and trust in oppression and perverseness and rely on them, therefore this iniquity shall be to you like a breach in a high wall, bulging out, and about to collapse, whose breaking comes suddenly, in an instant; and its breaking is like that of a potter's vessel that is smashed so ruthlessly that among its fragments not a shard is found with which to take fire from the hearth, or to dip up water out of the cistern. (Isa 30:9–14)

---

38. The biblical narrative makes clear that Jesus gave up his life on his own accord (e.g., John 10:13, 17–18 and Phil 2:8), but this is to view the death of Jesus "from above," from the divine perspective. The examination of the Word of God in this chapter approaches his death from the human perspective, "from below."

When Jesus began his prophetic ministry he was acting in continuity with the long line of prophets who had come before him. Like the prophets of old he called the people to repent of their sins and obey the commands that God had given. In his first sermon Jesus affirmed the Law they had spoken:

> Do not think that I have come to abolish the Law or the Prophets; I have not come to abolish them but to fulfill them. For truly, I say to you, until heaven and earth pass away, not an iota, not a dot, will pass from the Law until all is accomplished. Therefore whoever relaxes one of the least of these commandments and teaches others to do the same will be called least in the kingdom of heaven, but whoever does them and teaches them will be called great in the kingdom of heaven. For I tell you, unless your righteousness exceeds that of the scribes and Pharisees, you will never enter the kingdom of heaven. (Matt 5:16–20)

When the people's righteousness was lacking, Jesus spoke words of judgment and condemnation:

> Then he began to denounce the cities where most of his mighty works had been done, because they did not repent. "Woe to you, Chorazin! Woe to you, Bethsaida! For if the mighty works done in you had been done in Tyre and Sidon, they would have repented long ago in sackcloth and ashes. But I tell you, it will be more bearable on the day of judgment for Tyre and Sidon than for you. And you, Capernaum, will you be exalted to heaven? You will be brought down to Hades. For if the mighty works done in you had been done in Sodom, it would have remained until this day. But I tell you that it will be more tolerable on the day of judgment for the land of Sodom than for you. (Matt 11:20–24)

Of all his words of judgment, Jesus reserved his harshest attacks for his own religious leaders. Although they knew (and even taught) the law that God had spoken through Moses, they failed to obey it. Jesus explains, "The scribes and the Pharisees sit on Moses' seat, so practice and observe whatever they tell you—but not what they do. For they preach, but do not practice" (Matt 23:2–3). His condemnation of their hypocrisy was clear and to the point: "Woe to you . . ." (Matt 23:19–36).

Jesus' proclamation of God's judgment offended the religious leaders. But that is not the only (or even the primary) reason they sought to kill him. More offensive than his words of judgment were his claims to speak words of forgiveness. Luke records:

> On one of those days, as he was teaching, Pharisees and teachers of the law were sitting there, who had come from every village of Galilee and Judea and from Jerusalem. And the power of the Lord was with him to heal. And behold, some men were bringing on a bed a man who was paralyzed, and they were seeking to bring him in and lay him before Jesus, but finding no way to bring him in, because of the crowd, they went up on the roof and let him down with his bed through the tiles into the midst before Jesus. And when he saw their faith, he said, "Man, your sins are forgiven you." And the scribes and the Pharisees began to question, saying, "Who is this who speaks blasphemies? Who can forgive sins but God alone?" When Jesus perceived their thoughts, he answered them, "Why do you question in your hearts? Which is easier, to say, 'Your sins are forgiven you,' or to say, 'Rise and walk'? But that you may know that the Son of Man has authority on earth to forgive sins"—he said to the man who was paralyzed—"I say to you, rise, pick up your bed and go home." And immediately he rose up before them and picked up what he had been lying on and went home, glorifying God. (Luke 5:17–25)

Jesus' words of forgiveness to the paralytic were unacceptable to the religious leaders because, by claiming the ability to forgive sins, Jesus was claiming to be God himself. They knew that God alone is able remove the sin and guilt of those who disobey his commands. They knew, in Wolterstorff's terms, that God is the only "qualified party" who is able to forgive those who have failed in their "moral obligation" to obey his law. And this was not the only time Jesus claimed identity with God. In John 5 he healed a man on the Sabbath who had been lame for thirty-eight years by telling him to pick up his mat and go home. When the religious leaders saw the healed man and learned that Jesus was the one who had healed him, they attacked Jesus for working on the Sabbath. Jesus responded to their criticism by saying that he was doing the work of his Father. John records their reaction: "For this reason the Jews tried all the harder to kill him; not only was he breaking the Sabbath, but he was even calling God his own Father, making himself equal to God" (John 5:17–18; see also John 10:33).

Jesus was not the first prophet to be rejected and killed for speaking the Word of God (see Luke 11:47–51).[39] But he was the first prophet who

---

39. Neither was Jesus the last deputized speaker of the Word of God to be killed. In Acts 7:51–3 Stephen, full of the Spirit, was stoned for proclaiming God's law. Stephen reminds us that those who proclaim the Word of God can expect rejection, marginalization, and persecution. As Peter writes, "Beloved, do not be surprised at the fiery trial when it comes upon you to test you, as though something strange were happening to

claimed to be the Son of God, one with the Father from the beginning (John 8:58) with authority to forgive sins and grant eternal life. It was this claim that led the Jews to pick up stones (John 8:59) and finally to demand his crucifixion. As the Jews insisted to Pilate: "We have a law, and according to that law he must die, because he claimed to be the Son of God" (John 19:7; see also Mark 2:7 and Luke 5:20–21).

The Resurrected and Vindicated Word

Earlier in this chapter we considered the *locus classicus* of the biblical prophet from Deuteronomy 18. The end of that passage bears repeating: "And if you say in your heart, 'How may we know the word that the Lord has not spoken?'—when a prophet speaks in the name of the Lord, if the word does not come to pass or come true, that is a word that the Lord has not spoken; the prophet has spoken it presumptuously" (Deut 18:21–22). The opposite is also true: if what a prophet says comes to pass, then it follows that he is a true prophet (see Jer 28:19). Jesus' identity as the personal Word of God depends on the truth of his prophecy. After his anointing with the Spirit in the Jordan, Jesus began his ministry of speaking and acting in the name of the Father. He taught and spoke as one who had authority and performed miraculous deeds to support his claims. But the ultimate test for his claims came with his death on the cross. If Jesus had remained in the tomb, his claims to be the Son of God who was one with the Father from eternity, to fulfill the prophetic writings, and to forgive the sins of those who repent and believe in him, would have been proved false. Paul's summarizes what was at stake on Easter morning: "If Christ has not been raised, your faith is futile and you are still in your sins" (1 Cor 15:17).

But in fact, Paul continues, Jesus rose (1 Cor 15:20).

As all four of the canonical gospels report, Jesus rose from the dead three days after suffering death on a cross. In doing so he fulfilled the promise he had made at the very beginning of his ministry: "Destroy this temple and in three days I will raise it up" (John 2:19; cf. Matt 26:61 and Mark 14:58). After his resurrection the disciples remembered this promise and realized that he was talking about his body (John 2:21). John records, "When therefore he was raised from the dead, his disciples remembered that he had said this, and *they believed the Scripture and the word that Jesus had spoken* (John 2:22,

---

you. But rejoice insofar as you share Christ's sufferings, that you may also rejoice and be glad when his glory is revealed. If you are insulted for the name of Christ, you are blessed, because the Spirit of glory and of God rests upon you" (1 Peter 4:12–14).

emphasis added). The significance of this verse must not be missed. It was only *after* the resurrection, *after* he had been vindicated by the Father in the power of the Spirit that the disciples "believed the Scripture and the word that Jesus had spoken." Here is the only foundation for the Christian theology of Scripture. In his resurrection from the dead Jesus was vindicated as *the* Son and deputy of God. He proved the truth of his entire ministry and message, including his claim to be one with the Father and capable of forgiving sins (John 10:30; Luke 5:24); his self-description as the way, the truth, and the life (John 14:6); his affirmation that the Word of God is true (John 17:17); his assertion that he fulfilled the prophetic writings (Luke 24:44); his confirmation of the truth of the prophetic Scriptures (John 10:35); his insistence that he speaks the truth (John 8:45; John 18:37); and his promise to send the "Spirit of truth" to guide his apostles (John 15:26; John 16:13; 1 John 5:6). "Had Christ not risen," Wingren explains, "there would have been no risen Lord to send these preachers forth, no Spirit would have been given, and no life bestowed in the Word."[40]

At this point a word must be said about the doctrine of inspiration and its attempt to defend the historical truthfulness of the Scriptures. Proponents of the doctrine of inspiration are correct to insist on the absolute necessity of God speaking truthfully. As Wolterstorff points out, interpersonal communication depends on the trustworthiness of those who make promises. If God cannot be trusted to speak truthfully, humankind's relationship with him falls apart and the Christian faith becomes nothing more than wishful thinking. Quenstedt is on the mark: "Through His infinite knowledge God the Holy Spirit cannot be ignorant of anything, can forget nothing; through his infinite truthfulness and infallibility it is impossible for Him to err, deal falsely or be mistaken, not even in the smallest degree; and finally, through His infinite goodness He is unable to deceive anyone, neither can He lead anyone into offence or error."[41] As Werner Elert puts it, "The Gospel stands or falls with God's truthfulness and reliability."[42]

Problems arise in the doctrine of inspiration, however, when the reliability of the *written* Word of God is not rooted in the reliability of *personal* Word of God. Instead of following the logic of the biblical narrative and basing the truth of the Scriptures in Jesus' resurrection (see 1 Cor 15), the doctrine of inspiration grounds the truth of the Scriptures in the *testimonium*

---

40. Wingren, *The Living Word*, 123–24.
41. Quoted in Preus, *Inspiration*, 80.
42. Elert, *The Structure of Lutheranism*, 86.

Spiritus Sancti internum.[43] This is a tenuous and subjective foundation.[44] Although it is correct in affirming the historical truthfulness of the Scriptures, the doctrine of inspiration falls short for failing to establish the historical truthfulness of the Scriptures on the resurrection of Jesus Christ from the dead.

"Co-missioned" Apostles

God spoke his Word *definitively, ultimately, decisively,* and *for all time* in Jesus Christ, the Spirit-filled personal Word of God. But God did not stop speaking at Jesus' ascension. On the evening of his resurrection Jesus appeared to his disciples and said, "'Peace be with you. As the Father has sent me, even so I am sending you.' And when he had said this, he breathed on them and said to them, 'Receive the Holy Spirit. If you forgive the sins of any, they are forgiven them; if you withhold forgiveness from any, it is withheld'" (John 20:21–23). The resurrected and vindicated personal Word of God exercised his divine authority by "co-missioning" his disciples to speak *his* Word with *his* Spirit in *his* name."[45] "All authority in heaven and on earth has been given to me. Go therefore and make disciples of all nations, baptizing them in the name of the Father and of the Son and of the Holy Spirit, *teaching them to observe all that I have commanded you.* And behold, I am with you always, to the end of the age'" (Matt 28:18–20, emphasis added). In continuity with

---

43. Robert Preus writes, "The Spirit testifies through Scripture that Scripture is divine" (*Inspiration*, 108). Again, "The divinity of Scripture is proved by its supernatural effect" (110).

44. The work of the Spirit, according to Jesus, is to "bring to remembrance all that I have taught you" (John 14:26) and to "glorify me, for he will take what is mine and declare it to you" (John 16:14). The doctrine of inspiration limits the work of the Spirit to assuring the truth of the biblical account with little or no connection to Jesus and his work of salvation. Robert Preus recognizes this danger: "The manner in which the old dogmaticians have treated the *testimonium Spiritus Sancti internum* is perhaps unfortunate. They have taken this doctrine almost exclusively in reference to the authority of Scripture, and they speak of it far less often in reference to Christ as the object of saving faith or in reference to the believer's personal assurance of faith" (*Inspiration*, 115). He concludes, "It is quite clear that the dogmaticians' emphasis upon the testimony of the Spirit witnessing to the authority of Scripture cannot be found in Luther" (*Inspiration*, 118).

45. As far as I am aware, "co-mission" in this context is a neologism. I use it to emphasize the fact that Jesus sent his apostles to continue *his* mission. Jesus sent them to do the same work of calling to repentance and forgiving sins that the Father had sent him to do. In this sense they shared in and continued the mission of the personal Word of God.

his own prophetic ministry, Jesus sent his disciples to do two things: to call the people to repentance for failing in their moral obligation to obey God's commands, and to speak words of forgiveness and life to those who repent.

> Then he said to them, "These are my words that I spoke to you while I was still with you, that everything written about me in the Law of Moses and the Prophets and the Psalms must be fulfilled." Then he opened their minds to understand the Scriptures, and said to them, "Thus it is written, that the Christ should suffer and on the third day rise from the dead, and that *repentance and forgiveness of sins should be proclaimed in his name to all nations*, beginning from Jerusalem. You are witnesses of these things. And behold, I am sending the promise of my Father upon you. But stay in the city until you are clothed with power from on high." (Luke 24:44–49, emphasis added)

Among those sent by Jesus is one who was "untimely born" (1 Cor 15:8).

> Paul, a servant of Christ Jesus, called to be an apostle, set apart for the gospel of God, which he promised beforehand through his prophets in the holy Scriptures, concerning his Son, who was descended from David according to the flesh and was declared to be the Son of God in power according to the Spirit of holiness by his resurrection from the dead, Jesus Christ our Lord, through whom we have received grace and apostleship to bring about the obedience of faith for the sake of his name among all the nations. (Rom 1:1–5)

The apostle Paul was "sent by Jesus Christ" (Gal 1:1) and "set apart for the Gospel" (Rom 1:1) according to the "will of God" (1 Cor 1:1; 2 Cor 1:1; Eph 1:1; Col 1:1) to "preach him among the Gentiles" (Gal 1:16; see 1 Thess 2:4). Together with the other apostles he spoke as one who had been sent by the personal Word of God with the "full authority" of the one who sent him.

Sent with the Word and the Spirit

The commission received by the apostles to continue the work of Christ consisted primarily of preaching and teaching the Word they had heard from Jesus. David Lotz writes, "God's speaking and acting in Christ would remain *meaningless and ineffectual* without the oral witness to the Word made flesh, namely, the apostolic preaching or publishing of Christ to the world, the gospel or 'good news' of Christ as 'God for us.' Hence, the personal Word cannot be considered apart from the *spoken Word*."⁴⁶ In order to accomplish this work of proclaiming the Word of God, Jesus gave his apostles his Spirit.

It is helpful at this point to recall that the words of Jesus are "spirit and life" (John 6:63). It is also helpful to remember that Jesus did not begin his prophetic ministry until he had been anointed by the Spirit in the Jordan (see Luke 4:18–19). As the Father had sent the Son with the Spirit (John 3:34), Jesus was now sending his apostles with the same Spirit he had received from the Father.⁴⁷ With this Spirit they would continue the work of Jesus by speaking in his name and with his authority. Porsch explains, "Sie handeln niemals im eigenen Namen und eigener Autorität, sondern nur im Namen des Senden."⁴⁸ Wolterstorff summarizes John's description of the relationship between Jesus and his apostles, including the central role of the Spirit:

> In John, from chapter 13 through chapter 17, we get Jesus' final address to his disciples. It too, is a commissioning address; and the undertone, clear though mainly unspoken, is that the disciples are to be Jesus *representatives*. The words that the Father gave to Jesus, Jesus gave to his disciples. They have received them, and know in truth that Jesus came from the Father. They are now to give those words, and that knowledge, to others. They are able to do so because they have been with Jesus from the beginning, and because they will receive the Advocate, the Spirit of truth, who will guide them into all truth; the Advocate will remind them of all that Jesus said to them. "Very truly, I tell you," says Jesus, "whoever receives one whom I send receives me; and whoever receives me receives him who sent me." (13:20)⁴⁹

From the very beginning of their mission the apostles focused their efforts on proclaiming the Word they received from Jesus and the Spirit. This began on the day of Pentecost. After receiving the Spirit and speaking the wonders of God in many languages, Peter stood up and preached the first recorded Christian sermon (Acts 2). This preaching continued throughout the book of Acts as Luke described the work of the apostles as a "ministry of the word" (Acts 6:4). The "ministry of the Word" was also a "ministry of reconciliation." Paul describes, "All this is from God, who through Christ

---

46. Lotz, "Proclamation of the Word," 346. His emphasis.

47. In this sense "sending with the Spirit" is synonymous with having the authority to speak the Word of God and retain and forgive sins *in his name* (John 20:20–23).

48. "They never act in their own name or authority, but rather only in the name of their sender" (Porsch, *Pneuma und Wort*, 366).

49. Wolterstorff, *Divine Discourse*, 293.

reconciled us to himself and gave us the ministry of reconciliation; that is, in Christ God was reconciling the world to himself, not counting their trespasses against them, and entrusting to us the message of reconciliation. Therefore, we are ambassadors for Christ, God making his appeal through us. We implore you on behalf of Christ, be reconciled to God" (2 Cor 5:18–20). The apostles' reception of the Spirit also meant guidance and direction for their teaching of the Word (John 14:25–26). Jesus told his apostles, "I still have many things to say to you, but you cannot bear them now. When the Spirit of truth comes, he will guide you into all the truth, for he will not speak on his own authority, but whatever he hears he will speak, and he will declare to you the things that are to come. He will glorify me, for he will take what is mine and declare it to you. All that the Father has is mine; therefore I said that he will take what is mine and declare it to you" (John 16:12–15). Through his sending of the Spirit Jesus promised the truth of the apostolic message. So Barth says of the Spirit: "He is simply the Teacher of the Word: of that Word which is never without its Teacher."[50] As the "Teacher of the Word" the Spirit revealed to the apostles the fullness of who Jesus is and what he has done. Porsch explains that the Spirit "führt nicht in eine abstrakte Wahrheit, in eine Welt der Ideen; er vermittelt nicht neues Wissen, noch unbekannte 'Wahrheiten.' Sein 'Führen in die Füllen der Wahrheit' ist eine 'Reden,' ein Offenbaren . . . dessen, was vor Jesus 'hört,' was er vom 'Eigenen' Jesu 'emphängt,' also eine Fortführung der Offenbarung Jesu."[51] The fullness of this truth was centered in Jesus' sacrificial death and resurrection. Paul insists that he preaches nothing other than "Jesus Christ and him crucified" (1 Cor 2:2; 1 Cor 1:18). Luther emphasizes the same point: "At its briefest, the gospel is a discourse about Christ, that is the Son of God who became man for us, that he died and was raised, that he has been established as a Lord over all things."[52] All the Scriptures point to Christ, which is what Luther means when he describes the Old Testament writings as "the swaddling clothes" and "manger" in which Christ lies.[53]

---

50. Barth, *CD* 1/2:244.

51. The Spirit "does not lead them into an abstract truth, to a world of ideas; he supplies neither new knowledge nor unknown 'truths.' His 'leading into the fullness of truth' is a speaking, a revelation . . . of what he hears from Jesus, what he receives from Jesus himself, therefore a continuation of the revelation of Jesus" (Porsch, *Pneuma und Wort*, 302).

52. Luther, *LW* 35:118.

53. Ibid., 35:122.

Although the apostolic office came to an end with the death of the last apostle, the apostolic mission of proclaiming the Word of God in the power of the Spirit has continued in the church to the present day. Paul points in this direction: "How then will they call on him in whom they have not believed? And how are they to believe in him of whom they have never heard? And how are they to hear without someone preaching? And how are they to preach unless they are sent? As it is written, "How beautiful are the feet of those who preach the good news!" . . . So faith comes from hearing, and hearing through the word of Christ (Rom 10:14–17). Jesus similarly pointed toward the continual sending of preachers: "Repentance and forgiveness of sins should be proclaimed in his name *to all nations*, beginning from Jerusalem" (Luke 24:47, emphasis added). Wingren writes, "*The Word exists to be made known; only when it is preached is its objective content fully disclosed.*"[54]

Because the preaching of the Word of God stands at the heart of the church's mission to continue the work of Christ, Luther identifies the Word of God as the first and most important mark of the church.[55] He writes:

> The Church is a mouth-house [*Mundhaus*], not a pen-house [*Federhaus*], for since Christ's advent that Gospel is preached orally which before was hidden in written books. It is the way of the Gospel and of the New Testament that it is to be preached and discussed orally with a living voice. Christ himself wrote nothing, nor did he give command to write, but to preach orally. Thus the apostles were not sent out until Christ came to his mouth-house, that is, until the time had come to preach orally and to bring the Gospel from dead writing and pen-work to the living voice and mouth. From this time the church is rightly called Bethphage, since she has and hears the living voice of the Gospel.[56]

Rather than trying to comprehend God with our eyes (in the rationalistic mode of believing only what can be seen), Luther emphasizes the necessity of *listening* to the Word: "Sieh ihn nicht mit den Augen an, sondern stecke die Augen in die Ohren!"[57]

Because of the importance of the preached Word of God in the ongoing mission of the church, Luther holds in highest esteem the work of the

---

54. Wingren, *The Living Word*, 13.
55. Luther, *LW* 41:148–51.
56. Luther, *Complete Sermons*, 1:44.
57. "Do not look at him with your eyes, but rather stick your eyes in your ears!" (Mühlhaupt, *Luthers Evangelien Auslegung*, 704).

preacher. Again and again he emphasizes that the Word spoken by the faithful Christian preacher is the Word of God himself. "Listen, brother: God, the creator of heaven and earth, speaks with you through his preachers."[58] Through the faithful preacher God continues to speak—not because of the person of the preacher, but because of the Word that he has been sent to speak. The risen Christ continues to send his people to speak his Word and give his Spirit in the here and now to forgive the sins of those who repent and believe. Luther summarizes, "Denn unser Herr Gott hat vergebung der sünden inn kein Werk gelegt, das wir thün, sonder in das einnige werk, das Christus gelitten hat unnd aufferstanden ist. Das selb werk aber hat durch das wort inn der Apostlen und seiner Kirchen diener, ja zur not, in aller Christen mund gelegt, das sie dadurch vergebung der sünden aufstehlen und allen, die es begeren, verkundigen sollen."[59]

The Spoken Word and the Sacraments

The preacher's sermon is a primary instance of God's spoken Word, but it is not the only way in which God delivers his spoken Word. His Word is also proclaimed through specific churchly acts instituted by Jesus himself. The church calls these unique acts "sacraments."

The sacraments have played an important role in the church since its earliest days. In obedience to Jesus final command, the earliest church made new disciples by baptizing people in the name of the Father and the Son and the Holy Spirit. In remembrance of the last supper he ate with his disciples, the church has celebrated the Lord's Supper as a central part of the Christian life. In both of these instances, God's Word is spoken in conjunction with physical elements—water, bread, and wine. The key to these churchly acts is not the physical elements, however, but the spoken Word. Augustine highlights this in his definition of a sacrament: "Accedat verbum ad elementum et fit sacramentum" ("When the Word is added to the element, it becomes a sacrament").[60] The sixteenth-century reformers picked up on Augustine's definition as they tried to understand the significance of the sacraments.

---

58. Luther, *Tisch Reden WA* TR 4:531, no. 4812.

59. "For our Lord God has bestows the forgiveness of sin, not through work we do, but rather through the unique suffering and resurrection of Christ. This same work, however, is done through the word of the apostles and his church's ministers, and when necessary, through the mouth of all Christians, so that all who need and desire the forgiveness of sins shall hear it proclaimed" (Luther, *Hauspostille* 1544, in WA 52.273).

60. *Tractate* 80, *NPNF*, ser. 1, 7:344.

They continued his emphasis on the spoken Word in the sacraments, describing them as instances of the "visible word," the "picture of the Word" in which the Word of God is received with the eyes.[61] Like the preached Word, God is the one who speaks in these unique acts. In his explanation of baptism, for instance, Luther pointed to the Word: "For without the Word of God the water is just plain water and not a baptism, but with the Word of God it is a baptism."[62] He spoke similarly of the Lord's Supper: "The chief thing is God's Word and ordinance or command."[63] The Lord's Supper is "set within God's Word and bound to it."[64] With baptism and the Lord's Supper (as well as confession and absolution), God's Word of forgiveness in Christ makes the difference. Luther explains: "Wherever God's Word is, whether in baptism, absolution, the Sacrament, or in the preaching of the Gospel, God is speaking with us. In absolution, he himself is releasing us from sin; in the Sacrament, or Lord's Supper, Christ himself nurtures us with his body and blood. Similarly we have God's Word in the church, yes, in the home. When the pastor speaks God's Word to us in the church, or the father at home, God himself is speaking to us."[65]

Inseparable from the spoken Word (in preaching as well as the sacraments) is the life-giving Spirit of God. This was clearly seen on the day of Pentecost. After leading the people to confess their sins through the preached Word, Peter gave them this command and promise related to the baptismal Word: "Repent and be baptized every one of you in the name of Jesus Christ for the forgiveness of your sins, and you will receive the gift of the Holy Spirit" (Acts 2:38). The spoken Word (in baptism, in this case) and the reception of the Holy Spirit went hand in hand. So the Augsburg Confession identifies the preached Word and the sacraments as the means by which God gives his Spirit: "Through the Word and the sacraments as through instruments the Holy Spirit it given, who effects faith where and when it pleases God in those who *hear* the gospel."[66] J. T. Mueller summarizes Luther's emphasis on the Word of the Gospel: "It is the Word, the Gospel, that does everything, nothing else, nothing added by men: the Gospel proclaimed, the Gospel read, the Gospel symbolically presented, the Gospel applied in absolution, the Gospel

---

61. "For just as the Word enters through the ear in order to strike the heart, so also the rite enters through the eye in order to move the heart" (*Ap* XIII.5).

62. Luther, *SC* Baptism, 9–10.

63. Luther, *LC* V.4.

64. Luther, *LC* V.9.

65. Luther, *Sermon on Luke 18:31–43* (1534). Lenker, 5:308.

66. *CA* V.2. Latin text. Emphasis added.

in Baptism, the Gospel in the Lord's Supper, the Gospel in the 'mutual conversation and consolation of the brethren.'"[67]

In whichever form it is spoken—through preaching or in the sacraments—the Word of God remains the living and active instrument through which God kills and makes alive through his Spirit. His Word of law and judgment cuts to the heart (Acts 2:37); it incites rage among those who refuse to repent (Acts 5:33; 7:54); and it is the instrument by which God promises to overthrow the man of lawlessness (2 Thess 2:8). His Word of forgiveness and life is the "power of salvation for those who believe" (Rom 1:16); it comes "in power and in the Holy Spirit" (1 Thess 1:5); and it delivers the Holy Spirit into the hearts of those who hear and believe (Acts 10:44). Regin Prenter emphasizes the cruciform character of this spoken Word: "In every word of the *law*, which humbles us and reduces us to nothing, God is uniting us with the *crucified* Christ; and in every word of the *gospel*, which gives us Christ as our righteousness, God is uniting us with the *risen* Christ."[68]

From Spoken to Written Word

Up to this point in our examination of the Word of God in the divine economy, I have said very little about the Scriptures themselves. I have focused on the Word that God spoke through his Spirit-led deputized prophets. I have emphasized that God spoke *definitively, ultimately, decisively,* and *for all time* through Jesus, the Spirit-filled personal Word of God. I have highlighted Jesus' co-missioning of the apostles to continue speaking his Word under the guidance of his Spirit as they and their associates (the church) continue teaching his commands and forgiving sins in his name. Here, within the context of the trinitarian economy of salvation, we are finally ready to consider the *written* form of the Word. Indeed, the underlying claim that I am making throughout this book is that the written Word of God is only properly understood when it is approached in relation to the spoken and personal forms of the Word of God. N. T. Wright points in this direction when he describes the role of the Word in the economy of salvation:

> Here we have the roots of a fully Christian theology of scriptural authority: planted firmly in the soil of the missionary community, confronting the powers of the world with the news of the kingdom

---

67. Mueller, "Notes," 599. Cf. *SA* III.4.
68. Prenter et al., *More About Luther*, 2:72.

of God, refreshed and invigorated by the Spirit, growing particularly through the preaching and teaching of the apostles, and bearing fruit in the transformation of human lives as the start of God's project to put the whole cosmos to rights. God accomplishes these things, so the early church believed, through 'the word'; the story of Israel now told as reaching its climax in Jesus, God's call to Israel now transmuted into God's call to his renewed people. And it was this 'word' which came, through the work of the early writers, to be expressed in the writing of the New Testament as we know it.[69]

As Wright suggests, much of what needs to be said about Scripture has already been said about the personal and spoken forms of the Word of God. After all, the written Word is nothing more than the prophetic and apostolic proclamation put down into writing. As Barth puts it, the written Word is "the deposit of what was once proclamation by human lips."[70] Joachim Ringleben calls the transition of the Word from speech to script as the "Schriftwerdung des Wortes Gottes"—the "becoming-text of the Word of God."[71] He writes, "Die mündliche Predigt von Christus zur heiligen Schrift wurde, und das besagt: Das Wort ward Text."[72]

Martin Chemnitz offers a detailed account of this movement from spoken to written Word in his *Examination of the Council of Trent*. In order to defend against Rome's claim that post-apostolic tradition is equally authoritative as the apostolic Word, he emphasizes that the writings of both the prophets and apostles are one and the same as their proclamation. Regarding the Old Testament: "In order that the Word, which is the only organ of the Spirit, may not be corrupted, or it become uncertain what the Word is, God in the Old Testament commanded that it be comprehended in writing."[73] Chemnitz notes that the Word God spoke through Adam, Noah, Abraham, and the other patriarchs was not initially written down. Instead, it was passed down from generation to generation "by a living voice."[74] As the centuries passed this oral tradition was in danger of losing its purity and becoming corrupt. So with Moses God provided a more permanent form of his Word. Chemnitz explains:

69. Wright, *Scripture*, 37.
70. Barth, *CD* 1/1:102.
71. "The oral proclamation of Christ became Holy Scripture; in other words, the Word became text" (Ringleben, "Die Bibel," 31).
72. Ringleben, "Die Bibel," 32.
73. Chemnitz, *Examination*, 76.
74. Ibid., 51.

> We have thus shown two things from the most ancient sacred history: (1) the purity of the heavenly doctrine was not preserved always and everywhere through tradition by the living voice but was repeatedly corrupted and adulterated; (2) in order that new and special revelations might not always be necessary for restoring and retaining purity of the doctrine, God instituted another method under Moses, namely, that the doctrine of the Word of God should be comprehended in writing.[75]

After the Word of God had been written down by Moses "the church of the children of Israel was a pillar and ground of the truth, because to them had been entrusted the oracles of God (Rom. 3:2)."[76] The written Word of the prophets became the "norm and rule of faith, and of decisions in controversies and disputes concerning religion."[77] This view of the Old Testament was operative until the personal Word began his prophetic ministry.

About the New Testament Chemnitz notes agreement between the Lutherans and Romanists in the sixteenth century: "The doctrine of the New Testament . . . is what Christ in the time of his flesh during his ministry proclaimed with His own mouth, and what the apostles, once they had been led by the Holy Spirit into all truth, preached to every creature in all the world."[78] This doctrine was originally proclaimed both by Christ and the apostles "unwritten and orally," but was afterward written down by the apostles.[79] Chemnitz points to Irenaeus, who said:

> That alone is the true and living faith which the church has received from the apostles and communicated to her children. For the Lord of all gave His apostles the power of the Gospel, and through them we also have come to know the truth, that is, the doctrine of the Son of God; to whom also the Lord said, "He who hears you hears Me, and he who rejects you rejects Me and Him who sent Me." For through no others do we know the plan of salvation except through those by whom the Gospel has come to us. That, indeed, which they then preached, they afterward delivered to us in the Scriptures by the will of God, that it should be the foundation and pillar of our faith.[80]

---

75. Ibid., 54.
76. Ibid., 55.
77. Ibid., 62.
78. Ibid., 77.
79. Ibid.
80. Irenaeus, *Against Heresies* 3.1, quoted in Chemnitz, *Examination*, 80–81.

As their preaching and teaching was challenged and corrupted by false teachers (Gal 1:6–9), the apostles put into written form the Word they had been proclaiming orally. Lotz explains, "Christ's own preaching and that of the apostles eventually assumed written form, owing to the exigent need to preserve this preaching in its original purity and to protect it from the vagaries of false teachers and heretics."[81]

Chemnitz cites numerous examples of early church fathers who viewed the apostolic writings in this way. Chrysostom explained, "Matthew wrote when the believers in Christ from the Jews had approached him and asked that he would send them in writing what he had taught them by word of mouth, that it might be preserved."[82] Eusebius had a similar view:

> When the Gospel had come to the West, such a great light of devotion illumined the minds of those who had heard Peter that they could not be content with the unwritten teaching of the divine proclamation or remain steadfast in the things which they had learned of the divine Word without writing; but they implored Mark with great earnestness that he would leave them a written account of that doctrine which they had received orally . . . And they say that the apostle Peter, when he knew this by inspiration of the Holy Spirit, was delighted by the wish of these men, in a formal statement approved this writing, confirmed it, and ordained that it should be read in the churches.[83]

Much like the "Schriftwerdung" of the prophets and the gospels, the letters of Paul are nothing other than the written form of his original proclamation of the Word. Again Chemnitz: "The epistles of Paul were written so that they might be 'reminders,' embracing in a compendium the very same things which he had clearly transmitted orally and personally."[84] This resonates with Paul's words to the Thessalonians: "So then, brothers, stand firm and hold to the traditions that you were taught by us, either by our spoken word or by our letter" (2 Thess 2:15). Sasse summarizes: "All proclamation that is to be preserved must be written down. The written Word may lack the freshness of oral proclamation, but its contents remain the same, and it gains the advantage of remaining unchanged and being preserved for future generations."[85]

---

81. Lotz, "Proclamation," 347.
82. Chysostom, *Homily 1 on Matthew*, quoted in Chemnitz, *Examination*, 86.
83. Eusebius, 2.15, quoted in Chemnitz, *Examination*, 88.
84. Chemnitz, *Examination*, 106.
85. Sasse, "Luther and the Word of God," 71–72.

Because they were deputized and co-missioned by God himself, the prophets and apostles occupy a unique position in the divine economy. The Word they wrote became the standard by which all subsequent preaching and teaching would be measured. As Barth points out, the prophets and apostles occupy a "singular and unique position and significance."[86] Their writings have "supremacy" and "absolute constitutive significance"[87] for present day preaching. He quotes Luther:

> Now when He says, Ye also shall bear witness, for ye have been with me from the beginning, He thereby specially depicts the apostles for all preachers and confirms their preaching so that all the world should be bound to their word, and believe the same without any contradiction and be certain that all they preach and teach is right doctrine and the Holy Ghost's preaching which they have heard and received from Him . . . Such witness have no preachers on earth save the apostles only, for the others are hereby commanded that they should all follow in the apostles' footsteps, abide by the same doctrine and preach nothing more or otherwise.[88]

Because of the unique position of the prophets and apostles in the economy of salvation, those who speak the Word of God *after* them have nothing more and nothing less than the Word that they have received *from* them. This is what it means to be an apostolic church.[89] Paul points in this direction when he says the church is "built on the foundation of the apostles and prophets, Christ Jesus himself being the cornerstone" (Eph 2:20; see also 2 Pet 3:2). It is the continuing work of the church at all times and in all places to proclaim the same Word of Christ that the personal Word gave the apostles in the power of his Spirit. H. S. Wilson summarizes, "According to Luther, the preacher has nothing *new* to say other than what has already been spoken and written by the apostles."[90]

In his study of the apostolic fathers, H. M. Scott observes that the early church fathers recognized the unique authority of the apostolic message. He explains, "It is plain from direct and indirect references to apostolic

---

86. Barth, *CD* 1/2:495.

87. Barth, *CD* 1/1:102.

88. Luther, *Crucigers Sommerpostille*, quoted in Barth, *CD* 1/1:103.

89. Barth writes, "Apostolicity is one of the decisive notes of the true Church" (*CD* 1/1:103), and "The apostolic succession of the Church must mean that it is guided by the Canon, that is, by the prophetic and apostolic word as the necessary rule of every word that is valid in the Church" (*CD* 1/1:104).

90. Wilson, "Luther on Preaching," 67.

writers that their successors shrank from all comparison of position, looked to them as having peculiar authority from Christ, especially endowed by the Holy Ghost, and considered their oral and written instruction as of final character."[91] Scott cites numerous early fathers to show how they separated themselves from the apostolic Word. Ignatius: "Shall I reach such a height of self-esteem . . . as to issue commands to you as if I were an apostle?"[92] Polycarp: "Brethren, I write these things to you . . . not assuming anything to myself, but because ye besought me to do so. For neither I nor any other like me can equal the wisdom of the blessed and glorious Paul."[93] Barnabas insisted that he speaks "not as an apostle but as your teacher, as one of yourselves."[94] Clement: "The apostles were made preachers of the gospel to us by the Lord Jesus Christ. Jesus Christ was sent by God. So Christ is from God, and the apostles from Christ."[95] While the distinctions between that which is apostolic and that which is patristic may not always be as clear as have sometimes been suggested,[96] the early fathers explicitly separated their own writings from those of the apostles, striving to conserve, continue, and ground their ministry in the apostolic message. Scott concludes, "The apostolic writings were not to [the early fathers] the survival of the fittest, the cream of primitive Christian literature, differing only in degree, but not in kind of excellence from post-apostolic works. They were the lively oracles of God, spoken and written once for all to guide the Church in all ages."[97]

John Behr notes this understanding of the Word of God in Irenaeus, who "begins by affirming categorically that the revelation of God is mediated through the apostles."[98] For Irenaeus "the locus of revelation, and the medium for our relationship with God, is precisely in the apostolic preaching of him, the Gospel which, as we have seen, stands in an interpretative engagement with Scripture. The role of the apostles in delivering the Gospel is definitive."[99] By virtue of their commission from Christ himself, the Word of God proclaimed by the apostles forms the foundation for all subsequent Christian proclamation. Irenaeus writes, "We have learned from no others

---

91. Scott, "The Apostolic Fathers," 485–86.
92. Ibid., 480.
93. Ibid.
94. Ibid.
95. Ibid., 481.
96. Williams, *Evangelicals and Tradition*, 52–53.
97. Scott, "The Apostolic Fathers," 488.
98. Behr, *Way to Nicea*, 38.
99. Ibid., 38–39.

the plan of our salvation than from those through whom the Gospel has come down to us, which they did at one time proclaim in public, and at a later period, by the will of God, handed down to us in the Scriptures, to be the ground and pillar of our faith."[100] As D. H. Williams summarizes, "Any of the ancient church fathers would have been horrified to find their written legacy placed on a par with Holy Scripture."[101]

Summary

I began this chapter by agreeing with Karl Barth that the proper context for the Christian theology of Scripture is a trinitarian theology of the Word of God. Unlike Barth's account of the Word, however, I offered an account of the Word that recognizes God's use of deputized discourse and takes into consideration the central significance of Jesus' death and resurrection. This account of the Word of God begins with the recognition that Jesus is the Spirit-empowered, crucified, and risen Word sent by the Father to proclaim repentance and forgiveness of sins. It continues with the recognition that God has spoken his Word in many and various ways, through prophets, apostles, preachers, and ultimately through all Christians. It concludes with the recognition that the prophetic and apostolic Scriptures are the written form of the Word of God—the final authority and standard by which all Christian proclamation is to be measures. Wingren explains the economy of this Word: "The Word was not just God once upon a time, did not just once upon a time become flesh (John 1:1, 14), but the Word *is* God and now *becomes* flesh. It comes with the reading of the passages of Scripture, with the advance of the *kerygma* as a living Word, with Christ's divinity hidden in the ordinary human voice that proclaims the Word."[102]

While there are many ways in which this threefold Word of God might be summarized, at its most basic it could be said that the Word of God saves. The personal Word was sent by the Father in the Spirit to save the world through his life, death, resurrection, and promised return (1 John 4:14); the spoken Word has the power of salvation as it bestows life, forgiveness, and

---

100. *Against the Heresies*, 3.1.1, in *ANF* 1:414.

101. Williams, *Evangelicals and Tradition*, 60. Augustine writes, "What more shall I teach you than what we read in the apostle? For Holy Scripture fixes the rule of our doctrine, lest we dare to be wiser than we ought. Therefore I should not teach you anything else except to expound to you the words of the Teacher" (quoted in Chemnitz, *Examination*, 152).

102. Wingren, *The Living Word*, 213.

salvation to those who believe (Rom 1:16); the written Word is the prophetic and apostolic proclamation put down into writing so that we might believe that Jesus is the Christ and have life in his name (John 20:31). This written Word is profitable for salvation and useful for teaching and correcting, and in these terms it is described as *theopneustos* (2 Tim 3:16). In whatever form it appears, the Word of God accomplishes the saving will of the Father in the power of the Holy Spirit. Roehrs summarizes, "God speaks before and after the incarnation in the Word and words uttered and written by human beings, also in His determined manner, in order to bring to men the good news of this eternal plan of redemption and its accomplishment, and in order to create in men the faith which accepts this accomplished salvation through the power with which he has invested these words."[103] Or as Paul says to the Corinthians, "For God, who said, "Let light shine out of darkness," has shone in our hearts to give the light of the knowledge of the glory of God in the face of Jesus Christ" (2 Cor 4:6). Martin Franzmann captures this understanding of the saving Word of the Triune God in his hymn, "Thy Strong Word":

> Thy strong Word did cleave the darkness;
> At Thy speaking it was done.
> For created light we thank Thee,
> While Thine ordered seasons run.

> Lo, on those who dwelt in darkness,
> Dark as night and deep as death,
> Broke the light of Thy salvation,
> Breathed Thine own life-breathing breath.

> Thy strong Word bespeaks us righteous;
> Bright with Thine own holiness,
> Glorious now, we press toward glory,
> And our lives our hopes confess.

> From the cross Thy wisdom shining
> Breaketh forth in conquering might;
> From the cross forever beameth
> All Thy bright redeeming light.

> Give us lips to sing Thy glory,
> Tongues Thy mercy to proclaim,
> Throats that shout the hope that fills us,
> Mouths to speak Thy holy name.

---

103. Roehrs, "The Word in the Word," 105.

> God the Father, light-creator,
> To Thee laud and honor be.
> To Thee, Light of Light begotten,
> Praise be sung eternally.
> Holy Spirit, light-revealer, glory, glory be to Thee.
> Mortals, angels, now and ever praise the Holy Trinity![104]

---

104. Franzmann, "Thy Strong Word," in *Lutheran Service Book*, 578.

4

One Word, Many Forms

It takes only a casual reading through the prologue of John's Gospel to notice that the phrase "Word of God" has foundational significance for the Christian faith. As I tried to demonstrate in chapter 3, the Word of God is a deep and multifaceted concept with number of distinct, yet closely related referents. Karl Barth recognized this, which is why his *Church Dogmatics* was a significant contribution to the modern debate. Because of his influence in contemporary thinking, therefore, it is surprising that so few have continued his focus on the theology of the Word of God. Wolterstorff observes, "In the first half of [the twentieth] century there was a great deal of talk among *theologians* about the 'Word of God.' That talk, so far as I can tell, has withered on the vine in recent years."[1] This lack of attention to the Word of God in contemporary theology has contributed to a widespread lack of clarity when it comes to talk about the Word of God. Fifty years ago Walter Roehrs lamented this confusion: "One frequently finds the term 'Word' used so vaguely in contemporary theology that all distinctions are blurred."[2] Roehrs' concern remains valid today as theologians continue to say important things about the Word of God without unpacking what they mean. This can be found even among those working on the contemporary theology of Scripture.[3]

1. Wolterstorff, *Divine Discourse*, 9.
2. Roehrs, "The Word," 81.
3. The title of Telford Work's book on the theology of Scripture is a good example. Presumably drawn from Hebrews 4:12, the book is called *Living and Active: Scripture in the Economy of Salvation*. But in Hebrews 4:12 it is the *Word of God* that is "living and active."

Among theologians who *have* tried to articulate a more precise understanding of the Word of God, a variety of structures and proposals have been offered. Paul Tillich, for example, speaks of six forms of the Word.[4] Robert Kolb narrows the list to four,[5] and we have already discussed the three forms of the Word in Barth.[6] The purpose of this chapter is to think dogmatically about the Word of God and consider some of the ways in which theologians have related these forms to each other. My goal is to identify a dogmatic framework that is consistent with the biblical narrative and useful for teaching in the church.

The Analogy of the Word

One of the most popular ways in which theologians have tried to make dogmatic sense of the Word of God in the biblical narrative is to highlight the ontological similarities between Jesus and the Scriptures. Known as the "Analogy of the Word," this approach compares the hypostatic union of the two natures of Christ to the relationship between the divine and the human attributes of the Scriptures. Clark Pinnock explains the idea:

> It is natural to see an analogy between the incarnational character of revelation and the Bible. As the Logos was enfleshed in the life of Jesus, so God's Word is enlettered in the script of the Bible. In both cases there is some kind of mysterious union of the divine and the human, though of course not the same kind. But in each case both the divine and the human are truly present. The analogy helps us to defend the true humanity of the Bible against Docetism and to defend its divine authority against the Ebionitism of liberal theology.[7]

Carl Braaten makes a similar comparison for biblical interpretation. He calls for a "Chalcedonian hermeneutic" that takes into consideration the similarities between the written and incarnate Word. "The relevance of the

---

4. Tillich's six forms include: (1) the principle of divine self-manifestation, (2) the medium of creation, (3) the manifestation of divine life in the history of revelation, (4) Jesus, (5) the Bible, and (6) church proclamation through preaching and teaching (*Systematic Theology*, 1:174–6).

5. In addition to Jesus, Kolb identifies three other forms of the Word: written, oral, and sacramental (*The Christian Faith*, 184–85).

6. It would also be possible to consider the Word of God in two forms: created and uncreated.

7. Pinnock, *The Scripture Principle*, 97.

incarnation to biblical interpretation is spelled out in terms of the Chalcedonian model of explaining the meaning of the 'Word made flesh' . . . Just as the Word became flesh—without one being changed into the other or separated from each other, as Chalcedon taught—so we have treasures of divine revelation in vessels of human language and history."[8] More recently Peter Enns has assigned paradigmatic significance to this incarnational analogy for the theology of Scripture in his book, *Inspiration and Incarnation*. He maintains the only way to make sense of the inspiration of the Scriptures is to understand them as a "necessary consequence of God incarnating himself."[9]

A sophisticated account of the Analogy of the Word can be found in Telford Work's *Living and Active*. Work identifies the Analogy of the Word as the key dogmatic framework for considering the nature and function of the Scriptures. In order to make his case he enlists a vast array of historical and contemporary theological proposals. He begins by recalling Athanasius' writing on the incarnation of the *logos* together with Augustine's emphasis on the analogy between human speech and "the enfleshment of the Word."[10] He brings in Barth's threefold form of the Word as "a resource for expanding it into a properly Trinitarian account of the Bible,"[11] and then turns to Hans Urs von Balthasar's understanding of *kenosis* of the Word to strengthen the correspondence between the hypostatic union and verbal union. There he finds a "quasi-sacramental ontology for Scripture."[12] Finally, he adds the insights of Spirit-Christology to articulate a version of the Analogy of the Word that he refers to as a "bibliology of Word and Spirit."[13]

Work's version of the Analogy of the Word goes beyond most casual comparisons of the similarities between Jesus and the Bible. It is rooted in the history of the church and creatively incorporates many insights from many sources. Despite its ingenuity, however, there remain significant concerns with thinking of the Word of God in this way. Like the doctrine of inspiration, the Analogy of the Word is not necessarily *wrong*. But there are at least three reasons for suggesting that it might not be the most helpful way of thinking about the ways in which the biblical narrative speaks of the Word of God. The first concern with the Analogy of the Word is the effect that it has

---

8. Braaten, "A Chalcedonian Hermeneutic," 20.
9. Enns, *Inspiration and Incarnation*, 20.
10. Work, *Living and Active*, 52.
11. Ibid., 67.
12. Ibid., 100.
13. Ibid., 122.

on Christology. Despite the apparent similarities between the two natures of Jesus and the divine/human aspects of Holy Scripture, there is simply no true analogy for what God has done in Christ. The incarnation is entirely unique. For this reason the Lutheran dogmaticians were reluctant to make too much of the comparison. They were convinced that it would "almost certainly do violence to the doctrine of the personal union," which was "unique and without analogy."[14] John Webster agrees: "Like any extension of the notion of the incarnation . . . the result can be christologically disastrous, in that it may threaten the uniqueness of the Word's becoming flesh by making 'incarnation' a general principle or characteristic of divine action in, through, or under creaturely reality."[15] Because of God's unequivocal act of condescension in the person of Jesus, it is best to reserve "incarnational" language for the personal Word of God alone. The second reason for questioning the usefulness of the Analogy of the Word is that it conceives of the Scriptures (and Christ) in primarily static and objective terms. This is related to a helpful criticism that Spirit-Christology makes of classic Logos-Christology. While it was necessary for the church of the first four centuries to unpack the inner constitution of Jesus' two natures in order to defend against heresy, Logos-Christology's focus on the hypostatic union tends to obscure the work of Christ together with the Spirit in completing his mission of salvation. The result was an imbalanced view of the person and work of Jesus.[16] In a similar way, the Analogy of the Word and its focus on the "two natures" of the Scriptures tends to limit the role of the Spirit to the composition of the biblical writings. When the Scriptures are viewed primarily as a finished product to be studied and analyzed, the ongoing role of the Spirit in relation to the Scriptures in the divine economy is often left out of the discussion.[17] The final and most compelling reason to steer away from the Analogy of the Word is that it leaves out a crucial form of the Word of God. This form provides the link between Christ and the Scriptures in the biblical narrative: the spoken Word. As I tried to show in chapter 3, the Word that God speaks through his prophets, his Son, his apostles, his preachers, and ultimately all Christians is foundational for the theology of Scripture. Christ sent his apostles first to speak, and only

---

14. Preus, *Inspiration*, 201–2.

15. Webster, *Holy Scripture*, 22–23.

16. For a critique of Logos-Christology and a helpful discussion of a Spirit-Christology that restores this balance, see Sánchez M., "Receiver, Bearer, and Giver," 42–102 and 187–213.

17. Telford Work's account of the Analogy of the Word avoids this particular problem by incorporating the insights of Spirit-Christology.

subsequently did they put that Word into writing. When the spoken Word is left out of the conversation, the Scriptures are forced to do the work that Jesus originally entrusted (and continues to entrust) to preachers. Additionally, the incorporation of the spoken Word into the church's thinking and teaching about Christ and the Scriptures provides a natural safeguard against viewing the Scriptures and the Word of God in static and objective terms. Unlike the written and personal forms of the Word, the spoken Word does not exist apart from its proclamation.

Because of these problems (and potential problems) with the Analogy of the Word, it seems more helpful and more consistent with the biblical narrative to operate with a dogmatic framework that accounts for all three forms of the Word that God speaks in his divine economy. This requires a return to (and a revision of) Barth's threefold form of the Word of God.

BARTH: THE THREEFOLD FORM REVISITED

The usefulness of Barth's threefold form of the Word of God is its ability to summarize the variety of ways in which God speaks throughout the biblical narrative. But as I argued in chapter 2, there are some significant problems with his conception of the Word of God in all three of its forms. To understand where Barth went wrong, it is helpful to recall one of his favorite illustrations for describing God's work through his written Word.

The Scriptures, says Barth, are like the Pool of Bethesda.[18] From time to time God stirred the waters in the Pool of Bethesda so that the lame and the sick who gathered at its edge could be healed. In a similar way, God occasionally "stirs" the reading of the Scriptures so that he might encounter the hearer or reader with his saving presence. Through this encounter God reveals himself as the Word of God and reconciles the hearer (or reader) to himself. Just as there was nothing sacred about the water in the Pool of Bethesda, neither is there anything sacred in the Scriptures themselves. *Deus dixit* and *Paulus dixit* are two different things.[19] The uniqueness of the Scriptures (and church proclamation) for Barth is that God, in his sovereign and gracious freedom, chooses on occasion to reveal himself through them.

Here is the key to Barth's doctrine of the Word of God. The Word of God (who is God himself) only comes to human beings *where and when* it pleases God. Barth repeatedly returns to Article V of the Augsburg

---

18. Barth, *CD* 1/1:111; 1/2:530.
19. Barth, *CD* 1/1:113.

Confession: "To obtain such faith God instituted the office of preaching, giving the gospel and the sacraments. Through these, as through means, he gives the Holy Spirit who produces faith, where and when (*ubi et quando*) he wills, in those who hear the gospel."[20] Barth highlights this phrase (*ubi et quando*) to protect God from being coerced or controlled into revealing himself. He will not allow God to be pinned down in Scripture or in the proclamation of the church: "The freedom of God's grace is the basis and the boundary, the presupposition and the proviso, of the statements according to which the Bible and proclamation are the Word of God."[21] This insistence on maintaining the freedom of God governs Barth's view of the Scriptures, proclamation, and even Jesus himself. Wolterstorff notes, "Barth regarded the claim that God speaks by way of authoring Scripture as compromising the freedom of God. God and God alone speaks for God."[22] In Barth's words:

> That the Bible is the Word of God cannot mean that with other attributes the Bible has the attribute of being the Word of God. To say that would be to violate the Word of God which is God Himself—to violate the freedom and sovereignty of God. God is not an attribute of something else, even if this something else is the Bible. God is the Subject. God is Lord. He is Lord even over the Bible and in the Bible. The statement that the Bible is the Word of God cannot therefore say that the Word of God is tied to the Bible. On the contrary, what it must say is that the Bible is tied to the Word of God. But that means that in this statement we contemplate a free decision of God.[23]

As Wolterstorff points out, Barth's emphasis on the freedom of God actually ends up limiting God. Barth does not allow God to restrict his own freedom. Again Barth: "It is quite impossible that there should be a direct identity between the human word of Holy Scripture and the Word of God, and therefore between the creaturely reality in itself and as such and the reality of God the Creator. It is impossible that there should have been a transmutation of the one into the other or an admixture of the one with the other. *This is not even the case in the person of Christ.*"[24] Barth's insistence on defending the freedom and sovereignty of God keeps him from allowing the

---

20. *CA* V.1–3.
21. Barth, *CD* 1/1:117.
22. Wolterstorff, *Divine Discourse*, 73–74.
23. Barth, *CD* 1/2:513.
24. Ibid., 1/2:499. Emphasis added.

infinite God to identify himself directly with finite creatures *in any way*. Not only does Barth prohibit God from deputizing the prophets and apostles to speak his Word, but he also prohibits God from speaking through *Jesus*. Work criticizes him for this limitation: "Since Jesus is truly the Word made flesh, his words (whether preserved in writing or not) *are* truly the Word of God in human words, without qualification."[25] Ironically, in his effort to defend the freedom of God, Barth actually ends up limiting God's ability to speak *where and when* he has decided to speak![26]

Luther: Spoken and Written Word

If the theology of Scripture is most appropriately considered under the theology of the Word of God, it follows that a dogmatic account of the Scriptures should draw from theologians who have made the most significant contributions to the theology of the Word. That is what makes Karl Barth an important voice in this conversation. He is the most significant "theologian of the Word" in the twentieth century. But he is not the first theologian to focus on the Word of God, and a close look at the small print in the first volume of *Church Dogmatics* shows that much of his thinking on the subject came from a "theologian of the Word" who lived four hundreds earlier.[27] Jaroslav Pelikan describes him:

> The theology of Martin Luther was a theology of the Word of God. "The Word they still shall let remain, Nor any thanks have for it; He's by our side upon the plain With His good gifts and Spirit"— this is not only the concluding stanza of Luther's hymn, "A Mighty Fortress is our God"; it is the theme and the motto of his whole life and thought. He lived *by* the Word of God; he lived *for* the Word of God. It is no mistake, then, when interpreters of Luther take his doctrine of the Word of God as one of the most important single keys to his theology.[28]

---

25. Work, *Living and Active*, 84.

26. Barth is right that the Word of God is based on God's own decision. But according to the biblical narrative God *decided* to speak his Word through prophets, apostles, preachers, Christians, and most importantly, Jesus.

27. Barth praises the sixteenth-century reformers for their understanding of Scripture, which was an "honouring of God" (*CD* 1/2:522). He gives credit for this to Luther and Calvin, but he specifically notes that Luther spoke more "clearly and acutely" (*CD* 1/2:521).

28. Pelikan, *Luther the Expositor*, 48.

Despite the fact that Luther never wrote a dogmatic account of the Word of God (or the Scriptures), his understanding of the Word of God has been well documented. Uuraas Saarnivaara, for example, notes two important forms of the Word of God in Luther's writing: the written Word and the spoken Word. Although it is well known that Luther spent considerable time translating the written Word, it was the spoken Word that received particular emphasis in his writing. He believed God forgives sins and creates faith primarily through the message he has given his people to *proclaim*. He emphasized Jesus' commission to the disciples to forgive sins (John 20:23 and Matt 18:18); he highlighted Paul's insistence that "faith comes through hearing" (Rom 10:17); and he recognized the proclamation of the Gospel as the power of salvation for those who believe (Rom 1:16). There was no question in Luther's mind that when the Gospel is faithfully preached, God himself is speaking.[29]

Luther's emphasis on the proclamation of the Word fit well with his insistence that the Scriptures are the written Word of God and therefore the "highest norm and standard of our faith and life."[30] Although he recognized that the Scriptures were written by sinful human beings, Luther believed that the Scriptures ultimately come from God and are completely faithful and true. Unlike many proponents of the doctrine of inspiration, Luther did not try to resolve apparent discrepancies that occasionally appear in his reading of the Scriptures. When he came across something in the Scriptures that he could not harmonize, he would suggest that we simply "let it pass."[31] Because fallen human beings are limited in their understanding, he reasoned, it should not surprise us if we do not see how certain parts of the Scriptures fit together. But this should not lead us to question their truthfulness or reliability. Instead, Luther suggests, "Give the Holy Ghost the honor of being wiser than yourself, for you should so deal with Scripture that you believe that God himself is speaking."[32] With childlike faith Luther simply believed that the Scriptures are "from God."[33] Saarnivaara summarizes Luther's understanding of the mutually dependent relationship between the written and spoken forms of the Word:

---

29. See Wilson, "Luther on Preaching," 63–75.
30. Saarnivaara, "Written and Spoken Word," 167.
31. Ibid., 168.
32. Quoted in Reu, *Luther and the Scriptures*, 92.
33. Saarnivaara, "Written and Spoken Word," 168.

> Luther did not see any conflict between his conviction that Scripture is the normative word of God, and that God bestows His grace and forgives sins by means of the spoken word and sacraments. All preaching and administration of the sacraments have their source in the written word of God and must take place according to it. Therefore, the proclamation of the word (in sermons and in personal absolution and counseling) and the administration of the sacraments is inseparably connected with the Scriptures. Only a scriptural teaching, preaching, and consolation leads men to the knowledge of Christ and salvation in Him.[34]

In dogmatic terms, Saarnivaara describes Luther as working with a "revelation-Word" and a "means-of-grace Word." He explains, "Luther gives both to Scripture (and the written word in general) and the oral testimony and preaching of the word their proper places in the Christian church: the written Word of God is primarily a 'revelation-word,' which is the norm and standard of all faith, life and teaching. The spoken word (in preaching, absolution, and sacraments) is the 'means-of-grace-word,' through which God forgives sins, works faith, and imparts His Holy Spirit."[35] As the "means-of-grace-word," Luther emphasized that God actually speaks through human beings when they proclaim the gospel of Christ crucified. Unlike Barth, Luther would have been very comfortable with Wolterstorff's definition of "deputized discourse." This spoken form of the Word is the means by which God normally creates faith in the hearts of sinful human beings (Rom 10:17).[36] As the "revelation-word," Luther understood the writings of the prophets and apostles to be perfectly true despite occasional appearances to the contrary. The written Word of God alone is the final rule and norm in the church. This is what *sola scriptura* means. Like Chemnitz after him, Luther suggests that the apostolic Word was written "to provide against the false doctrines and to keep Christians in the divine truth."[37]

Whether he was speaking about the "revelation-word" (Scripture) or the "means-of-grace-word" (gospel proclamation), Luther always understood the Word of God in christological and soteriological (that is, cruciform) terms. Scripture exists to serve the proclamation of the gospel, and

---

34. Ibid., 169.

35. Ibid., 174. "Revelation-word" and "means-of-grace-word" are Saarnivaara's terms.

36. Saarnivaara points out that, on occasion, Luther would also refer to Scripture as a "means-of-grace-word." But this was not his normal way of speaking. He usually emphasized the need for the oral proclamation of the Word, as well as Paul's comment that faith comes through "hearing" (Rom 10:17).

37. Saarnivaara, "Written and Spoken Word," 171.

the gospel is nothing other than Christ crucified for our forgiveness and salvation.

A New (and Improved) Threefold Form of the Word

Luther grants God the freedom to speak his living and active Word through sinful human beings, and in this way he follows the biblical narrative more consistently than Barth. Barth's structure remains helpful, however, for the biblical narrative clearly speaks of three forms of the Word of God in the divine economy. With Luther correcting Barth's deficiencies, the following might be seen as a revised threefold form of the Word of God.

Any discussion of the Word of God must begin with the recognition that God is a speaking God. He is a "God of Word"[38] from the very beginning—and a trinitarian Word at that. Through his Word and his Spirit the Father brought all things into existence at creation. Through his Word and in his Spirit the Father issued commands that morally obliged his human creatures. Through his Word and in his Spirit the Father made promises that he morally obligates himself to keep. This eternal Word of God, John says in his prologue, became a human being by the power of the Holy Spirit in the person of Jesus of Nazareth. He is the personal, Spirit-anointed Word who speaks the Father's commands and fulfills the Father's promises of forgiveness, life, and salvation. "All the promises of God find their Yes in him" (2 Cor 1:20). It was precisely because of his speaking, however, that the personal Word of God was rejected and put to death on a cross. Three days later the Father vindicated his identity, message, and mission by raising him from the dead in the power of the Spirit (Rom 1:4), just as Jesus had promised (John 2:22). This first form of the Word of God is the *personal* Word, Jesus Christ, through whom God spoke *definitively, ultimately, decisively,* and *for all time.*

In the biblical narrative God usually speaks his Word through someone other than himself. He deputizes individuals to speak in his name and with his authority. In the Old Testament these deputies are known as prophets. God sent them to speak his Word, and he led them with the Spirit of Christ (1 Pet 1:10–11). In the New Testament Jesus sent apostles with his Spirit to speak his Word with his authority. The Spirit of truth guided them in their proclamation of the Word to ensure the reliability of their message (John 16:13). In the church God continues to send his people with his Spirit to forgive sins (John 20:21–23; 2 Cor 5:18–19) and proclaim the Word of Christ

---

38. Work, *Living and Active*, 33.

for the salvation of those who believe (Rom 1:16). The church's proclamation of the gospel takes place in a variety of settings, including public preaching, confession and absolution, the administration of the sacraments, and the mutual conversation and consolation of believers.[39] The church continues its apostolic mission as it continues to speak the Word of God in the power of the Spirit. The second form of the Word of God is the *spoken* Word. Three aspects of the spoken Word arise from the biblical narrative. First, the spoken Word points to the personal Word. The prophets testified to the death and resurrection of Jesus (Luke 24:44–46), the apostles proclaimed nothing but "Jesus Christ and him crucified" (1 Cor 1:23), and preachers are sent to proclaim the "word of Christ" (Rom 10:17). Second, the spoken Word is living and active (Heb 4:12). Luther calls it a "means-of-grace-word" through which God judges those who are sinful and forgives those who are repentant. It is primarily through this form of the Word that God creates saving faith in Christ (Rom 10:17). Third, the spoken Word of God is reliable and true. Those who originally heard the apostolic proclamation recognized that it was God's Word (1 Thess 2:13), and that it was completely trustworthy (John 19:35; 21:24).

After considering the personal and spoken forms of the Word, it becomes obvious that much of what needs to be about the Scriptures has already been said. The writings of the prophets and apostles are nothing other than definitive versions of the Word they were sent to proclaim. These writings make up the third form of the Word of God—the *written* Word. As the written form of the Word, the same conclusions may be made about the Scriptures that were made about spoken Word. Like the spoken Word, the Scriptures are living and active. God works through the Scriptures to judge and comfort, to kill and make alive. Also like the spoken Word, the written Word is true. Jesus affirmed the truth of the Old Testament (John 10:35) and he promised the Spirit of truth to those who would eventually produce the New Testament (John 16:13). To describe the written Word as "living and active" and "true" is to say important things in the theology of Scripture. But perhaps the most important thing to be said about the written Word of God is what John says at the end of his gospel. "These are written so that you may believe that Jesus is the Christ, the Son of God, and that by believing you may have life in his name" (John 20:31). With these words John provides both the starting point and the ultimate goal of the Christian theology of Scripture.

---

39. Cf. *SA* part III, article IV.

5

Meeting the Postmodern Challenge
Canon, Authority, Interpretation

"CHRISTIANS ARE A 'PEOPLE of the book,'" write Stanley Grenz and John Franke.[1] The book they are talking about is the Bible, of course, and many Christians—especially those who want to separate themselves from the critical side of the modern debate—embrace this description of what it means to be a Christian. "People of the book" also tend to identify themselves as "Bible believers." They worship at "Bible chapels," send their children to "Vacation Bible School," and encourage their young adults to enroll in "Bible colleges." When they confess what they believe, the first and most prominent article of faith is usually an affirmation of the inspiration and inerrancy of the Bible, which they confidently identify as the foundation of their faith. As the children's song puts it, "Oh, the B-I-B-L-E, yes that's the book for me. I stand alone on the Word of God, the B-I-B-L-E!"

I have argued throughout this book that the Christian faith is inseparable from the writings of the prophets and apostles, and that the reliability of the Scriptures is fundamentally important for the continuity of historic Christianity. But I do not think describing themselves as "people of the book" (or "Bible believers") is the most helpful way for Christians to identify themselves. John Barton makes this point in *People of the Book? The Authority of the Bible in Christianity*. Barton argues that Christians who identify themselves as "people of the book" misunderstand the nature and function

---

1. Grenz and Franke, *Beyond Foundationalism*, 57. See also Willimon, *Shaped*, 11 and Bruce, *The Canon*, 18–19.

of the Scriptures.² Rather than seeing themselves in relation to the Scriptures, says Barton, Christians should understand and identify themselves in relation to Jesus. Joachim Ringleben makes a similar point. Christianity is not "eine Buchreligion," he says. Rather, "Christentum ist besser als *Wortreligion* zu kennzeichnen."³ That would make Christians "people of the Word."

It is as "people of the Word" that I am suggesting Christians should approach the theology of Scripture. "People of the Word" believe first of all in Jesus Christ, the Spirit-filled personal Word who was sent by the Father. This personal Word became flesh and lived among us; he proclaimed repentance and forgiveness of sins as *the* deputy of God; he suffered and died on the cross for claiming to speak *in the name of* the Father; he was vindicated as the eternal Son of God through his resurrection; and he has promised to return in glory on the last day. This personal Word of God is the church's one foundation, the one through whom God who spoke *definitively, ultimately, decisively,* and *for all time*.⁴ In addition to this personal Word, God spoke "in many ways and at many times" in the biblical narrative. He spoke through deputized prophets and co-missioned apostles, and he continues to speak as he sends preachers to proclaim the gospel of Christ crucified. Through his spoken Word God calls sinners to repent (Acts 2:36–41), forgives sins (John 20:21–23), and creates faith in the hearts of those who believe (Rom 10:17). Finally, "people of the Word" believe that the writings of the prophets and apostles are the written Word of God. They believe this *because* they believe in Jesus, the personal Word. After his vindicating resurrection Jesus sent his apostles to teach everything he had commanded them and gave them the Spirit to guide them into all truth. The apostles proclaimed the Word of God by speaking and by writing (2 Thess 2:15) so that all would believe that Jesus is the Christ and have life in his name (John 20:31).

The problem with modern approach to the Bible is that it fails to locate the Scriptures in the context of this theology of the Word of God. This has made it difficult for Christians to speak confidently and consistently about a number of important issues related to the Scriptures, namely the canon, authority, and interpretation. As long as the Scriptures were assumed to be central to the life, witness, and reflection of the church, some of these issues

---

2. Barton notes that "people of the book" is more descriptive of people of Islamic and Jewish beliefs (*People of the Book?*, 1).

3. Christianity is not "a book religion." Instead, "Christianity is better characterized as a *Word*-religion" (Ringleben, "Die Bible," 29, emphasis added).

4. Perhaps the children's song should be revised to conclude: "I stand alone on the Word of God, J-E-S-U-S!"

could be passed over. But when that assumption was exposed and criticized, previously held assumptions about the canon, authority, and interpretation came into question as well. When it came to the canon, for instance, the conception of the scriptural writings as inspired assumed that they were canonical and therefore authoritative. When it came to interpretation, the conception of the scriptural writings as inerrant assumed that a certain kind of interpretation (namely, literal) was inevitable and sufficient. In today's postmodern context these assumptions may no longer be taken for granted.

This fifth and final chapter is my attempt to demonstrate, in preliminary ways, how a theology of Scripture that is grounded in the theology of the Word of God responds to today's questions and challenges. These questions include, "What is the purpose of the New Testament canon in the first place?" "How does God exercise his authority through these particular writings?" "What does it mean to read (and therefore also interpret) the written Word of *God*?" These are not the only questions that must be addressed in the theology of Scripture. But they help point in some important directions, and therefore chapter 5 should be seen as the beginning of the discussion.

Canon

For a thousand years Christian theology has developed in a "Christendom" or "Constantinian" situation in which "church" and "world" are not clearly distinguished. As a result certain basic issues have been taken for granted. One such issue has been the "canon" of the Scriptures.[5]

Times have changed. Today basic questions about the canon can no longer be ignored. Indeed, it is enough to mention a few names to raise questions: Dan Brown, Elaine Pagels, Bart Ehrman. They (and others) have challenged the identity of Jesus, the development of early Christianity, and, of particular interest for this study, the formation of the New Testament canon. They have made urgent the canonical *crux theologorum*: "Why some and not others?" Or "Why were *these* particular writings included in the canon and others left out?" Those who challenge the traditional canon typically answer this question by arguing that many "Scriptures" were wrongly excluded from the New Testament. Ehrman, for instance, insists that "ancient Christians knew of far more Gospels than the four that eventually came to be included in the New Testament."[6] These other writings had "equally

---

5. My focus in this chapter will be primarily on the New Testament canon.
6. Ehrman, *Lost Christianities*, 13.

impressive pedigrees"[7] and equal claims to the truth about Jesus. They were left out of the canon, not because they were somehow less than Scripture, but because they supported positions that ended up on the losing side of ecclesio-political power struggles. When advocates of what would become "orthodoxy" gained control of the church, these "lost Scriptures" were (unfairly) marginalized, rejected, and destroyed.

This conception of the formation of the New Testament calls into question more than the usual issues associated with the biblical canon. It also suggests that the very idea of a New Testament has to be reconsidered. Once we start questioning the canon so radically, there is no reason to stop with the suggestion that other (noncanonical) writings should be included in the New Testament. We must not only ask, "Why some and not others?" but also, "Why are there any authoritative writings at all?" This question means that an adequate theology of Scripture must also consider the question, "What is the purpose of the New Testament canon?" The appropriate answers to these questions are grounded in the mission that Jesus gave to his apostles and the church after his resurrection. They are found in the continuation of the economy of salvation into the first two centuries.

Before we answer these questions, however, there is an important dogmatic issue to consider. Modern theology has made an account of the canon hard to imagine properly, because, as John Webster points out, modern theology has conceived of the canon—Old Testament and especially New Testament—wrongly. It has "mislocated" the canon in dogmatic theology. This mislocation has been brought about by two powerful considerations. The first involves the migration of the theology of Scripture to the prolegomena of dogmatic theology. Transplanted out of its original soil (namely, "the saving economy of the triune God"[8]), the canon became detached from the rest of the Christian confession. Webster explains, "Instead of being a consequential doctrine (consequential, that is, upon logically prior teaching about the provenience of God in God's dealing with the creation), it shifts to become a relatively isolated piece of epistemological teaching."[9] He is referring to the doctrine of inspiration. Its treatment of the Scriptures in the prolegomena has forced inspiration to provide the epistemological warrant for the rest of the Christian confession as an *a priori* foundation for the other articles of faith.[10] This has resulted in an isolation of "*sola scriptura*

7. Ibid., 3.
8. Webster, "Dogmatic Location," 17.
9. Ibid.
10. Webster does not discuss how the migration of Scripture to the prolegomena came about. Robert Kolb investigates this shift in dogmatic structure in his study of the

from the other Reformation exclusive particles *solus Christus, sola gratia,* and *solo verbo*."[11] A second consideration contributing to the dogmatic mislocation of the canon comes from the other side of the modern debate. Critical theologians often regard the formation of the canon as a act of the church solely within the realm of religious history (*Entstehungsgeschichte*), having little (if anything) to do with God's providential direction. The canon is merely another instance of ecclesiastical decision-making—it is "product, not norm."[12] This view is attractive, Webster admits, because it recognizes that the church did, in fact, make decisions to include or exclude the books that belong in the Bible. The result of this conception of the canon, however, is that it becomes nothing more than any other ecclesiastical decision. It is "(at best) an arbitrary or accidental factor in Christian religious history or (at worst) an instrument of political wickedness."[13] This view raises fundamental questions about the ability of the canon to exercise any meaningful authority in (and over) the church. "In the end," says Webster, "the canon does not transcend us; we transcend the canon."[14]

With these two considerations in mind, Webster helps clarify the task at hand. First, we must locate the canon in the dogmatic theology of the church in a way that allows for us to deal with questions about the composition, collection, and purpose of the New Testament canon. Second, we must answer these questions.

Locating the Canon Dogmatically

Webster shows that the question of the canon belongs neither in the prolegomena nor solely within the realm of religious history. But where *is* the proper dogmatic location of the canon? It is helpful to consider Webster's own answer. He points to some fundamental Christian concepts: Trinity, soteriology, pneumatology, and sanctification. Ultimately, Webster says, the question of the canon belongs under the doctrine of God and divine revelation. Similar to Barth, Webster views revelation as God's reconciling triune self-manifestation: "As Father, God is the root or origin of revelation

---

ordering of Melanchthon's *Loci Communes* and the tradition that followed. See "The Ordering," 317–37.

11. Webster, "Dogmatic Location," 17.
12. Ibid., 22.
13. Ibid., 18.
14. Ibid., 22.

as saving self-manifestation: in him is grounded revelation's sheer gratuity and sovereign freedom. As the incarnate, crucified and glorified Son, God is the agent through whom the saving history of God with us is upheld against all opposition and denial. As Spirit, God is the agent of revelation's perfection, its being made real and effective in the community of the church as the reconciled assembly of the saints."[15] With this starting point, Webster understands the process of canonization in terms of its historical *and* theological dimensions. The canon is not simply a "list or code," but rather a "specification of those instruments where the church may reliably expect to encounter God's communicative presence, God's self-attestation."[16] The formation of the canon is a unique kind of churchly historical act. "There can be no recourse to denials of the element of human decision-making in the process of canonisation," he explains. "What is needed, by contrast, is *a theological account of the church's action* at this point."[17]

Webster begins with a conception of the church as an "assembly around the self-bestowing presence of the risen Christ."[18] The church is, properly speaking, a *hearing* church before it is a speaking church. It speaks only what it has heard (ultimately) from Jesus himself. As Spirit-led hearers of this apostolic Word, the early church made "compliant judgments" about the canon. These judgments exhibit four distinct characteristics. First, canonical decisions are more properly understood as acts of confession rather than acts of selection. Early Christians confessed what they heard (namely, the *viva vox Jesu Christi* mediated through the apostolic testimony). This message preceded and imposed itself on the church.[19] As acts of confession the church's canonical decisions have "noetic but not ontological force, acknowledging what Scripture is but not making it so."[20] Second, canonical judgments are acts of submission. The authority exercised by the church in making canonical decisions was nothing more than an acknowledgment that it stands under the very Scriptures it canonized. Third, as acts of confession and submission, canonical judgments have a "backward reference." More than anything else, canonization *recognizes* the apostolicity of a given writing. It *looks backward* to God's saving activity in Jesus Christ and to the witness of this salvation by Jesus' co-missioned apostles. Fourth, canonical

15. Ibid., 29.
16. Ibid., 30.
17. Webster, *Holy Scripture*, 58. Emphasis added.
18. Webster, "Dogmatic Location," 35.
19. Webster, *Holy Scripture*, 62.
20. Webster, "Dogmatic Location," 38.

judgments in the church are a "pledging of itself to be carried by this norm in all its actions."[21] When the church canonized certain writings it committed itself to be normed by them in its preaching and teaching. Taken together, Webster identifies these four characteristics to depict the church's act of canonization as "properly passive, a set a human activities, attitudes, and relations which refer beyond themselves to prevenient divine acts of speaking and sanctifying."[22]

This account of the canon is helpful in a number of ways. Most directly relevant, it relocates the canon within the context of a trinitarian and soteriological economy. Moreover, the conception of the church as a "hearing community" takes into account the fact that God communicates with his creation through his Word. This explains more fully the nature of churchly judgments about the shape of the canon and provides a way of taking seriously the historical decisions made by the church without relegating the canon to another piece of ecclesiastical tradition. Webster's theological account of canonization is still more helpful, however, when compared to other contemporary accounts of the New Testament canon. Before exploring the direction he puts us on, therefore, we will take a brief look at these advantages.

The Criteria Question

A central feature of many contemporary discussions about the New Testament canon is the *criteria* question. Which characteristics of a given writing are necessary to warrant its inclusion in the canon? The answers that follow often focus on abstract criteria. Lee McDonald gives a typical response. He suggests that, in the process of developing the New Testament canon, the church considered four key criteria: apostolicity, orthodoxy, antiquity, and use. *Apostolicity* meant: "If a writing was believed to have been produced by an apostle, it was eventually accepted as sacred scripture and included in the New Testament canon."[23] Apostolicity in this sense refers to the origin of a writing. The *orthodoxy* criterion meant that a writing had to conform to the rule of faith that governed the Christian confession. Bishop Serapion (ca. 200), for example, was asked if the *Gospel of Peter* could be read during worship. Initially he agreed on the basis of its supposed apostolic origin. But

21. Ibid.
22. Ibid., 39.
23. McDonald, "Identifying Scripture," 424.

later, after learning more about its content, he reversed his decision on the basis of its false teaching: "I have now learnt, from what has been told me, that [the author's] mind was lurking in some hole of heresy."[24] The *antiquity* criterion meant that, for a writing to be considered canonical, it must have been composed in close chronological proximity to Jesus' life. McDonald writes, "For the church, the ministry of Jesus had become the defining moment in history. Consequently, the church's most important authorities were those closest to this defining moment."[25] The Muratorian Fragment, for example, spoke against the canonicity of the *Shepherd of Hermas* because it was not written during the apostolic age: "It cannot be read publicly to the people in the church either among the prophets, whose number is complete, or among the apostles, for it is after [their] time."[26] The fourth criterion of canonicity that McDonald identifies is *use*. In order for a writing to be judged canonical, it must have been used in the worship and educational life of the church. This is what Eusebius was getting at in his distinction between the *homolegoumena* (agreed upon) and *antilegomena* (spoken against). The former were read as Scripture throughout the church of the fourth century, whereas some Christian communities questioned the latter.

McDonald's account of the canon gives reasons that explain its present form, but it does not explain the development of the canon that took place during the first several centuries. Indeed, McDonald (like many others) approaches the criteria question retrospectively: he assumes the existence of a New Testament. The problem with this can be seen when we take a close look at several of these criteria. The "antiquity" criterion assumes a chronological distance that did not exist in the earliest years of the church. Already in the first century the church faced the need to identify which *contemporary* writings faithfully presented the true apostolic gospel. A similar problem exists for McDonald's conception of the "use" criterion. Certainly the writings that were canonized had been in use throughout the first few centuries, but McDonald's understanding follows Eusebius' fourth-century distinctions between *homolegoumena* and *antilegomena*. This is anachronistic, for the historical observations made by Eusebius were based on the canonical decisions that had been made several centuries earlier. Another inadequacy in McDonald's account is his conception of the "apostolicity" criterion, in which the apostolicity of a writing is based on its *origin*. If a writing was

---

24. Eusebius, *Hist. eccl.* 6.12.4, quoted in McDonald, "Identifying Scripture," 428.

25. McDonald, "Identifying Scripture," 431.

26. *Muratorian Fragment*, lines 73–74, quoted in McDonald, "Identifying Scripture," 431.

believed to have been produced by an apostle it was eventually included in the New Testament. Although McDonald is correct in emphasizing that the apostles were sent to proclaim the Word of God, there are two problems with his conception of what makes a particular text "apostolic." First, it does not account for canonical writings that were *not* written by apostles (e.g., Mark and Luke). Even if we extend the conception of "apostolicity" to include these writings under something like "apostolic supervision," there remains another problem. The equation of apostolic origin and canonicity would suggest that every writing produced by an apostle would have been included in the canon. It is hard to dispute, however, that some letters of Paul were not included in the New Testament (see 1 Cor 5:9; Col 4:16).

McDonald's account is not *dogmatic*, so it would be misleading to speak of it as another instance of what Webster identifies as a "dogmatic mislocation" of the canon. But this way of considering canonical criteria falls short because it does not account for the theological considerations that lie behind the development of the New Testament canon. Furthermore, McDonald's account operates with a conception of the New Testament that was unknown to the church of the first two centuries. Neither the apostolic authors nor the original recipients and readers conceived of the New Testament canon in the same way as the church of the fourth century. We can overcome the inadequacies of McDonald's account of the canon by reconsidering what is means for a writing to be "apostolic." This requires two things: first, a fresh consideration of his first and second criteria (apostolicity and orthodoxy); second, an explanation of how the theology of the Word of God provides direction for the question of the canon. In other words, we need, as Webster suggests, a properly *dogmatic* account of the canon.

The Canon in Dogmatic Perspective

An appropriate starting point for a dogmatic account of the canon is a redefinition of what it means for a writing to be "apostolic." For this, Webster offers a more adequate explanation than McDonald. "Canonisation is recognition of apostolicity, not simply in the sense of the recognition that certain texts are of apostolic authorship or provenance, but, more deeply, in the sense of the confession that these texts, 'grounded in the salvific act of God in Christ which has taken place once for all,' are annexed to the self-utterance of Jesus Christ. The canon and the apostolicity (and so apostolic succession) of the church are inseparable here."[27] Webster notes that canonization has more to

---

27. Webster, *Holy Scripture*, 64.

do with the Word Christ sent his apostles to proclaim than with the persons of the apostles themselves. He emphasizes the "presence of the risen Christ," the "self-utterance of Jesus Christ," the "*viva vox Jesu Christi*" mediated through the apostolic testimony. This is helpful for understanding how God works through his spoken and written Word. But it does not get us very far towards understanding how the early church identified *which writings* were apostolic. Despite his helpful account of the canonical decisions made by the early church, Webster begs *the* contemporary canonical question: "Why were some writings included in the canon and not others?"

Lacking in Webster's account is a consideration of the "orthodoxy" criterion.[28] This criterion is the key to understanding apostolicity (and canonicity), and therefore a properly dogmatic consideration of the canon necessitates a closer look at the *content* of the Word that Jesus spoke through his co-missioned apostles. This requires a return to the economy of salvation we examined in chapter 3.

The trinitarian economy of salvation begins with Jesus, the personal Word of God who was born of Mary and anointed with the Spirit at his baptism in the Jordan. He was sent by the Father in the power of the Spirit and proclaimed a message of repentance and forgiveness of sins. This led to faith in some hearers, but to his rejection and crucifixion in others. After God vindicated his message and mission by raising him from the dead, Jesus sent his apostles (literally, "sent ones") to continue his mission by preaching and teaching his Word in his name. He breathed on them his Spirit, bestowed on them the authority to forgive, and promised (through his Spirit of truth) to remind them of everything he had taught them. Their living and active *message* was constitutive for their mission, and this message is what separated them from all others. Martin Luther emphasizes the importance of *what* they proclaimed: "Now it is the office of a true apostle to preach of the Passion and resurrection and office of Christ, and to lay the foundation for faith in him, as Christ himself says in John 15[:27], 'You shall bear witness to me.' All the genuine sacred books agree in this, that all of them *preach and inculcate Christ*. And that is the true test by which to judge all books, when we see whether or not they inculcate Christ."[29] Luther's insight was that apostolicity

---

28. Here Barth's influence on Webster seems clear. To Barth the important thing is *that* God speaks. It does not matter so much what he says, because God's speaking is itself his self-revelation and reconciliation. Webster's emphasis on the "self-utterance of Jesus" and the "presence of the risen Christ" follows Barth's understanding of revelation as reconciliation.

29. Luther, *LW* 35, 396. Emphasis added.

was actually a *dogmatic* criterion. The message of the apostles was not simply the Word of Christ in a subjective sense (a Word that Christ himself speaks, as Webster emphasizes). It was also the Word of Christ in an objective sense (a Word spoken *about* Christ, as Luther emphasizes). In terms of the canon, this makes the criteria question a question about *content*. The only way for the early church to determine which writings were truly apostolic was to examine their content to see if they conformed to the Spirit-led message the apostles had proclaimed from the beginning. Luther's understanding of apostolicity did not "by-pass the historic apostolate in favor of a dogmatic one, but rather invites the reader to focus on the *message*, instead of the *person*, of the apostle."[30]

The message of the apostles, Luther rightly emphasized, centered on the cross. They repeatedly highlighted the death and resurrection of Jesus as the center and foundation their preaching. Paul summarizes, "For I delivered to you as of first importance what I also received: that Christ died for our sins in accordance with the Scriptures, that he was buried, that he was raised on the third day in accordance with the Scriptures" (1 Cor 15:3–4; see also Rom 6:1–11, Phil 2:6–10). Peter concludes, "This Jesus, delivered up according to the definite plan and foreknowledge of God, you crucified and killed by the hands of lawless men. God raised him up, loosing the pangs of death, because it was not possible for him to be held by it" (Acts 2:23–24; see also 1 Pet 3:18–22). When it came to identifying which writings were apostolic, the church looked to writings that faithfully proclaimed *this* gospel, for this was the message the earliest Christians heard, believed, and were shaped by from the beginning. In obedience to Paul's exhortation in Galatians 1:6–9, the early Christians measured everything they heard against this gospel.

The recognition of "Christ crucified" as *the* criterion of canonicity helps explain the standard by which the early church identified which writings were apostolic. But there remain several other important questions about the formation of the New Testament canon: "What was the purpose of the New Testament in the first place?" and "Why were some writings included and not others?" In order to answer these questions we must take a closer look at the ministry of the Word in the first two centuries. As Larry Hurtado notes, "It has been clear for some time that the second century was a (indeed, perhaps *the*) crucial period in the development of the New Testament."[31]

---

30. Bohlmann, "The Criteria of Biblical Canonicity," 116–17 n. 56.
31. Hurtado, "The New Testament," 3.

Canons in the Early Church

In Jesus' day there was already a collection of writings that ruled and normed the faith and life of God's people: the writings which would later become known as the Old Testament. Although there remains some dispute about exactly which books belonged in this collection,[32] there was clearly a collection of writings that the people of God recognized as the written Word of God. Jesus described this collection as "the Law and the Prophets" (Matt 5:17; 7:12; 11:13; Luke 16:16), "Moses and all the Prophets" (Luke 24:27), or "the Law of Moses, the Prophets and the Psalms" (Luke 24:44). Together they were acknowledged as "all the Scriptures" (Luke 24:27, 45) which, Jesus said, "cannot be broken" (John 10:35). The existence of an established canon in Jesus' day raises a fundamental question about the reasons for the existence of a New Testament canon. If there was already an authoritative collection of Scriptures among the first Christians, what need was there for a "new" canon? If we can answer this question adequately, then we can also answer the question: "Why some and not others?"

Before answering these questions it is helpful to take a closer look at the way in which the word "canon" has been used in religious discussions. Eugene Ulrich points out that there are two important but different ways in which the term "canon" has been understood. The first definition is known as "canon 1." Ulrich describes it as "the *rule* of faith that is articulated by the Scriptures."[33] This understanding of the canon refers to the general contours of the gospel Jesus sent the apostles to proclaim. It outlines God's plan of salvation and provides boundaries that separate faithful Christian proclamation from false teaching. "Canon 1" matches the early church's conception of the *regula fidei*. At the end of the first century Clement of Rome wrote about the "glorious and venerable rule (*kanona*)."[34] Irenaeus (ca. 130–200) spoke of the "rule of truth,"[35] Clement of Alexandria (ca. 150–215) pointed to a "rule of faith,"[36] and Tertullian (ca. 150–220) referred to the "rule" that was

---

32. Questions remain, for example, about the canonicity of the apocryphal writings in the Roman Catholic canon. There are also questions about the differences between the Masoretic Text and the Septuagint and the implications these differences have for the question of the canon. For an overview of the contemporary discussion about both of these (and other Old Testament canonical issues), see McDonald, *The Canon Debate*, 21–263.

33. Ulrich, "The Notion," 28.

34. 1 Clement 7 in *ANF* 9:231.

35. *Against Heresies* I.9.4 in *ANF* 1:330; I.22.1 in *ANF* 1:337.

36. *Stromata* 6.15 in *ANF* 2:510.

taught by Christ.[37] While the exact wording and specific details of these *regulae* varied, they shared a common understanding of the trinitarian gospel of Christ crucified for the forgiveness of sins. Robert Wall explains, "These 'rules' summarized the heart of Christian faith and served as theological boundary markers for Christian identity."[38]

The second way the term "canon" has been used refers more directly to a list of distinctive writings. It is known as "canon 2." According to Ulrich this is "the *list* of books accepted as inspired scripture."[39] Unlike "canon 1" which provides boundaries for what is apostolic, "canon 2" lists writings that the early church recognized as definitive instances of apostolic proclamation. This second definition of the canon is usually in effect when it comes to discussions about the biblical canon. "Though the adjective 'canonical' is used legitimately in both senses, the noun 'canon [of Scripture]' is predominantly used in the second sense . . . In such cases, the proper meaning of the canon is the definitive list of inspired, authoritative books which constitute the recognized and accepted body of sacred scripture of a major religious group, that definitive list being the result of inclusive and exclusive decisions after serious deliberation."[40]

With this distinction between "canon 1" and "canon 2," we can return to the relationship between the personal Word of God and the question of the New Testament canon in the first two centuries. Prior to the appearance of concrete versions of the *regula fidei* or a definitive New Testament, the church in its earliest years simply lived according to this gospel that Jesus and his Spirit-led apostles preached and taught. Whether it was proclaimed by word of mouth or sent by letter (2 Thess 2:15), the early Christians conformed their faith and life to the message of Christ crucified. At the same time, however, false teachers arose and introduced distortions, contradictions, and confusions to the church's message and mission (Gal 1:6–9). This made it necessary for the church to identify a standard by which it could judge and regulate faithful preaching and teaching. As the first century ended and the second began, both "canon 1" (in the sense of a *rule* of faith) and "canon 2" (in the sense of a *list* of writings) arose to serve this purpose.

"Canon 1" provided boundary lines for separating the true proclamation of the apostolic Word from false teachers who proclaimed a different "gospel." It was an outline, a roadmap of the basic components of the

---

37. *On the Prescriptions of Heretics* 13 in ANF 3:249.
38. Wall, "Reading the Bible from within Our Traditions," 89.
39. Ulrich, "The Notion," 29.
40. Ibid.

trinitarian economy of salvation. Preaching and teaching that upheld and was consistent with the features of God, Christ, and the Spirit in the *regula fidei* were recognized as "apostolic." They were apostolic not simply (or even primarily) because of their relation to the *persons* of the apostles, but because they conformed to the apostolic message that had formed and shaped the early church. This *regula* was passed along in and gave shape to the early church's confessions of faith, hymns, and liturgical practices, and it was central to the form, content, and function of the church's official creeds. "Canon 2" also provided a boundary between true and false preaching and teaching, but in a different way. Rather than outlining general boundaries for faithful preaching and teaching, this canon arose as a list of writings that were recognized as clear and paradigmatic expressions of the apostolic Gospel. They were faithful and definitive versions of the apostolic proclamation of Christ, the doctrine based on his life, death, and resurrection, and the warnings and exhortations for his disciples.

This answers our first question: "What is the purpose of the New Testament?" The New Testament was gathered together to *regulate* the preaching and teaching of the church. It did this by *preserving* definitive versions of the Word which had been spoken and written by the Spirit-led apostles of Jesus Christ. This also begins to answer our second question: "Why some and not others?" The writings included in "canon 2" were recognized as definitive versions of the apostolic proclamation by virtue of their faithfulness to the gospel of Christ crucified. This is what it means for apostolicity to be a *dogmatic* criterion of canonicity. Writings that proclaimed a message conflicting with this apostolic gospel were recognized by the early church as distortions and imposters. This includes Gnostic gospels that proclaimed a different Christ, "a different gospel" (Gal 1:6). These writings did not present Jesus as the incarnate Son of God, born of Mary; as the one crucified and risen on the third day; as the one who ascended into the heavens and who will return in glory to judge the living and the dead. Their deviation from the recognized apostolic message, which was summarized by Paul as "Christ crucified," meant their disqualification from canonical consideration.

Collections within the Collection

Agreement with the gospel of Jesus Christ was *the* criterion by which writings were judged apostolic (and therefore "canonical") in the early church. This helps explain why Gnostic gospels were not (and cannot today be) included in the New Testament canon. But it does not fully explain why some writings were canonized and others were not. In order to complete our answer we must take a closer look at how these specific books were identified by the church of the first and second century. These first generations of Christians were in the unique position of identifying which writings belonged in the developing New Testament canon.

There are a variety of ways in which scholars have sought to determine which writings the early church recognized as apostolic. Traditionally, ancient lists have played an important role. The Muratorian Fragment, the Eusebian distinctions between *homolegoumena* and *antilegomena*, and the great uncials have each, in their own way, listed the canonical writings. These sources shed significant light on the shape of the canon, but they are not as helpful as is often assumed. The reason is that each of them (with the possible exception of the Muratorian Fragment[41]) dates from the fourth and fifth centuries. While they help us understand the canon four centuries after Jesus, they do not help us understand what was happening during the earliest generations of the church—the time during which the apostolic writings were originally written and collected. A second way of trying to identify which books were recognized as genuinely apostolic has been to examine the citations of the early fathers.[42] We can know which writings were apostolic, the thinking goes, by examining which writings the earliest fathers cited. The problem with this approach is twofold. First, it is difficult to determine with certainty what counts as a citation. An allusion to a text is different from a loose citation, which is different still from an exact quotation. Second, the significance of a citation is difficult to measure. The citation of a text—even an exact quotation—does not necessarily mean that the text cited was recognized as genuinely apostolic and canonical. As Hurtado notes, it is "dubious" to look for evidence explaining canonical judgments on the basis of which writings the early church fathers cited.[43]

Recently scholars have taken a third approach of investigating which writings were recognized as apostolic in the early church. Instead of focusing on lists or citations, they have looked at the ways in which texts were collected and circulated among the first few generations of Christians. Long before what we know as the "New Testament" came into existence as a single entity, several smaller collections of writings were gathered together and read in the

---

41. Traditionally it had been thought that the Muratorian Fragment was a second century document, but that view has recently been challenged. Cf. Hahneman, "The Muratorian Fragment," 405–15.

42. See Hurtado, "The New Testament," 15–19.

43. Ibid., 17.

church as genuinely apostolic. This makes the New Testament "a collection of prior collections."[44] Today it is possible to divide the writings in the New Testament into three distinct collections: the gospels, the letters of Paul, and the catholic (or general) epistles. Of these three collections, the first two circulated at a very early date. Again Hurtado: "We know that at some point the four canonical Gospels came to be thought of as complementary renditions of the gospel story of Jesus, and came to form a closed circle enjoying distinctive regard in many Christian circles. We know also that collections of Pauline epistles were circulating, probably from the late first century, and were likewise treated as scripture in at least some circles."[45] J. K. Elliott suggests that these smaller collections functioned canonically by drawing boundaries around books that were unquestionably apostolic. "When each book circulated as a separate entity, obviously there was no limit to the number of texts that could be received. When certain, approved, texts were gather into small collections this had the effect of ostracizing and isolating texts which were not deemed suitable for inclusion."[46]

The earliest known collection of genuinely apostolic writings was a collection of Paul's letters. Toward the end of the first century his letters were already recognized as "Scriptures" (see 2 Pet 3:16). It is likely that Paul kept a collection of his letters during his own lifetime, which may have been what he was referring to when he asked Timothy to bring along his "books" and "parchments" (2 Tim 4:13). Gamble explains, "It would correspond better with the circumstances and methods of the Pauline mission if the earliest edition of Paul's collected letters had been based on copies retained by Paul and preserved after his death by his associates."[47] This means that a collection of Pauline letters would have been in circulation already by AD 100.[48] Stanley Porter concludes, "There is reasonable evidence to see the origin of the Pauline corpus during the latter part of Paul's life or shortly after his death, almost assuredly instigated by a close follower if not by Paul himself, and close examination of the early manuscripts with Paul's letters seems to

---

44. Ibid., 21.

45. Ibid., 19. The catholic epistles did not circulate as a firm collection until the fourth century. Harry Gamble notes that, of the catholic epistles, only 1 Peter and 1 John appear to have been known and used widely during the second century. 1 Peter was known and used by Papias, Polycarp, Irenaeus, Clement of Alexandria, Tertullian and Origen; 1 John was known and used by Papias, Irenaeus, Clement of Alexandria, and Origen (Gamble, "The New Testament Canon," 287).

46. Elliott, "Manuscripts, the Codex, and the Canon," 106.

47. Gamble, *Books and Readers*, 100.

48. Hurtado, "The New Testament," 21.

endorse this hypothesis."[49] The existence of a first-century Pauline collection is important for the question of the canon because it shows that Paul's message was widely agreed upon by the first generations of Christians.

In addition to the Pauline collection, a second collection of apostolic writings arose early in the second century. These writings were known as "gospels," and various pieces of evidence suggest that there were four (and only four) gospels from the very beginning. Martin Hengel points to the superscriptions that identified the four gospels ("The Gospel according to . . ."), as well as the existence of commentaries on these four gospels before the time of Irenaeus (around AD 180).[50] It is also significant that these four gospels appeared together in the form of a codex early on, and that they never appeared in a codex together with other gospels. Elliott explains, "The Gospels that were rejected from that fourfold collection were never bound together with any or all of those four. There are no manuscripts that contain say Matthew, Luke and Peter, or John, Mark and Thomas. Only the Gospels of Matthew, Mark, Luke and John were considered as scriptural and then as canonical."[51] By the time of Irenaeus, the existence of a fourfold collection of gospels was a given. Hengel notes, "[Irenaeus] certainly did not invent this collection himself; it had already existed for quite a long time in the mainstream of the church, largely recognized and used in worship."[52] Together with the Pauline epistles (and 1 Pet and 1 John), the four gospels were recognized as definitive versions of the apostolic preaching and teaching by, at the latest, the middle of the second century.[53]

We have already discussed why writings that deviated from the apostolic gospel were not included in the New Testament canon. But what about other first-century writings that were consistent with the true apostolic message? Why were there four true gospels, and not five, or one? Why were these (and *all* these) particular letters of Paul collected, and not other letters he (or the other apostles) may have written, such as the letter to the Laodiceans (Col 4:16; see also 1 Cor 5:9)? We can speculate about these questions, but any answers will probably always be speculation. That is not a problem, however. As I noted above, the purpose of the early collections of apostolic

---

49. Porter, "When and How Was the Pauline Canon Compiled?," 126–27.

50. Hengel, *Four Gospels*, 48–60. Hurtado notes that no commentaries were written in the second century on any books that did not eventually become included in the twenty-seven book New Testament we have today ("The New Testament," 25).

51. Elliott, "Manuscripts," 107.

52. Hengel, *Four Gospels*, 10.

53. Hurtado, "The New Testament," 20.

writings was to *regulate* the preaching and teaching of the Word that Christ gave to the church. The early Christians did not seem to find it necessary to preserve a comprehensive or exhaustive list that included *every* faithful apostolic writing. The collections that were forming seemed more like "good enough" collections that remained somewhat fluid or "open" (similar to the composition of the *regula fidei*, which also exhibited some flexibility). When the time came at the end of the fourth and beginning of the fifth century to make explicit the contents of a "New Testament" canon, the writings that had already been collected and were already in circulation among the first Christians were obvious candidates for inclusion.

Up to this point I have said very little about Eusebius' fourth-century distinctions between writings that were read and recognized as Scripture throughout the church (*homolegoumena*) and those that were questioned in some places (*antilegomena*). Neither have I mentioned Athanasius' festal letter of AD 367 (the first known list that corresponds exactly to the twenty-seven books that are found in today's New Testament)[54] or the Third Council of Carthage in AD 397 (the first church council on record for listing the contents of the New Testament canon).[55] These help us understand the New Testament as we know it today. But they do not help us understand the formation of the New Testament canon in the first and second century. By the end of the fourth century the existence of a New Testament canon was a matter of fact. The questions that occupied Eusebius, Athanasius, and the Third Council of Carthage had to do with the exact contents of the New Testament that was already in existence. In the first and second century, however, it was not obvious that there would even be a "New Testament." Paul and the apostles recognized that they were speaking (and writing) the Word of God (see 1 Thess 2:13), but they probably did not envision a New Testament canon as we know it today (or as the church of the fourth century knew it). Neither did they seem to need it. The apostles simply proclaimed the gospel Jesus (and his Spirit) had given them to proclaim. The church heard, believed, and was shaped by the preaching and teaching of this gospel. As the church faced the need to distinguish between the true apostolic message and others that were false, they gathered together and circulated definitive versions of the apostolic message. These initial first- and second-century decisions (to write, collect, and circulate) provide the foundation for answering questions about the canon in subsequent centuries—whether they arise in the fourth, sixteenth, or twenty-first century.

54. See Bruce, *The Canon*, 208–10.
55. Ibid., 232–33.

Summary

There are two fundamental canonical questions that must be addressed in a comprehensive theology of Scripture: "What is the purpose of the New Testament canon?" and "Why were some writings included and not others?" The answers to these questions are rooted in the trinitarian economy of salvation that was accomplished in and centered around the life, death, and resurrection of Jesus. This economy continued as the risen Christ sent his apostles and the church with his Spirit to continue his proclamation of the Word for the salvation of the world. The New Testament canon (as well as the *regula fidei*) developed within this economy as the church testified to Jesus of Nazareth. This Jesus was born of Mary and baptized in Jordan; he preached with authority and did signs and wonders; he called sinners to repentance and faith; he was rejected and crucified; he was raised from the dead on the third day and ascended into the heavens with the promise to return in glory. The writings eventually included in the New Testament *regulated* the church's preaching and teaching by *preserving* definitive versions of this apostolic message. Writings that proclaimed a different Jesus (such as the Gnostic gospels) were rejected for being inconsistent with the true apostolic message. By the end of the first century the church had recognized a collection of Paul's letters as the standard for apostolic preaching and teaching, and by the middle of the second century a fourfold collection of gospels had been recognized throughout the church as definitive and true.

Recent challenges to the formation of the New Testament canon reflect the scandal of particularity. Why *this* Jesus? In dealing with this question, I have tried to emphasize that this problem belongs first of all to Jesus himself. Recent attacks against the traditional Christian canon are ultimately attacks against the mission and identity of the personal Word of God. Still, it seems that there could have been other legitimate, that is, orthodox, candidates for inclusion in the canon. What about them? When the purpose of the canon is seen as *regulative*, it becomes clear that it was unnecessary to include *every* faithful apostolic writing. The list of definitive versions only had to be "good enough" rather than exhaustive, and its composition could remain somewhat flexible.[56]

---

56. This conception of the canon rules out the possible inclusion of a hypothetical letter or gospel that might be discovered in the future—even if its apostolic authenticity could be proved beyond "reasonable doubt." There is simply no need for any further canonical writings.

In his criticism of the Council of Trent, Martin Chemnitz maintained, "The church does not have such power, that it can make true writings out of false, false out of true, out of doubtful and uncertain, certain, canonical and legitimate."[57] This criticism applies still today. Writings that were not identified as definitive versions of the apostolic Word during the pivotal first and second centuries (e.g., Ehrman's "lost scriptures") cannot seriously be considered canonical today. They testify to a different gospel, which is precisely why they were rejected (or "lost") in the first place. The criticism of Chemnitz also applies, however, to defenders of the traditional canon. Many proponents of the doctrine of inspiration have short-circuited the historical processes involved in the formation of the New Testament canon, speaking as though the church made no decisions about the contents of the canon. This is seen most obviously in the widespread avoidance of the questions in the early church about the canonicity of several of the New Testament books. Throughout the world Bibles continue to roll off the press with little mention of the early uncertainties surrounding Hebrews, James, 2 Peter, 2 and 3 John, Jude, and Revelation. If the church is to take seriously the question of the canon and its complex history, it must acknowledge that some of the writings in today's Bibles were not universally recognized as definitive versions of the apostolic Gospel in the first several centuries.

Authority

In the first chapter I noted that biblical authority has been viewed as *the* issue in the modern battle for the Bible. Proponents of the doctrine of inspiration insist that the Bible is the final authority in the church, and critics dismiss the authority of the Bible as a casualty of the Enlightenment. Although many nuances and qualifications apply, this has been the extent of the modern debate over biblical authority. To the present day theologians continue to disagree about inspiration and inerrancy, and subsequently whether or not the Bible continues to be "authoritative" in the church. But despite all the arguing over biblical authority, there has been little consideration of *how* the authority of the Scriptures functions in the economy of salvation. Such an explanation is necessary for a comprehensive theology of Scripture in our postmodern context. This calls for a closer look at the notion "authority" in the first place.

---

57. Chemnitz, *Examination*, 181.

Authority as a Functional Concept

In chapter 1 we considered David Kelsey's study of the authority of the Scriptures in modern theology. He notes that authority is a functional and relational concept. "If scripture is authority," he suggests, "it is always authority *for* somebody or somebodies, and authority for them *in regard* to something else."[58] Stephen Fowl agrees: "The authority of Scripture, then, is not so much an invariant property of the biblical texts, as a way of ordering a set of textual relationships. To call scripture authoritative also establishes a particular relationship between that text and those people and communities who treat it as authoritative."[59] This means that (contra Lindsell) the authority of the Scriptures do *not* stand or fall with inspiration and inerrancy. On the contrary, authority is inherent in the description of a writing as "Scripture." Kelsey's explanation bears repeating:

> "Authoritative" is part of the meaning of "scripture"; it is not a *contingent* judgment made about "scripture" on other grounds, such as their age, authorship, miraculous inspiration, etc. . . . To call certain texts "scripture" is, in part, to say that they ought to be *used* in the common life of the church in normative ways such that they decisively rule its form of life and forms of speech. Thus part of what it means to call certain texts "scripture" is that they are authoritative for the common life of the church. It is to say of them that they *ought* to be used in certain ways to certain ends in that life.[60]

As long as Christian communities continue to read the Bible as *Scripture* (whether or not they regard it as inspired and inerrant), it will continue to function among them with at least some degree of authority.

Kelsey helps identify the problem with modernity's conception of biblical authority. His own account, however, has other problems. Rather than grounding the function of the biblical authority in the work of God through his Word, Kelsey locates biblical authority solely in its *ecclesial* function. "Scripture's authority specifically for theology, we said, is a function of its authority for the common life of the church. Its authority for the common life of the church consists in its being used in certain rulish and normative ways so that it helps to nurture and reform the community's self-identity and the personal identities of her members . . . In short, the doctrine of 'scripture and

---

58. Kelsey, *Proving Doctrine*, xi.
59. Fowl, *Engaging Scripture*, 6.
60. Kelsey, *Proving Doctrine*, 97–98.

its authority' is a postulate of practical theology."[61] For Kelsey the authority of the Scriptures is an instance of the *church's* use of these particular writings—not *God's* use of them. Webster identifies the problem: "In such proposals, definition of the character, purpose and interpretation of Scripture is regarded as inseparable from the place occupied by Scripture in the life and practices of the Christian community. Scripture is thus neither a purely formal authority to be invoked in theological deliberation, nor a collection of clues to help us reconstruct its religious and cultural background, nor a symbolic deposit of experience; it is a book of the church, a community text best understood out of its churchly determinism."[62] The problem with thinking of the Scriptures solely as a book *of* the church is that, in the end, it has no ability to exercise authority *over* the church. As Webster notes, "Scripture is not the word of the church; the church is the church of the Word."[63]

Divine Authority in the Divine Economy

At this point N. T. Wright's account of the authority of the Scriptures becomes very helpful. Wright suggests that biblical authority begins with the authority that God exercises in and among his people. Authority is not so much an ontological property of the biblical writings, and neither is it an instance of ecclesiastical authority. It is an *activity* of the Triune God. In other words, the authority of the Scriptures is an instance of the Father working through his Son and his Spirit.

> All authority is from God, declares Paul in relation to governments (Romans 13:1); Jesus says something very similar in John 19:11. In Matthew 28:18, the risen Jesus makes the still more striking claim that all authority in heaven and on earth has been given to *him*, a statement echoed elsewhere, for instance in Philippians 2:9–11. A quick glance through many other texts in both Old Testament (e.g. Isaiah 40–55) and New (e.g. Revelation 4 and 5) would confirm this kind of picture. When John declares that "in the beginning was the word," he does not reach a climax with "and the word was written down" but "and the word became flesh" . . . Since these are themselves "scriptural" statements, that means that scripture itself points—authoritatively, if it does indeed possess authority!—away

---

61. Ibid., 208.
62. Webster, *Holy Scripture*, 43.
63. Ibid., 44.

from itself and to the fact that final and true authority belongs to God himself, now delegated to Jesus Christ."[64]

As Wright notes, the proper starting point for all thinking about authority in the church is the authority of God as he exercises it through Jesus, the personal Word. In him God acts authoritatively to forgive, teach, heal, and save.

Wright begins his account of the authority of the Scriptures by thinking about the God who acts to rescue his people and renew his fallen creation. In the face of radical evil God establishes his kingdom within his fallen creation. The means by which he does this saving work, Wright suggests, is the Scriptures. Through these writings the children of Israel discovered who God was and how his purposes were achieved. Through them the kingdom of God was "breaking into the world, and to Israel's life, in judgment and mercy."[65] Wright notes that behind this work of God through the Scriptures is an "elusive but powerful idea of God's 'word.'"[66] This "word" is not synonymous with the prophetic writings, he says, but is rather a "strange personal presence, creating, judging, healing, recreating."[67]

> This view of YHWH's "word" in the Old Testament is very instructive. It is as though, to put it one way, "the word of YHWH" is like an enormous reservoir, full of creative divine wisdom and power, into which the prophets and other writers tap by God's call and grace, so that the word may flow through them to do God's work of flooding or irrigating his people. Or, to put it another way, the creator God, though utterly transcendent over and different from the world which he has made, remains present and active within that world, and one of the many ways in which this is so is through his living and active word.[68]

Wright summarizes the entire Old Testament narrative as the story of Israel who "heard God's word—in call, promise, liberation, guidance, judgment, forgiveness, further judgment, renewed liberation and renewed promise."[69]

In the person of Jesus God brought this saving work to a completion. Jesus was the fulfillment of the prophetic writings, and through him God performed the same work that he had been doing through the Scriptures

---

64. Wright, *Scripture*, 24. His emphasis.
65. Ibid., 27.
66. Ibid., 28.
67. Ibid.
68. Ibid.
69. Ibid., 29.

of old. "The work that God had done through Scripture in the Old Testament is done by Jesus in his public career, his death and resurrection, and his sending of the Spirit."[70] In this sense John describes Jesus as the Word of God made flesh. When Jesus "fulfilled" the Scriptures (e.g., Mark 14:49) he did much more than fulfill isolated verses. Instead, he brought to completion the entire "storyline" of God's authoritative work among his people. Jesus is the "living embodiment of Israel's God, the God whose Spirit had inspired the scriptures in the first place."[71] When it comes to the apostolic church, Wright highlights the fact that the apostles proclaimed the Word before a single New Testament book was ever written. This Word can be summarized as the "story of Jesus (particularly his suffering and death), told as the climax of the story of God and Israel."[72] He concludes, "The early church was centrally constituted as the people called into existence, and sustained in that existence, by the powerful, effective and (in that sense and many others) 'authoritative' word of God, written in the Old Testament, embodied in Jesus, announced to the world, taught in the church."[73]

There is much that is helpful in Wright's account of the authority of the Scriptures. Like Webster, he recognizes that the people of God have always been constituted by the Word God speaks—that Christians are most properly understood as people who hear the voice of God.[74] He also notes that Jesus' death and resurrection was the message proclaimed by the apostles, and that through this message God brings his authoritative Word to the entire world. He summarizes: "The apostolic writings, like the 'word' which they now wrote down, were not simply *about* the coming of God's kingdom into the world; they were, and were designed to be, part of the *means whereby* that happened."[75]

Despite these helpful contributions, Wright's account lacks clarity in its conception of the Word of God. Although he recognizes the Word of God behind the authority of the Scriptures, he does not distinguish between the various forms of the Word of God in the biblical narrative. For example, when speaking about the work God accomplishes among his people through the Scriptures, Wright says that God used the Scriptures to perform works of

70. Ibid., 32.
71. Ibid.
72. Ibid., 36.
73. Ibid., 37.
74. As Luther put it, Christians are "little sheep who hear the voice of their shepherd" (SA III.12).
75. Wright, *Scripture*, 38. His emphasis.

judgment and mercy, to equip them for service, and to shape them according to his will. It is true that God did these things through the Scriptures. But long before a single Scripture was written (and long after they were written), God was accomplishing these things through the Word he *spoke* through his deputized prophets. But Wright has no account of the spoken Word. A second example of this lack of clarity can be seen in Wright's suggestion that the incarnation is a continuation of the work that God had been doing through the Old Testament Scriptures. By construing the work of Jesus as a continuation of the work God had been doing through the Scriptures (rather than speaking about the Scriptures in terms of the work that God was accomplishing in Christ), Wright gives dogmatic priority to the written Word over the personal Word—as if Jesus were one form of the Scriptures.[76] He speaks about the power of the Word to change lives, but he remains vague about how God actually makes these changes.[77]

In order to provide some clarity and completion to Wright's account of the authority of the Scriptures, it is helpful to take a closer look at the authority of the Word of God in the divine economy. This begins with a look at the authority God exercised through his personal Word, Jesus Christ.

Authority to Save and Authority to Teach

Of all the people who encountered Jesus during his earthly ministry, it may have been a Roman soldier who best understood the authority God exercises through his Word. In Matthew 8 we read about a centurion who asked Jesus to heal his servant. Jesus offered to come to his home, but the centurion stopped him. "Lord," he said, "I am not worthy to have you come under my roof, but only say the word, and my servant will be healed. For I too am a man under authority, with soldiers under me. And I say to one, 'Go,' and he goes, and to another, 'Come,' and he comes, and to my servant, 'Do this,' and he does it" (Matt 8:8–9). Jesus responded by addressing the crowd, "Truly, I tell you, with no one in Israel have I found such faith" (Matt 8:10). Then he addressed the centurion, "Go; let it be done for you as you have believed,"

---

76. Wright's book is about Scripture and not Jesus. Perhaps that is the problem. I am arguing that any theological account of Scripture should begin (and end) with God's saving work through the personal Word of God. Wright's inattention to Christ as the personal Word may also explain why he makes no mention of God speaking his Word at creation. It appears as though he makes the Word "stranger" and more "elusive" than necessary.

77. Wright, *Scripture*, 28.

and Matthew reports that the servant was healed at that very moment (Matt 8:13). As the centurion correctly understood, the personal Word was capable of accomplishing his will simply by speaking. Jesus did this throughout his ministry in two specific ways. First, he exercised authority over sin, death, and the power of the devil by forgiving sins (Matt 9:6; Luke 5:24), casting out demons (Mark 3:15; Luke 4:36), healing the sick (Matt 4:23), and raising the dead (Mark 5:35–42; John 11:1–44). In these ways he acted with "authority to save." Jesus also exercised authority through his teaching. He taught with unique authority as he proclaimed the truth about God. "When Jesus finished these sayings, the crowds were astonished at his teaching, for he was teaching them as one who had authority" (Matt 7:28–29; see also Mark 1:22, 29; Luke 4:32). Through his speaking, the personal Word of God exercised his authority in two specific ways—authority to save and authority to teach.

In chapter 4 we considered Luther's understanding of the written and spoken Word of God. These categories are helpful again as we consider the authority of the Word of God. Jesus' "authority to save" and "authority to teach" correspond to two forms of the Word that Luther emphasized. Saarnivaara describes the spoken form of the Word as the "means-of-grace-word." Through this form of the Word God works to forgive sins, create life, and grant eternal salvation. Luther explains:

> There is no other way to have sins forgiven than through the Word . . . The Lord, our God, has not promised to forgive our sins through any work that we do, but He has connected it with the unique work of Christ who has suffered and risen from the dead. This work he has, through the word, placed in the mouth of the apostles and the ministers of the Church, and in the cases of emergency of all Christians, to the end that they through it would distribute and proclaim the forgiveness of sins to those who desire it.[78]

The proclamation of this "means-of-grace-word" is the first and most important mark of the church for Luther, which is why he describes the church as a "mouth-house" rather than a "pen-house."[79] In addition to the spoken Word, Luther emphasized that the Scriptures were the written Word of God. They teach the truth about God and his expectations for his people. Luther writes in his commentary on Genesis, "When we hear that God says something, we must simply hold to it, so that we believe it without any argument

---

78. Luther, WA 52.273, quoted in Saarnivaara, "Written and Spoken," 167.
79. Saarvnivaara, "Written and Spoken," 174.

and bring our reason into captivity to the obedience of Christ."[80] Although he occasionally spoke of the Scriptures themselves as a "means-of-grace-word,"[81] Luther did not look to the written Word as the means by which God normally accomplishes his saving work. Instead, he viewed the Scriptures primarily as the "revelation-word" that guide and rule the teaching and preaching of the church as "the highest norm and standard of our faith and life."[82]

For Luther the written Word and the spoken Word both function authoritatively, but in different ways. Saarnivaara explains:

> Luther gives both to Scripture (and the written word in general) and the oral testimony and preaching of the word their proper places in the Christian Church: the written word of God is primarily a "revelation-word," which is the norm and standard of all faith, life, and teaching. The spoken word (in preaching, absolution, and sacraments) is the actual "means-of-grace-word," through which God forgives sins, works faith, and imparts his Holy Spirit. Luther never says that Scripture has the office or ministry of reconciliation, or that Christ has given the power of the keys to the written Word; neither does Scripture itself contain any such statement. The ministry of reconciliation and the power of the keys are given to the living Christians of each generation, not to Scripture. God may work faith through the written word, namely faith in Him and His truth and promises, so that the penitent sinner can seek the Gospel in the Church from the ministry of reconciliation and be justified in believing it. In Luther's view, Scripture is not given for the purpose that a person by means of it, independently from the Church, might care for the salvation of his soul.[83]

In Luther's view the Scriptures function primarily as the "revelation-word," while proclamation of the Gospel functions primarily as the "means-of-grace-word." These two forms of the Word must be distinguished, but they cannot be separated. Saarnivaara summarizes, "The proclamation of the word (in sermons and personal absolution and counseling) and the administration of the sacraments are inseparably connected with the Scriptures.

---

80. Luther, *WA* 42.118, 11, quoted in Saarvnivaara, "Written and Spoken," 170.
81. Saarvnivaara, "Written and Spoken," 172–74.
82. Ibid., 167.
83. Ibid., 174.

Only a scriptural teaching, preaching, and consolation leads men to the knowledge of Christ and salvation in Him."[84]

Jesus' "authority to save" corresponds to the spoken Word of God. He gave this authority to his disciples as he sent them to forgive sins (Matt 18:18; John 20:23) and proclaim the gospel, which is the power of salvation (Luke 24:47; Rom 1:16). Jesus continues to exercise this authority as his people speak the "means-of-grace-word" throughout the world for the forgiveness of sins and salvation of the world. Jesus' "authority to teach" corresponds to the written Word of God. Jesus gave authority to his disciples to teach everything that he had commanded them (Matt 20:18), and he sent them his Spirit of truth to guide them (John 16:13). He continues to exercise this authority as his people continue read and hear the written Word of the apostles.

In this context the Reformation slogan *sola scriptura* is best understood. The primary function of the written Word of God is to provide the rule and norm for the church's preaching and teaching. This is what it means for the Scriptures to have "authority to teach." As Webster notes, the written Word of God means the end of "free speech" in the church.[85] Preachers are not at liberty to proclaim their own ideas about God. They are bound to preach and teach in conformity to the definitive versions of the Word proclaimed by the apostles. When there are disagreements about what it is that the church believes, teaches, and confesses, the final judge for what is truly apostolic is the written Word. As Paul warns the Romans, "Watch out for those who cause divisions and create obstacles contrary to the doctrine that you have been taught" (Rom 16:17; see also 1 Tim 6:3–4). *Sola scriptura*, therefore, refers to the written Word's role as "eine Appellationinstanz im innerkirchlichen Autoritätenkonflikt."[86] As the definitive versions of the apostolic message, the Scriptures are the only judge for sorting out disagreements in the church.[87] Thus the Formula of Concord declares, "We confess our adherence to the prophetic and apostolic writings of the Old and New Testaments, as to the pure, clear fountain of Israel, which alone is the *one*

---

84. Ibid., 169.

85. Webster, *Holy Scripture*, 65.

86. "An appeals court in inner-churchly conflicts of authority" (Slenczka, "Schrift—Tradition—Kontext," 45).

87. The seventeenth-century dogmaticians noticed this kind of biblical authority at work in the biblical narrative itself. Robert Preus explains, "The reforms of Hezekiah and Josiah were both brought about by a return to the Word of God as the only norm of doctrine and life. Both Christ and his disciples appealed to the written Word in times of controversy (Matt 4:4; 19:4; 22:29; Mark 9:12: Luke 10:26; 24:26; Acts 3:22; 7:2; 13:33; 26:22)" (*Inspiration*, 118).

true guiding principle, according to which all teachers and teaching are to be judged and evaluated."[88] With the theology of the Word of God as our foundation, we might summarize the relationship between the authority of spoken Word and the authority of the written Word in this way:

> The Gospel was the "power of God unto salvation" (Rom 1:16) even before holy men of God committed it to writing. To say that the Scriptures are the authority for *the way we express* the Gospel is not to say that the Gospel derives its authority or power from the Scriptures. The *normative* authority of Scripture does not make the Gospel the living Word of God (1 Pet 1:23–25), but the formal principle, Holy Scripture, *does* tell us authoritatively what Gospel truly is *God's* living Word and pronounces a curse upon anyone who preaches a different gospel (Gal 1:8–9).[89]

The Old Authority and the New

The primary authoritative function of the written Word of God is to provide the rule and norm for faith and life. But as we observed in the previous section on the canon, the Bible is not a single book. It is a collection of books—and a collection of collections at that. The most basic division within the Bible, which we did not explore earlier, is the division between the Old and New Testaments. These two collections differ in fundamental ways, including the way in which they function authoritatively in the life of the church. Wright observes, "Our relationship to the New Testament is not the same as our relationship to the Old, and . . . we can say this with no diminution of our commitment to the Old Testament as a crucial and non-negotiable part of 'holy scripture.'"[90]

The key to understanding the difference between the authority of the Old Testament and the authority of the New Testament is to view them in terms of their relationship to the personal Word of God. Because all authority belongs to him (Matt 28:18), the authority of both testaments is relative to Jesus. A consideration of Jesus' own biblical practice is essential at this point. The personal Word of God recognized the writings of the prophets as

---

88. *FC SD*, Basis, Rule and Guiding Principle, 3. This norming function of the Bible in the Formula of Concord is similar to the view of Josef Ratzinger in his commentary on Vatican II. See Dunn, "Has the Canon a Continuing Function?," 574 n. 42.

89. Commission on Theology and Church Relations, "Gospel and Scripture," 17.

90. Wright, *Scripture*, 92.

the written Word of God and submitted to them as the standard for faithful living under the law. But he also fulfilled them (Matt 5:17) and insisted that they testify to himself (John 5:39). Through his life, death, and resurrection Jesus was establishing a *new* covenant with the people of God (see Luke 22:20; 2 Cor 3:6), and this new covenant involved a change in their relationship to the law God had given in the Old Testament Scriptures. Wright explains:

> The ancient Jewish purity laws are seen as no longer relevant to a community in which Gentiles are welcome on equal terms (Mark 7; Acts 15; Gal 2). The Temple in Jerusalem, and the sacrifices that took place there, were no longer the focal point of God's meeting with his people (Mark 12:28–34; Acts 7; Rom 12:1–2; Hebrews 8–12) . . . The sabbath is no longer mandatory (Rom 14:5–6), and indeed if people insist on such observances they are cutting against the grain of the gospel (Gal. 4:10). There is now no holy land: in Paul's reinterpretation of the Abrahamic promises in Romans 4:13, God promises Abraham not just one strip of territory but the whole world, anticipating the renewal of all creation as in Romans 8. Perhaps most importantly, the dividing wall between Jew and Gentile has been abolished (throughout Paul, and summarized in Ephesians 2:11–22).[91]

As Wright points out, Jesus' fulfillment of the Old Testament Scriptures changed the way they functioned authoritatively in the life of the church. Jesus explained some of these changes through his own proclamation of the Word, and he left the rest to be taught by his apostles as they were led by his Spirit. Their preaching and teaching set forth his expectations for living in the new covenant, and these expectations were ultimately codified in the formation of the New Testament canon.

What does this mean for the Old Testament today? In accordance with Jesus' own biblical practice, Christians are bound to live according to the Old Testament law *only insofar as* Jesus (and his apostles) continued to teach it.[92] This does not mean that the prophetic writings no longer function authoritatively in the church, however. To the contrary, the Old Testament continues to play an important role in the economy of salvation because they

---

91. Ibid., 41.

92. In "How Christians Should Regard Moses," Luther writes, "The sectarian spirits want to saddle us with Moses and the commandments. We will just skip that. We will regard Moses as a teacher, but we will not regard him as our law-giver—unless he agrees with both the New Testament and the natural law" (*LW* 35.165).

provide the context for God's saving work through Christ. Luther referred to the prophetic writings as the "swaddling clothes" and "manger" in which Christ is wrapped. They provide the context for understanding the identity and work of the personal Word of God, and as such provide a normative framework for understanding God and his creation, beginning with the creation of all things up to the redemption of all things in his Son.[93] Without them it is simply impossible to understand the life and mission of the personal Word of God. As Elizabeth Achtemeier writes, "Jesus Christ is, in the New Testament, the Word of the Old made flesh—the new promised action of God (Isa. 43:19) that nevertheless gathers up the promises of the Old Testament and brings them to their final interpretation and conclusion."[94]

Summary

Biblical authority has been a central front in the modern battle for the Bible. But rather than arguing about *how* the Scriptures function authoritatively, both sides have focused their attention on debating *if* the Scriptures are authoritative. As a result, false dichotomies have dominated the discussion. Proponents of the doctrine of inspiration have argued *either* the Bible is inspired, inerrant, and authoritative *or* its authority is lost. Critical theologians, on the other hand, have set the Scriptures against some other conception of the Word of God (e.g., the gospel, Christ, or an existential "I-Thou" encounter). *Either* the Scriptures are authoritative *or* the Word of God is authoritative. Carl Braaten, for example, writes, "The ultimate authority of Christian theology is not the biblical canon as such, but the gospel of Jesus Christ to which the Scriptures bear witness—the 'canon within the canon.'"[95]

---

93. The Old Testament also remains necessary for teaching about and understanding God's nature and work. It gives good examples from which to learn, and it contains the promises of God that were fulfilled in Christ. Luther writes, "I have stated that all Christians, and especially those who handle the word of God and attempt to teach others, should take heed and learn Moses aright. Thus were he gives commandment, we are not to follow him except so far as he agrees with the natural law ... We have our own master, Christ, and he has set before us what we are to know, observe, do, and leave undone. However it is true that Moses sets down, in addition to the laws, fine examples of faith and unfaith—punishment of the godless, elevation of the righteous and believing—and also the dear and comforting promises concerning Christ which we should accept" (*LW* 35.173–74).

94. Achtemeier, "The Canon as the Voice," 125. By now it is clear that the authority of the Old and New Testaments is bound up with their interpretation. Achtemeier's observation points us toward the final section in this chapter.

95. Braaten, *Christian Dogmatics*, 1:61.

In contrast to both sides of the modern debate, the authority of the Scriptures must be grounded in the authority of God. More precisely, it must be grounded in Jesus, the personal Word of God who received all authority from the Father (Matt 28:18). He exercised "authority to save" by forgiving sins, casting out demons, healing the sick, and raising the dead. He also exercised "authority to teach" by proclaiming the truth about God and his expectations for human faith and life. This personal Word of God co-missioned his apostles with his Word and his Spirit to continue his mission of speaking with authority. He gave them "authority to save" (Matt 18:18; John 20:23) and "authority to teach" (Matt 28:19; John 16:13), and subsequent generations of Christians have looked to their writings as definitive versions of what to preach and teach in the church. This written Word of God serves the spoken Word of God, and this is what it means for the Scriptures to be the only rule and norm for Christian faith and life.

Interpretation

Our reflection on the biblical canon helps us understand which writings are properly recognized as Scripture. Our reflection on biblical authority helps us think about how Christian faith and life is ruled and normed by these particular writings. Standing behind both canon and authority is the interpretation of the Scriptures. They were written to be read, and inherent in reading is interpretation. As Stephen Fowl notes, "Accepting that scripture is the standard for their faith, practice, and worship does not get Christians out of the hard tasks of scriptural interpretation."[96]

Because the Scriptures are the written Word of *God*, it follows that biblical interpretation is unlike any other act of literary interpretation. This requires that the theology of Scripture offer more than simply a theory of interpretation. It must give a *theological* account of what it means to interpret the Bible. Much like with the question of the canon and authority of the Scriptures, biblical interpretation is best understood when it is approached within the context of a cruciform theology of the Word of God. Before we get to that, however, we need to understand the postmodern hermeneutical context. Contemporary theology has witnessed an explosion of interpretive strategies and theories, leading many to conclude that "theology simply *is* hermeneutics."[97]

---

96. Fowl, *Engaging Scripture*, 2.
97. Kelsey, *Proving Doctrine*, xiv.

The Postmodern Hermeneutical Context

Stephen Fowl's *Engaging Scripture* offers a helpful summary of the current hermeneutical situation. He describes three "stories" or "accounts" of biblical interpretation. He calls the first story "determinate interpretation." In this story the goal of interpretation is "to produce, uncover, or illuminate the meaning of the biblical text."[98] Operating with the assumption that the meaning of the text is located in the text itself, a determinate view of interpretation treats the biblical text as a problem to be solved. "One might even say that the aim of this type of interpretation is to render interpretation redundant by making the meaning of the biblical text clear to all reasonable people of good will."[99] Benjamin Jowett, a pioneer of determinate interpretation, makes this aim explicit: "The true use of interpretation is to get rid of interpretation and leave us alone in company with the author."[100] Modern theologians, with their objectivistic attitudes about interpretation leading the way, have frequently approached the interpretive task in this way. By presuming to strip away all "interpretation," they seek to discover the stable and secure meaning of the text. Once this meaning has been uncovered, the difficult work of biblical interpretation is complete and the interpreter may move on to another text.

In reaction to this "determinate" account of biblical interpretation, some postmodern interpreters have offered an opposing conception of biblical interpretation. Fowl calls it "anti-determinate interpretation." It goes something like this: "Nobody's interpretation is better than anyone else's; everyone has a right to his/her own interpretation; it is rude and not inclusive to fail to accept someone's interpretation as true for that person."[101] In contrast to the determinate view of interpretation, which locates the meaning solely in the *text*, anti-determinate readings locate the meaning solely in the *reader*. The aim of anti-determinate interpretation is to "upset, disrupt, and deconstruct interpretive certainties."[102] Deconstructionism is a good example of this. Deconstructive interpretation is an on-going process characterized by a two-step approach to interpreting the text. It begins by identifying the dominant reading of text—the one that is generally agreed upon as right and true. Rather than accepting the consensus, the decon-

---

98. Fowl, *Engaging Scripture*, 32.
99. Ibid.
100. Quoted in Fowl, *Engaging Scripture*, 33 n. 1.
101. Fowl, *Engaging Scripture*, 40.
102. Ibid., 33.

structive interpreter challenges the traditional reading by highlighting a perspective that has been obscured by the dominant interpretation. From this new perspective the reader reinterprets the text and arrives at an alternate meaning. Anti-determinate interpretation disallows mastery of the text because the anti-determinate reader continually turns the dominant reading on its head.

Fowl points out that there are problems with both the determinate and the anti-determinate stories of interpretation. The problem with determinate interpretation is its assumption that it is possible to get beyond the need to interpret, as if we are capable of escaping our own perspective. Because there is no such thing as purely objective interpretation, determinate interpretation is a practical impossibility—the meaning of a text does not reside solely within the text itself.[103] The problem with anti-determinate interpretation is that there is no end to the deconstructive possibilities. As soon as the dominant reading becomes subverted by the deconstructive reader, the deconstructed reading itself becomes subject to deconstruction. The result is a text with no limit to possible meanings, which ultimately leads to a text with no meaning at all.

In contrast to determinate and anti-determinate stories of biblical interpretation, Fowl suggests what he calls "underdetermined interpretation." Rather than making absolute claims about the certainty of a text's meaning as a property of the text (determinate interpretation), and rather than reducing the meaning of a text to its context (anti-determinate interpretation), he suggests that "theological convictions, ecclesial practices, and communal and social concerns should *shape and be shaped* by biblical interpretation."[104] That is, proper interpretation involves more than just the text, and more than just the reader. It requires a community of the faithful as they live together

---

103. Several biblical examples illustrate this point. In Acts 8 we read about an encounter between Philip and an Ethiopian eunuch who was reading the prophecy of Isaiah. When Philip asked him if he understood what he was reading the eunuch said, "How can I, unless someone guides me?" (Acts 8:31). Philip responded by explaining to him the good news about Jesus. Paul explains the theology behind this encounter: "Now we have received not the spirit of the world, but the Spirit who is from God, that we might understand the things freely given us by God. And we impart this in words not taught by human wisdom but taught by the Spirit, interpreting spiritual truths to those who are spiritual. The natural person does not accept the things of the Spirit of God, for they are folly to him, and he is not able to understand them because they are spiritually discerned. The spiritual person judges all things, but is himself to be judged by no one. 'For who has understood the mind of the Lord so as to instruct him?' But we have the mind of Christ" (1 Cor 2:12–16).

104. Fowl, *Engaging Scripture*, 60.

under the text they are trying to interpret. "Biblical interpretation will be the occasion of a complex interaction between the biblical text and the varieties of theological, moral, material, political, and ecclesial concerns that are part of the contexts in which they find themselves."[105] Underdetermined interpretation appreciates the fact that the Scriptures were written within the context of the community of believers, and that faithful interpretation is only possible within that context.

The value of Fowl's description of these three stories of biblical interpretation is that he gives us a clear and concise view of the postmodern hermeneutical landscape. He identifies the practical impossibilities of a determinate account of biblical interpretation, but also recognizes the problems with the deconstructive approach. His own account only gets us so far, however, because he does not lay out concrete steps or boundaries to guide faithful underdetermined interpretation.[106] Instead, he offers examples of what he envisions this kind of interpretation to look like. In order to provide some concrete guidance for biblical interpretation, the following may be seen as further steps toward a faithful "underdetermined" account of biblical interpretation that is grounded in a cruciform theology of the Word of God.

Entering the Circle

"Interpretation is a circular process." Thus begins the first of seven theses on Reformation hermeneutics offered by Martin Franzman.[107] The circular process to which he is referring is a widely recognized hermeneutical principle: "Unless you know what a man is talking about, you will not make sense of his words." Or in Luther's words, "Qui non intelligit res non potest ex verbis sensum elicere."[108] An everyday example explains what he means. Everyone has experienced the situation in which someone enters into the middle of a conversation between several other people. The latecomer understands the words (*verba*) that are being said, but he does not know the subject matter (*res*) of what the group is discussing. So he asks, "What are you guys talking

---

105. Ibid.

106. Fowl is explicit and intentional about *not* trying to do this. After briefly identifying the "rule of faith" as a boundary setter for proper biblical interpretation he writes, "The arguments of this book are not as much concerned with establishing boundaries as with making constructive use of the interaction of Christian convictions, practices, and scriptural interpretation" (*Engaging Scripture*, 8).

107. Franzmann, "Seven Theses," 120.

108. "Whoever does not understand the subject cannot make sense of the words."

about?" If he wants to understand the messages that are being conveyed, he needs a clear understanding of the subject being discussed. This is true of spoken communication, and it is especially true of *written* communication where tone, inflection, and nonverbal communication are all absent. Franzmann explains, "To interpret adequately any portion of a text, a man must therefore have formed some conception of the text as a whole: this conception of the whole guides him in the interpretation of the individual words and unites and is in turn subject to correction, enrichment, and deepening by his study of the individual units. The process by which a genuine understanding of a text is gained is, therefore, 'circular'; from *verba* to *res* to *verba*, in continual and lively interaction."[109]

The implications for biblical interpretation are obvious. Faithful biblical interpretation requires more than just knowledge of what the words (*verba*) mean. It requires (at least some) prior understanding of the subject matter (*res*) of the Christian faith. That begs the question, "What is the *res* about which the Scriptures are talking?" A valid description of the subject matter of the Christian faith must find ample documentation in the biblical narrative itself, for the biblical narrative provides the framework for all Christian thought. The *res* will flow from the Scriptures even as it guides the interpretation of the Scriptures. Franzmann considers a number of possible descriptions of the Bible's subject matter. "Sovereignty of God" is a potential candidate, for the Scriptures depict a God who is in charge of his creation. But a description of God's nature leaves open questions about *how* he exercises his sovereignty. Other possibilities include "the God who acts" or the "self-disclosure of God." These descriptions help focus attention on what God does, but they remain vague and indefinite. They are too abstract to offer helpful interpretive direction. Still another possibility is to see the *res* of the Bible as the "verbally inspired, infallible Word." As we discussed in the first chapter, this is a popular choice among proponents of the doctrine of inspiration. But as Franzmann points out, this does not say enough. The affirmation that the Scriptures are perfect and true does not provide much direction for what a given biblical text *means*.

So how should we describe the subject matter of the Christian faith? Franzmann offers what he describes as "the radical Gospel." This is shorthand for, "God, to whom man can find no way, has in Christ creatively opened up the way which man may and must go."[110] This description of the *res* of the Scriptures "subsumes all that is good and true in the other *res* that have been

---

109. Franzmann, "Seven Theses," 120.
110. Ibid., 122.

proposed; and it puts them in right relation to the central *res*."¹¹¹ To get more specific, Franzmann identifies three aspects of the radical Gospel. First, it recognizes "the condemning law and wrath of God" and the "guilt and lostness" of humankind. Second, it recognizes the "sole working of God" in the salvation of his human creatures. Third, it recognizes the "transformation" of humankind's existence that is produced by God's saving acts in Christ. Franzmann concludes his account of the "radical Gospel" by showing how it manifests itself throughout the biblical narrative, from the beginning in Genesis to the end in Revelation.

The Image of the King

Long before Franzmann (or Luther) identified the circular nature of biblical interpretation and the interplay between the *res* and the *verba* of the written Word, Irenaeus engaged a group known as the Valentinians in a struggle over faithful biblical interpretation. He criticized the Valentinians in the first book of *Against Heresies* for perverting the Scriptures "to their baseless fictions."¹¹² The problem was not that they denied that the Scriptures were true and perfect. Rather, their interpretations were heretical because they approached the Scriptures with false ideas about the subject matter of the Christian faith.

> They endeavor to adapt with an air of probability to their own peculiar assertions the parables of the Lord, the sayings of the prophets, and the words of the apostles, in order that their scheme may not seem altogether without support. In doing so, however, they disregard the order and the connection of the Scriptures, and so far as in them lies, dismember and destroy the truth. By transferring passages, and dressing them up anew, and making one thing out of another, they succeed in deluding many through their wicked art in adapting the oracles of the Lord to their opinions.¹¹³

Instead of reading the Scriptures in light of their proper subject matter, the Valentinians rearranged the *verba* and ended up with a foreign and heretical *res*.

> Their manner of acting is just as if one, when a beautiful image of a king has been constructed by some skillful artist out of precious

---

111. Ibid., 130.
112. *Against Heresies* I.8.1 in *ANF* 1:326.
113. Ibid.

jewels, should then take this likeness of the man all to pieces, should re-arrange the gems, and so fit them together as to make them into the form of a dog or a fox, and even that but poorly executed; and should then maintain and declare that *this* was the beautiful image of the king which the skillful artist constructed, pointing to the jewels which had been admirably fitted together by the first artist to form the image of the king, but have been with bad effect transferred by the latter one to the shape of a dog, and by thus exhibiting the jewels, should deceive the ignorant who had no conception what a king's form was like, and persuade them that that miserable likeness of the fox was, in fact, the beautiful image of the king.[114]

Irenaeus' description of the Scriptures as an image of a king is helpful for identifying boundaries for faithful biblical interpretation. The gems in the picture of the king are like the many passages in the Bible. When viewed as they were arranged by the Spirit-led prophets and apostles they paint a beautiful picture of a king. But when taken out of context and read in ways that depart from their original order, they make up a picture of a fox—and a "poorly executed" fox at that.[115] To use Franzmann's language, when the *res* of the Scriptures is not held firmly in view, the *verba* can be manipulated in a destructive circle of interpretation to make the Scriptures themselves proclaim an entirely different gospel.

For Irenaeus the *res* of the Scriptures is an image of a king. This king is distinctively trinitarian and soteriological, similar to the *regulae fidei* ("canon 1") of many of the early church fathers (as well as Franzmann's "radical Gospel"). Irenaeus summarizes this image:

> The Church, though dispersed throughout the whole world, even to the ends of the earth, has received from the apostles and their disciples this faith: [She believes] in one God, the Father almighty, Maker of heaven, and earth, and the sea, and all things that are in them; and in one Christ Jesus, the Son of God, who became incarnate for our salvation; and in the Holy Spirit, who proclaimed through the prophets the dispensations of God, and the advents, and the birth from a virgin, and the passion, and the resurrection from the dead, and the ascension into heaven in the flesh of

---

114. Ibid.

115. Irenaeus' caution against reading individual passages of out context is particularly applicable today—especially among those who affirm that the Bible is the inspired and inerrant Word of God. Single passages of Scripture are frequently used as isolated truisms to support ideas that have very little to do with Christ and the gospel.

> the beloved Christ Jesus, our Lord, and His [future] manifestation from heaven in the glory of the Father "to gather all things in one," and to raise up anew all flesh of the whole human race, in order that . . . He should execute just judgment towards all.[116]

Irenaeus' image of a king is an appropriate description of the *res* of the Scriptures because the heart of the biblical message is that Jesus Christ, the trinitarian Word who became a man, ushered in the reign of God through his life, death, and resurrection. This "King of kings" will return on the last day to judge all people and begin his eternal reign over the new creation.

At the heart of Franzmann's "radical Gospel" and Irenaeus' image of the king is the life, death, and resurrection of Jesus. This "cruciform" conception of the Scriptures is consistent with Jesus' own understanding of the Scriptures, both Old and New Testaments. Jesus emphasized that the prophetic writings testified to him (John 5:39) and foretold his suffering and death (Luke 24:24, 47). He sent his apostles to proclaim a message that focused on his death and resurrection as the center and foundation of their faith. His passion is the central issue in the four canonical gospels and the cornerstone of the apostolic message in the New Testament epistles. Paul summarizes his proclamation: "Now I would remind you, brothers, of the gospel I preached to you, which you received, in which you stand, and by which you are being saved, if you hold fast to the word I preached to you—unless you believed in vain. For I delivered to you as of first importance what I also received: that Christ died for our sins in accordance with the Scriptures, that he was buried, that he was raised on the third day in accordance with the Scriptures" (1 Cor 15:1–4). To the Philippians he paints a similar picture:

> Christ Jesus, who, though he was in the form of God, did not count equality with God a thing to be grasped, but made himself nothing, taking the form of a servant, being born in the likeness of men. And being found in human form, he humbled himself by becoming obedient to the point of death, even death on a cross. Therefore God has highly exalted him and bestowed on him the name that is above every name, so that at the name of Jesus every knee should bow, in heaven and on earth and under the earth, and every tongue confess that Jesus Christ is Lord, to the glory of God the Father (Phil 2:5–10).

---

116. Irenaeus, *Against Heresies*, I.10.1. in *ANF* 1:330.

Peter continues this theme as he describes the personal Word of God in terms of his suffering and death in both his preaching (see Acts 2:22–36; 3:13–22; 10:39–42) and his writing (1 Pet 1:18–21; 2:21–25; 3:18–22).

To return to Irenaeus' illustration of the mosaic of jewels, the individual gems that make up the image of the king must be viewed as parts of a greater whole. All of them contribute in some way to the overall picture of the crucified and risen king. So it is with the Scriptures. The writings of the prophets and apostles paint a picture of Jesus Christ, the Son of God and Savior of the world who was born of Mary and baptized in the Jordan; who preached and taught and did miraculous signs in the power of the Spirit; who claimed to be one with the Father; who spoke words of forgiveness; who was rejected and crucified for what he said; who was vindicated by the Father through his resurrection; who sent apostles and their associates (the church) to continue his ministry until he returns in glory. It is this picture of Jesus, this *res*, that informs and is informed by the *verba* of the Scriptures. While many passages in Scripture have an indirect relationship to his death and resurrection—especially in the Old Testament—all biblical interpretation takes place in relation to the divine economy of salvation. Every faithful reading of the Scriptures contributes in some way to the image of the crucified and risen king. As Telford Work puts it: "Scripture surrounds the cross of Christ on all sides."[117] Or in Luther's words, "I, poor little creature, do not find anything in the Scriptures but Jesus Christ and him crucified."[118]

Reading the Written Word of God

The recognition that Christ crucified is the subject matter of the Scriptures is an important step. But the difficulty of faithful biblical interpretation remains. Colin Gunton suggests that to read the Bible is to engage in a conversation. It is a one-sided conversation, for God is the one who speaks through his deputized prophets and apostles, but it is a conversation nonetheless. As a participant in this conversation, the reader (or hearer) of the Scriptures stands in a "position of passivity."[119] In this "position of passivity" the reader engages in the active (and theological) work of biblical interpretation, and in doing so participates in the economy of salvation. John Webster recognizes this and responds by offering a "dogmatic depiction of *faithful reading in*

---

117. Work, *Living and Active*, 190.
118. Quoted in Prenter, *More About Luther*, 66.
119. Gunton, "Using and Being Used," 250.

the economy of grace."[120] He unpacks three ways of understanding the act of reading the Scriptures, and together he offers them as a "theological anthropology of the reader."[121]

> (1) Faithful reading of Holy Scripture in the economy of grace is an episode in the history of sin and its overcoming.

Reading the Scriptures is unlike any other reading. One who reads the Scriptures is involved in the story it tells—but not in the sense of getting "caught up in" a well-written novel. Rather, God addresses the reader of the Scriptures who, because of his or her sin, is estranged from him. "We do not read well, not only because of technical incompetence, cultural distance from the substance of the text, or lack of readerly sophistication, but also and most of all because in reading we are addressed by that which runs clean counter to our will."[122] This means that it is impossible to read the written Word of God as a neutral observer. "Reading Scripture is thus best understood as an aspect of mortification and vivification: to read Scripture is to be slain and made alive."[123] When sinful human beings read the commands of God in his written Word, they become aware of the fact that they fail to measure up to his standard of faith and life. Faithful reading in this context takes place "as a kind of brokenness, a relinquishment of willed mastery of the text."[124] It requires a "hermeneutical conversion" that is brought about through the work of the Spirit operating through the Word.

The proper theological categories for biblical reading, therefore, are soteriological and pneumatological. "Through the incarnate Word, crucified and risen, we are made capable of hearing the gospel, but only as we are at one and the same time put to death and raised to new life. Through the Spirit of the crucified and risen Christ we are given the capacity to set mind and will on the truth of the gospel and so read as those who have been reconciled to God."[125] As one who has been slain and made alive, the reader of the Scriptures emerges as one who has been restored to read responsibly, open to what God has said and continues to say in his Word. Such a reader approaches the text with a "focused attentiveness" to what it says and engages in a "deliberate directing of attention to the text and an equally de-

120. Webster, *Holy Scripture*, 86. His emphasis.
121. Ibid., 105.
122. Ibid., 87.
123. Ibid., 88.
124. Ibid.
125. Ibid., 89.

liberate laying aside of other concerns."[126] Faithful reading is achieved as the reader maintains the proper balance between "fear and trembling" before the Almighty and expectant confidence that the Holy Spirit will illuminate the reader to understand the written Word.

> (2) Faithful reading of Holy Scripture in the economy of grace is a faithful reading of the clear Word of God.

In the second part of his theological anthropology of the reader, Webster tries to add some theological precision to two standard features of the doctrine of inspiration: biblical perspicuity and the idea that the Scriptures are self-interpreting. He acknowledges that, on one level, these concepts arose as a protest against the "authority of interpretive traditions or élites."[127] But he cautions against viewing them with the kind of individualism and objectivism that has characterized modern biblical interpretation. "To reject the *a priori* authority of traditions and interpretations is quite different from giving free rein to the individual interpreter, making exegesis into yet another kingdom rule by unformed intellectual conscience."[128] Rather than advocating the kind of individualism that governs the modern approach to the Scriptures, faithful reading of the Bible is a collective work of the body of Christ to whom the Scriptures were written in the first place.

In order to unpack what it means for the Scriptures to interpret themselves, Webster focuses on God's use of the Scriptures. "Scripture is self-interpreting and perspicuous by virtue of its relation to God."[129] Through the Scriptures God addresses the reader and thereby mortifies and brings him or her to life. This can only make sense when it is seen in a soteriological context—"that is, in relation to God's act as Word and Spirit and the creature's act of faith."[130] For this reason the Scriptures do *not*, properly speaking, interpret themselves. As the written Word of the living God, God himself is the active agent in biblical interpretation. Faithful reading of the Scriptures occurs when "God who as Word interprets himself through the Spirit's work."[131] Biblical perspicuity, then, should not be regarded as an inherent property of the Scriptures that exists apart from the act of reading. Rather, "Scripture is clear because of the Spirit's work in which creaturely acts of reading are so

126. Ibid., 90.
127. Ibid., 93.
128. Ibid.
129. Ibid.
130. Ibid.
131. Ibid., 94.

ordered towards faithful attention to the divine Word that through Scripture the light of the gospel shines in its own inherent splendour."[132] Perspicuity is the gift and work of God through his Word and in his Spirit—not "the product of exegetical prowess or technique."[133] This does not remove the necessity for doing the hard "natural" work of reading the text with appropriate skills and tools. But "the mere technical deployment of these skills is insufficient, and may, indeed, mislead."[134] Webster summarizes, "Scripture's clarity is neither an intrinsic element of the text nor simply the fruit of exegetical labor; it is that which the text *becomes* as it functions in the Spirit-governed encounter between the self-presenting saviour and the faithful reader. To read is to be caught up by the truth-bestowing Spirit of God."[135]

> (3) Faithful reading of Holy Scripture in the economy of grace is not the work of masters but of pupils in the school of Christ.

"One of the chief fruits of the Spirit's conversion of the reader," Webster explains, "is *teachableness*, a teachableness which extends into the disposition with which Scripture is read. To read Scripture as one caught up by the reconciling work of God is to abandon mastery of the text, and, instead, to be schooled into docility."[136] To "abandon mastery" of the text is not to sacrifice confidence in hearing and confessing what God has spoken through his prophets and apostles. Nor is it to give up the hard work of struggling with the intricacies of the text. It is rather a humble disposition toward the entire practice of biblical interpretation. It recognizes that the written Word of God is, in fact, the written Word of *God*. Webster finds this attitude in Zwingli's approach to biblical interpretation, who writes, "It is not for us to sit in judgment on Scripture and divine truth, but to let God do his work in and through it, for it is something which we can learn only of God. Of course, we have to give an account of our understanding of Scripture, but not in such a way that it is forced or wrested according to our own will, but rather so that we are taught by Scripture."[137] It is as "pupils in the school of Christ" that we must judge whether or not critical tools and methods of investigation are

---

132. Ibid.

133. Ibid.

134. Ibid.

135. Ibid., 95. His emphasis. It is important to note that, unlike Barth, Webster is not saying here that Scripture becomes the *Word of God*. It becomes *clear* to the one who reads it through the power of the Holy Spirit (and often through the help of Christians who have been sent to proclaim it; see Philip and the Ethiopian eunuch in Acts 8:26–35).

136. Webster, *Holy Scripture*, 101. His emphasis.

137. Zwingli, *On the Clarity and Certainty*, 90.

appropriate for biblical interpretation. Rather than arguing for or against any particular method, Webster notices a glaring deficiency of "teachableness" among modern critical scholars. Rather than listening to what God says in his written Word, they judge for themselves whether or not God actually could have said and done the things that have been recorded. At its root, this is an *anthropological* problem. It "concerns the way in which an intellectual activity such as reading is understood. At the heart of that problem is a sense—often implicit but nevertheless real—of the sublimity of reason, expressed as a competence and adequacy, for which the term 'mastery' is hardly too strong."[138] Unlike the faithful reader of the Scriptures who defers to these writings as the written Word of God, critical interpreters presume the ability to transcend God's self-communication in the Scriptures and become the final judge of what God did or did not say and do.

Summary

In this final section I have argued that there are two ways in which the threefold form of the Word of God provides direction for a faithful account of "underdetermined" biblical interpretation in our contemporary context. First, Irenaeus reminds us that the subject matter (the *res*) of the Scriptures is Jesus, the personal Word of God who was crucified and raised for us. These Scriptures were written so that we might believe that he is the Christ and have life in his name (John 20:31). This understanding of the function of the Scriptures in the economy of salvation underscores and gives direction to all acts of faithful biblical interpretation. The key question that must be asked when interpreting any biblical text is how it fits into God's mission to save sinners through his Spirit-filled Word. Second, interpreting the Scriptures is most appropriately understood as listening to the Word that God has spoken through his prophets and apostles. Rather than presuming to exercise mastery over the biblical text (something which has been done by both sides of the modern debate), this view of biblical interpretation leads to a certain amount of humility. As the old rule says, "Wenn zur Theologie kommt, eine gewiße Bescheidenheit gehört dazu."[139] This humble disposition recognizes that the Scriptures are the written Word of *God*. As such, they require, at the very least, a "hermeneutic of trust."[140] The use of any method or tool of

---

138. Webster, *Holy Scripture*, 104.

139. "When it comes to theology, a certain amount of humility is appropriate." See Rosin, "Reformation Christology," 58.

140. Wright, *Scripture*, 100.

interpretation that puts the interpreter in a position of judgment over the Scriptures is incompatible with it as the written Word of God.

In the last words he wrote before his death, Luther exhibits the kind of humble disposition necessary for faithful biblical interpretation. After spending his entire thirty-four year career lecturing on the Scriptures, and after preaching more than two thousand sermons (approximately two per week),[141] Luther understood that he always remained a "pupil in the school of Christ." He writes:

> No one is able to understand Vergil in *Bucolics* unless he has been a shepherd for five years. No one is able to understand Vergil in *Georgics* unless he has been a farmer for five years. No one is able to understand Cicero in his letters (as I teach) unless he has worked under a distinguished government for twenty years. Know that no one has sufficiently tasted the sacred Scriptures unless he has governed churches for one hundred years with the prophets, such as Elijah and Elisha, John the Baptist, Christ and the apostles. Do not lay a hand on this divine Aeneid; rather, bow before its feet. We are beggars; this is true.[142]

---

141. Lotz, "Proclamation," 344.
142. Luther, WA *Tischreden* 5:168. (No. 5468). My translation.

Conclusion

In the chancel of the *Stadtkirche* in Wittenberg stands an altarpiece made by Lucas Cranach the Elder. The top half contains a triptych depicting three central aspects of the Christian life: baptism, the Lord's Supper, and confession. Underneath them all, serving visually as their foundation, is a picture that sums up the theology of Scripture that I have been trying to articulate throughout this book. Mark Edwards describes it:

> Luther stands in the pulpit with his left hand laid upon an open book of scripture and with the right gesturing to a central crucifix. The Wittenberg congregation faces the crucifix (and Luther) and responds in prayer. The crucifix to which Luther gestures and the congregation responds appears, as it were, within quotation marks. It represents the *message* drawn from scripture, not the utterance that conveys that message—and that message, Luther insisted, whether drawn from the Old Testament or the New, always points to Christ crucified. The good news of the crucified Christ as Luther understood it, and as depicted by Cranach, is both present and removed. It is present as the content of all scripture (it does not matter where scripture is opened under Luther's left hand) and it is the (pictorially literal) undergirding for the sacraments depicted in the surmounting triptych. It is simultaneously removed in the *theologia crucis* and *deus absconditus* of Luther's theology and in the uncertain mooring, unworldly lighting and aesthetic blandness of Cranach's painting. These images and actions are but visible, embodied signs of an invisible promise—"God so loved the world that he gave his only Son, so that everyone who believes in him may not perish but may have eternal life."[1]

---

1. Edwards, "The Power of a Picture," 31–32.

This scene in Cranach's altarpiece illustrates a cruciform account of the threefold form of the Word of God. The personal and crucified Word of God is at the center. The preacher proclaims the spoken Word of God by pointing to the cross. The written Word of God provides the content for and serves the proclamation of the Gospel. The hearers listen to the proclamation of the Word and believe. It does not matter where in the Scriptures Luther has placed his hand, for the Scriptures as a whole testify to Jesus. Still, it would have been fitting for preacher to be pointing to John 20:31: "These are written so that you may believe that Jesus is the Christ, the Son of God, and that by believing you may have life in his name."

I began this book with a sense of discomfort about the assumptions, concepts, and categories that have governed the modern debate over the Scriptures. Neither liberal criticism nor the doctrine of inspiration is sufficiently rooted in the gospel of Christ crucified; neither takes into consideration the various ways (including through written texts) that God has given his Word; neither flows from a fully trinitarian and soteriological reading of the biblical narrative as a whole. My dissatisfaction with the modern debate led me in the same direction that it led Karl Barth: back to the Word of God. In the biblical narrative the Word of God is, first and foremost, Jesus. He is the personal Word through whom all things were created; who became incarnate and proclaimed a message of repentance and forgiveness by the power of the Holy Spirit; who was crucified for claiming to be one with the Father with the authority to forgive sins; who was vindicated by the Father in his resurrection from the dead; and who promised to return in glory on the last day. Both the identity and the mission of the personal Word of God come together in the cross, making the Word of God in the divine economy a *cruciform* Word. The biblical narrative also centers around the spoken form of the Word of God. This living and active Word was proclaimed by God's deputized prophets and co-missioned apostles for the judgment and salvation of sinful human beings, and the church continues to proclaim this Word of repentance and forgiveness of sins in Jesus' name. In time this spoken form of the Word of God was written down, resulting in texts that the church recognizes as Holy Scripture. These writings were gathered together by the church as definitive versions of the Word that God gave his prophets and apostles to speak in the power and guidance of his Spirit of truth. In this context the Scriptures are properly recognized as the written Word of God and the final rule and norm for the preaching and teaching of the church.

This account of the Scriptures as one form of the Word of God does not answer every question in contemporary theology about the prophetic and

Conclusion

apostolic writings. Indeed, there are many aspects of the theology of Scripture that I have not even mentioned. Rather than trying to offer a comprehensive theology of Scripture, my goal has been to provide a foundation for the theology of Scripture that is grounded in and consistent with the biblical narrative and its focus on the cross.

Gustav Wingren suggests that the most basic decision a theologian makes is the answer to this question: "What is the essence of Christianity?"[2] The answer to this question, he says, determines the shape of one's theology, including the theology of Scripture. David Kelsey agrees: "A theologian's answer to that question, and the way he makes that decision, is decisive for the way he construes scripture and for the ways in which he uses scripture in the course of making his theological proposals."[3] In this book I have answered Wingren's question for the theology of the Scripture by pointing to Paul's words to the Corinthians. With Paul we preach "Christ crucified"—our theology of Scripture notwithstanding.

---

2. Wingren, *Theology in Conflict*, 163.
3. Kelsey, *Proving Doctrine*, 8.

Bibliography

Achetmeier, Elizabeth. "The Canon as the Voice of the Living God." In *Reclaiming the Bible for the Church*, edited by Carl Braaten and Robert Jenson, 119–30. Grand Rapids: Eerdmans, 1995.
Allen, Diogenes. *Philosophy for Understanding Theology*. Atlanta: John Knox, 1985.
Anderson, William P. *A Journey Through Christian History: With Texts from the First to the Twenty-First Century*. Minneapolis: Fortress, 2000.
Austin, John Langshaw. *How to Do Things With Words*. Cambridge, MA: Harvard University Press, 1962.
Barth, Karl. *Church Dogmatics*. Vol. 1, part 1–2. Translated by Geoffrey Bromiley. London: T and T Clark, 2004.
———. *The Word of God and the Word of Man*. Translated by Douglas Horton. New York: Harper and Row, 1957.
Barton, John. *People of the Book? The Authority of the Bible in Christianity*. Louisville: John Knox, 1988.
Behr, John. *Way to Nicea: The Formation of Christian Theology*. Vol. 1. Crestwood, NY: St. Vladimir's, 2001.
Bohlmann, Ralph. "The Criteria of Biblical Canonicity in Sixteenth-Century Lutheran, Roman Catholic and Reformed Theology." PhD diss., Yale University, 1968.
Borg, Marcus. *Reading the Bible Again for the First Time: Taking the Bible Seriously but Not Literally*. San Francisco: HarperCollins, 2002.
Braaten, Carl. "A Chalcedonian Hermeneutic." *Pro Ecclesia* 3 (Winter 1994) 18–22.
Braaten, Carl, and Robert Jenson, eds. *Reclaiming the Bible for the Church*. Grand Rapids: Eerdmans, 1995.
Bromiley, Geoffery. "The Authority of Scripture in Karl Barth." In *Hermeneutics, Authority and Canon*, edited by D. A. Carson and John Woodbridge, 276–82. Grand Rapids: Baker, 1995.
Brown, Dan. *The DaVinci Code*. New York: Doubleday, 2003.
Bruce, F. F. *The Canon of Scripture*. Downers Grove, IL: InterVarsity, 1988.
Carson, D. A. "Three More Books on the Bible: A Critical Review." *Trinity Journal* 27 (2006) 1–62.
Chemnitz, Martin. *Examination of the Council of Trent*. Part 1. Translated by Fred Kramer. St. Louis: Concordia, 1971.

Commission on Theology and Church Relations of the Lutheran Church-Missouri Synod. *Gospel and Scripture: The Interrelationship of the Material and Formal Principles in Lutheran Theology*. St. Louis: Concordia, 1972.

Cullman, Oscar. *The Christology of the New Testament*. Rev. ed. Translated by Shirley C. Guthrie and Charles A. M. Hall. Philadelphia: Westminster, 1963.

Cunningham, Mary Kathleen. "Karl Barth." In *Christian Theologies of Scripture: A Comparative Introduction*, edited by Justin S. Holcomb, 183–201. New York: New York University Press, 2006.

Ebeling, Gerhard. *The Word of God and Tradition: Historical Studies Interpreting the Divisions of Christianity*. Philadelphia: Fortress, 1968.

Ehrman, Bart. *Lost Christianities: The Battles for Scripture and the Faiths We Never Knew*. Oxford: Oxford University Press, 2003.

Elert, Werner. *Eucharist and Church Fellowship in the First Four Centuries*. Translated by Norman Nagel. St. Louis: Concordia, 1966.

———. *The Structure of Lutheranism*. Translated by Walter A Hansen. St. Louis: Concordia, 1962.

Elson, John. "Witness to an Ancient Truth." *Time*, April 20, 1962.

Elliott, J. K. "Manuscripts, the Codex, and the Canon." *Journal for the Study of the New Testament* 63 (1996) 105–23.

Enns, Peter. *Inspiration and Incarnation: Evangelicals and the Problem of the Old Testament*. Grand Rapids: Baker, 2005.

Feuerhahn, Ronald R., and Jeffery J. Kloha. *Scripture and the Church: Selected Essays of Hermann Sasse*. St. Louis: Concordia Seminary Monograph Series, 1995.

Forde, Gerhard. *On Being a Theologian of the Cross: Reflections on Luther's Heidelberg Disputation, 1518*. Grand Rapids: Eerdmans, 1997.

Fowl, Stephen E. *Engaging Scripture: A Model for Theological Interpretation*. Oxford: Blackwell, 1998.

———, ed. *The Theological Interpretation of Scripture: Classic and Contemporary Readings*. Oxford: Blackwell, 1997.

Frei, Hans. *The Eclipse of Biblical Narrative: A Study in Eighteenth and Nineteenth Century Hermeneutics*. New Haven, CT: Yale University Press, 1974.

Freitheim, Terrence E., and Karlfried Froehlich, eds. *The Bible as the Word of God in a Postmodern Age*. Minneapolis: Augsburg Fortress, 1998.

Funk, Robert, ed. *The Acts of Jesus: The Search for the Authentic Deeds of Jesus*. New York: Polebridge, 1998.

———. "The Issue of Jesus." In *Jesus Reconsidered: Scholarship in the Public Eye*, edited by Bernard Brandon Scott, 5–12. Santa Rosa, CA: Polebridge, 2007.

———. "The Once and Future New Testament." In *The Canon Debate*, edited by Lee Martin McDonald and James A. Sanders, 541–57. Peabody, MA: Hendrickson, 2002.

Gamble, Harry. *Books and Readers in the Early Church: A History of Early Christian Texts*. New Haven, CT: Yale University Press, 1995.

———. "The New Testament Canon: Recent Research and the Status Quaestionis." In *The Canon Debate*, edited by Lee Martin McDonald and James A. Sanders, 267–94. Peabody, MA: Hendrickson, 2002.

Geisler, Norman, ed. *Inerrancy*. Grand Rapids: Zondervan, 1979.

Grenz, Stanley J., and John R. Franke. *Beyond Foundationalism: Shaping Theology in a Postmodern Context*. Louisville: Westminster John Knox, 2001.

Gunton, Colin. "Using and Being Used: Scripture and Systematic Theology." *Theology Today* 47 (1990) 248–59.
Hahneman, Geoffery Mark. "The Muratorian Fragment and the Origins of the New Testament Canon." In *The Canon Debate*, edited by Lee Martin McDonald and James A. Sanders, 405–15. Peabody, MA: Hendrickson, 2002.
Hansen, Collin. "Rome's Battle for the Bible." *Christianity Today* (October 2008) n.p. Online: http://www.christianitytoday.com/ct/2008/octoberweb-only/143-11.0.html.
Hartwell, Herbert. *The Theology of Karl Barth: An Introduction*. Philadelphia: Westminster, 1964.
Harvey, Van Austin. *The Historian and the Believer: The Morality of Historical Knowledge and Christian Belief*. Reprint, Chicago: Illinois University Press, 1996.
Hauerwas, Stanley. *Unleashing the Scripture: Freeing the Bible from Captivity to America*. Nashville: Abingdon, 1993.
Hengel, Martin. *Four Gospels and the One Gospel of Jesus Christ*. Harrisburg, PA: Trinity, 2000.
Henry, Carl F. H. *God, Revelation, and Authority*. Vol. 4. Waco, TX: Word, 1979.
―――, ed. *Revelation and the Bible*. Grand Rapids: Baker, 1958.
Holcomb, Justin S. *Christian Theologies of Scripture: A Comparative Introduction*. New York: New York University Press, 2006.
Hughes, Philip Edgcumbe. *A Commentary on the Epistle to the Hebrews*. Grand Rapids: Eerdmans, 1977.
Hunsinger, George. *How to Read Karl Barth: The Shape of His Theology*. Oxford: Oxford University Press, 1991.
Hurtado, Larry. "The New Testament in the Second Century: Text, Collections and Canon." In *Transmission and Reception: New Testament Text-Critical and Exegetical Studies*, edited by Jeff. W. Childers and D. C. Parker, 3–27. Piscataway, NJ: Gorgias, 2006.
Kähler, Martin. *The So-Called Historical Jesus and the Historic, Biblical Christ*. Philadelphia: Fortress, 1964.
Kaufman, Gordon D. "What Shall We Do With the Bible?" *Interpretation* 25 (1971) 95–112.
Kelly, J. N. D. *Early Christian Creeds*. 2nd edition. London: Longmans, 1960.
Kelsey, David. *Proving Doctrine: The Uses of Scripture in Modern Theology*. Harrisburg, PA: Trinity, 1999.
Kolb, Robert. "The Ordering of the *Loci Communes Theologici*: The Structuring of the Melanchthonian Dogmatic Tradition" *Concordia Journal* 23 (October 1997) 317–37.
Lindsell, Harold. *The Battle for the Bible*. Grand Rapids: Zondervan, 1976.
Lotz, David. "The Proclamation of the Word in Luther's Thought." *Word and World* 3 (1983) 348–54.
Luther, Martin. *The Complete Sermons of Martin Luther*. Vol. 1. Edited by John Nicholas Lenker. Grand Rapids: Baker, 2000.
Lutheran World Federation. "Can the Bible Be Equated with the Word of God? Theologians in LWF Study Program Debate Contextual Realities of Biblical Authority" *Lutheran World Information* 2 (2006) 11.
Maier, Gerhard. *The End of the Historical-Critical Method*. Translated by Edwin W. Leverenz and Rudolph F. Norden. St. Louis: Concordia, 1977.
Matera, Frank J. *New Testament Christology*. Louisville: Westminster John Knox, 1999.

McCormack, Bruce L. "The Being of Holy Scripture is in Becoming." In *Evangelicals and Scripture: Tradition, Authority, Hermeneutics*, edited by Vincent Bacote, Laura C. Miguélez, and Dennis Okholm, 55–75. Downers Grove, IL: InterVarsity, 2004.

McDonald, Lee Martin, "Identifying Scripture and Canon in the Early Church: The Criteria Question." In *The Canon Debate*, edited by Lee Martin McDonald and James A. Sanders, 416–39. Peabody, MA: Hendrickson, 2002.

McDonald, Lee Martin, and James A. Sanders, eds. *The Canon Debate*. Peabody, MA: Hendrickson, 2002.

McGrath, Alister. *Christian Theology: An Introduction*. Oxford: Blackwell, 2006.

———. "Reclaiming Our Roots and Vision: Scripture and the Stability of the Christian Church." In *Reclaiming the Bible for the Church*, edited by Carl Braaten and Robert Jenson, 63–88. Grand Rapids: Eerdmans, 1995.

Metzger, Bruce. *The Canon of the New Testament: Its Origins, Development, and Significance*. Oxford: Clarendon, 1987.

Morrison, John D. "Barth, Barthians, and Evangelicals: Reassessing the Question of the Relation of Holy Scripture and the Word of God." *Trinity Journal* 25 (2004) 187–213.

Mueller, John Theodore. "Notes on Luther's Conception of the Word of God as the Means of Grace." *Concordia Theological Monthly* 20 (August 1949) 580–600.

Mühlhaupt, Erwin, ed. *Luthers Evangelien Auslegung*. Zweiter Teil, deuchgesehene Auflage. Göttingen. Ger.: Vandenhoeck & Ruprecht, 1973.

Nafzger, Samuel H. "Scripture and the Word of God." In *Studies in Lutheran Hermeneutics*, edited by John Reumann et al., 107–26. Philadelphia: Fortress, 1979.

Pagels, Elaine. *The Gnostic Gospels*. New York: Random House, 1979.

Pelikan, Jaroslav. *Luther the Expositor*. St. Louis: Concordia, 1959.

———. *Whose Bible Is It? A History of the Scriptures Through the Ages*. New York: Viking, 2005.

Pieper, Francis. *Christian Dogmatics*. Vol. 1. St. Louis: Concordia, 1950.

Pinnock, Clark H. *The Scripture Principle*. San Francisco: Harper and Row, 1984.

Pontifical Biblical Commission. "The Interpretation of the Bible in the Church." *Origins* 23 (January 6, 1994) 497–524.

Porsch, Felix. *Pneuma und Wort: Ein exegetischer Beitrag zur Pneumatologie des Johannesevangeliums*. Frankfurt, Ger.: Josef Knecht, 1974.

Porter, Stanley. "When and How Was the Pauline Canon Compiled? An Assessment of Theories." In *The Pauline Canon*, edited by Stanley Porter, 95–127. Boston: Brill, 2004.

Prenter, Regin, Jaroslav J. Pelikan, and Herman A. Preus. *More About Luther*. 2 Vols. Decorah, IA: Luther College Press, 1958.

Preus, J. A. O. "The New Testament Canon in the Lutheran Dogmaticians." *The Springfielder* 25 (1961) 8–33.

Preus, Robert D. *The Inspiration of Scripture*. 2nd ed. Concordia Heritage. St. Louis: Concordia, 1981.

———. "The Word of God in the Theology of Karl Barth." *Concordia Theological Monthly* 31 (1960) 105–15.

Rahner, Karl. *The Trinity*. New York: Herder and Herder, 1970.

Ratzinger, Joseph. "Foundations and Approaches of Biblical Exegesis." *Origins* 17 (February 11, 1988) 593–602.

Reu, Michael. *Luther and the Scriptures*. Dubuque, IA: Wartburg, 1944.

Ringleben, Joachim. "Die Bibel als Wort Gottes." In *Die Autorität der Heiligen Schrift für Lehre und Verkündigung der Kirche*, edited by Karl-Hermann Kandler, 15–32 . Neuendettelsau, Ger.: Freimund, 2000.

Roehrs, Walter. "The Word in the Word." *Concordia Theological Monthly* 25 (February 1954) 81–108.

Rosin, Robert. "Reformation Christology: Some Luther Starting Points." *Concordia Theological Quarterly* 71 (2007) 147–68.

Runia, Klaas. *Karl Barth and the Word of God*. Leicester, UK: Theological Students Fellowship, 1980–1986.

———. *Karl Barth's Doctrine of Holy Scripture*. Grand Rapids: Eerdmans, 1962.

Saarnivaara, Uuraas. "Written and Spoken Word." *Lutheran Quarterly* 2 (1950) 166–79.

Sánchez M., Leopoldo A. "Receiver, Bearer, and Giver of God's Spirit: Jesus' Life and Mission in the Spirit as a Ground for Understanding Christology, Trinity, and Proclamation." PhD diss., Concordia Seminary, 2003.

Sasse, Herman. "Luther and the Word of God" in *Accents in Luther's Theology: Essays in Commemoration of the 450th Anniversary of the Reformation*, edited by Heino Kadai, 47–97. St. Louis: Concordia, 1967.

———. *Sacra Scriptura: Studien zur Lehre von der Heiligen Schrift*. Edited by Friedrich Wilhelm Hopf. Erlangen, Ger.: Verlag der Ev.-Luth. Mission, 1981.

Scaer, David P. "Biblical Inspiration in Trinitarian Perspective." *Pro Ecclesia* 14 (2005) 143–60.

Schöne, Jobst. "Die Irrlehre des Fundamentalismus im Gegensatz zum lutherischen Schriftverständnis." In *In Treue zu Schrift und Bekenntnis: Festschrift für Wolfgang Büscher*, edited by Jürgen Diestelmann, 171–83. Braunschweig, Ger.: Evang-luth. Pfarramt St. Ulrici-Brüdern, 1994.

Scott, H. M. "The Apostolic Fathers and New Testament Revelation" *Presbyterian and Reformed Review* 3/11 (1892) 479–88.

Silva, Moises. *Has the Church Misread the Bible? The History of Interpretation in Light of Current Issues*. Vol. 1. Grand Rapids: Zondervan, 1987.

Slenczka, Reinhard. "Die Heilige Schrift, das Wort des dreieinigen Gottes." *Kerygma und Dogma* 51 (2005) 174–91.

———. *Kirchliche Entscheidung in theologischer Verantwortung: Grundlagen Kriterien Grenzen*. Göttingen, Ger.: Vandenhoeck & Ruprecht, 1991.

———. "Schrift—Tradition—Kontext." In *Grenzüberschreitende Diakonie: Paul Philippi zum 60. Geburtstag*, edited by Theodor Schober, 40–52. Stuttgart, Ger: Diakonie, 1984.

Smith, Wilfred Cantwell. *What Is Scripture? A Comparative Approach*. Minneapolis: Fortress, 1993.

Sproul, R. C. *Scripture Alone—The Evangelical Doctrine*. Phillipsburg, NJ: P and R, 2005.

Stout, Jeffery. *The Flight from Authority: Religion, Morality, and the Quest for Autonomy*. Notre Dame: University of Notre Dame Press, 1981.

Thompson, Mark. *A Sure Ground on Which to Stand: The Relation of Authority and Interpretive Method in Luther's Approach to Scripture.* Cumbria, UK: Paternoster, 2004.

Tillich, Paul. *Systematic Theology.* Vol. 1. London: Nisbet, 1953.

Trobisch, David. *Die Entstehung der Paulusbriefsammlung: Studien zu den Anfängen christlicher Publizistik.* Göttingen, Ger.: Vandenhoeck & Ruprecht, 1989.

Ulrich, Eugene. "The Notion and Definition of Canon." In *The Canon Debate*, edited by Lee Martin McDonald and James A. Sanders, 21–35. Peabody, MA: Hendrickson, 2002.

Valenti-Hein, Charles. "In All Senses of the Word: Scripture and Authority in Contemporary Theology." PhD diss., Marquette University, 1996.

Vanhoozer, Kevin. "Lost in Interpretation? Truth, Scripture, and Hermeneutics." *Journal of the Evangelical Theological Society* 48 (March 2005) 89–114.

Wall, Robert W. "Reading the Bible from within Our Traditions: The 'Rule of Faith' in Theological Hermeneutics." In *Between Two Horizons: Spanning New Testament Studies and Systematic Theology*, edited by Joel B. Green and Max Turner, 88–107. Grand Rapids: Eerdmans, 2000.

Watson, Francis. "The Bible." In *The Cambridge Companion to Karl Barth*, edited by John B. Webster, 57–71. New York: Cambridge University Press, 2000.

———. "A Response to Professor Rowand." *Scottish Journal of Theology* 48 (1995) 518–20.

Webster, John. "The Dogmatic Location of the Canon." *Neue Zeitschrift für Systematische Theologie und Religionsphilosophie* 43 (2001) 17–43.

———. "Hermeneutics in Modern Theology: Some Doctrinal Reflections." *Scottish Journal of Theology* 51 (1998) 307–41.

———. *Holy Scripture: A Dogmatic Sketch.* Cambridge: Cambridge University Press, 2003.

Wenz, Armin. *Das Wort Gottes—Gericht und Rettung: Untersuchungen zur Authorität der Heiligen Schrift in Bekenntnis und Lehre der Kirche.* Göttingen, Ger.: Vandenhoeck & Ruprecht, 1996.

Williams, D. H. *Evangelicals and Tradition: The Formative Influence of the Early Church.* Grand Rapids: Baker, 2005.

———. *Tradition, Scripture, and Interpretation: A Sourcebook of the Ancient Church.* Grand Rapids: Baker, 2006.

Willimon, William. *Shaped by the Bible.* Nashville: Abingdon, 1990.

Wilson, H. S. "Luther on Preaching as God Speaking." *Lutheran Quarterly* 19 (2005) 63–75.

Wingren, Gustav. *The Living Word.* Philadelphia: Muhlenberg, 1960.

———. *Theology in Conflict: Nygren—Barth—Bultmann.* Philadelphia: Muhlenberg, 1958.

———. "'The Word' in Barth and Luther." *Evangelical Quarterly* (1949) 265–85.

Witherington, Ben, III. "Why the 'Lost Gospels' Lost Out." *Christianity Today* (June 2004) 26–32.

Wolterstorff, Nicholas. *Divine Discourse: Philosophical Reflections on the Claim that God Speaks.* Cambridge: Cambridge University Press, 1995.

Work, Telford. *Living and Active: Scripture in the Economy of Salvation.* Grand Rapids: Eerdmans, 2002.

Wright, N. T. *Scripture and the Authority of God.* London: Society for Promoting Christian Knowledge, 2005.

www.ingramcontent.com/pod-product-compliance
Lightning Source LLC
Chambersburg PA
CBHW071454150426
43191CB00008B/1346